To Josie + Jean.

Best Wishes.

Bob Dolgan

10-21-04

HEROES, SCAMPS *and* GOOD GUYS

HEROES, SCAMPS *and* GOOD GUYS

101 COLORFUL CHARACTERS FROM **CLEVELAND SPORTS** HISTORY

Bob Dolgan

GRAY & COMPANY, PUBLISHERS • CLEVELAND

These writings were originally published as newspaper columns and feature stories in The Plain Dealer.

Gray & Company, Publishers
1588 E. 40th St.
Cleveland, OH 44103

Library of Congress Cataloging-in-Publication Data
Dolgan, Bob.
Heroes, scamps, and good guys : 101 colorful characters from Cleveland sports history / Bob Dolgan.
1. Athletes—Ohio—Cleveland—Anecdotes. 2. Athletes—Ohio—Cleveland—Biography. 3. Sports—Ohio—Cleveland—Anecdotes. I. Title.
GV697.A1D645 2003
796'.09771'32—dc21 2003009246

ISBN 1-886228-67-1

Printed in the United States of America

First Printing

For Cecilia, Ann and Bob

Contents

Preface

We are in the midst of a nostalgia craze in sports, with good reason. We pluck the strings of memory and it seems money wasn't quite as important in the old days.

It was a time when common fans and tycoons could sit side by side in $4 box seats.

It was the era of the reserve clause, when athletes could not leave teams and work for whomever offered the most money. It may not have been fair to the players, but it made life nicer for everybody else, especially the fans, who knew their best players would be on their team for years and years.

There were no agents then, no strikes. Few players became acquainted with the police blotter. Sportswriters could cover their games and people without sounding like accountants; they could concentrate on curve balls and long runs without having to discuss "option clauses" or "draft and follow free agents."

It was the day of the baseball doubleheader, "the bargain bill," and the star player who made $40,000, when locker rooms did not have couches, when players came to the games in streetcars or ordinary cars, rather than Hummers, and when teams announced a player's injury by saying, "His side hurts," rather than, "He has a strained oblique."

I have always liked writing about sports history, even when I was young. My first Plain Dealer article, back on July 31, 1957 (when I was 24), was on the 25th anniversary of the first Indians game at the old Municipal Stadium, when a sellout crowd saw Cleveland lose to the Philadelphia Athletics, 1-0.

During the years I was a columnist, I usually debated the current controversies of the sports world. But occasionally I would still reach back and do a nostalgia piece on some old athlete.

In the last decade or so, I have written more than 200 history articles. Readers have responded to them in the most generous terms. In many ways, this has been the most satisfying time of my sportswriting career. Instead of inflicting my opinions on people, I have enjoyed telling stories.

This book contains profiles of some of the most interesting athletes I have written about in The Plain Dealer over the last four decades. Their stories cover the span of Cleveland sports, from the 1890s to the 21st century, from Ray Chapman, Louis Sockalexis, and "Shoeless" Joe Jackson to Brian Sipe, Mark Price, and Albert Belle. Otto Graham, Jesse Owens, Bob Feller, Jim Brown, Lou Boudreau and Harrison Dillard are among the notables who stroll across these pages.

The stories are written from the perspective of a person who was born in Cleveland and spent most of his life here. I have either seen or covered almost everybody in the book.

Most of the chapters are about famed athletes, but there are also pieces about comparatively unknown people who lived extraordinary lives, had unusual traits, or especially enjoyed their 10 minutes of fame.

They all deserve to have their stories told. Whenever possible, I have tried to do it with a touch of humor, focusing on the human angle. Most of the book is aimed at bread-and-butter sports followers, but it also contains people stories that will hopefully please even readers who are not particularly interested in sports.

The purpose of this book is to entertain. It is a try for some fun, the way sports are supposed to be.

HEROES, SCAMPS *and* GOOD GUYS

Indians 1948

Lanky, Aged Reliever Played to the Crowd

LEROY "SATCHEL" PAIGE *Aug. 9, 1998*

Leroy Robert "Satchel" Paige was more than an outstanding pitcher. He was an entertainer in spikes and flannels. It wasn't enough for him to merely stifle enemy hitters. He wanted fans to have fun while watching him do it.

His show was never better than when he made his major-league debut July 9, 1948, in a two-inning scoreless relief stint for the Indians in the Stadium.

From the moment the tall, skinny black man walked out of the bullpen to face the St. Louis Browns, he had the crowd eating out of his hand.

He looked and behaved like an old man, an important part of his persona. He walked slowly. He looked unconcerned. When he finally arrived at the mound, he threw sidearm, submarine and overhand pitches. He used the triple windup, double windup, no windup and hesitation pitch.

He added a closing flourish to his performance when Ed Pellegrini lifted a routine fly to left fielder Dale Mitchell for the third out of the sixth, Paige's final inning. Knowing all eyes were on him, Paige ambled off the hill as soon as the ball was hit and didn't bother to watch Mitchell catch it. Fifty years later, a Cleveland fan who was present recalled the gesture: "The fans went crazy. We loved it."

Paige's act wasn't finished on the diamond. He liked to entertain writers after games, too. He would tell them about his repertoire of pitches, "the trouble ball, the bat dodger and the B-Ball." When a writer asked what the B-Ball was, Satch replied: "When I throw it, you be out."

"He liked to act like a country boy who outslicked the city slickers," said Larry Lester of Kansas City, a historian of black baseball.

"He knew when to bow down and say, 'Yassuh,' when it was to his benefit. He was fooling them as much as they were fooling him.

"He knew prejudice was real, but he acted like it wasn't there. He wasn't a pursuer of racial causes."

Unlike Jackie Robinson and Larry Doby, who were largely unknown to white fans when they entered the majors as the first black players, Paige was legendary when he arrived.

Most fans knew that he had pitched in the Negro Leagues since the 1920s and that he had pitched year-round in the Caribbean, South America and Mexico.

Paige had out-dueled Dizzy Dean and a team of major-leaguers, 1-0, in a 13-inning barnstorming game in 1934. Hall of Famers Connie Mack and Dean said that in his prime, the fast-balling Paige was the best pitcher ever. "He makes my fastball look like a change-up," Dean said.

But that prime was long past when Indians owner Bill Veeck gave Paige his first chance in the majors in 1948. The Indians' staff was a bit short-handed when Veeck asked player-manager Lou Boudreau to give Paige a tryout in the Stadium in early July. The skeptical Boudreau warmed up Paige himself. Boudreau liked his nice, easy delivery. Then, Paige handed Boudreau a handkerchief, folded into a four-inch square. "He told me to put it anywhere I wanted and he'd throw the ball over it," Boudreau, 81, recalled. Nine of every 10 pitches sailed over the hankie. Then Boudreau, who was hitting about .360, batted against Paige. "I hit only a couple of balls well," Boudreau said. "I told Veeck we could use him."

Veeck was attacked for signing Paige. "A lot of writers saw it as a cheap, tawdry box-office stunt," Veeck said in his autobiography, "Veeck as in Wreck."

J.G. Taylor Spink, publisher of the Sporting News, the baseball bible, said it demeaned baseball to sign a player of Paige's age, which was rumored to be anywhere from 40 to 60. "Veeck never would have signed him if he was white," Spink wrote. "He would have been in the majors 25 years ago if he was white," Veeck retorted.

Paige made Spink eat his words with his pitching and his ability to attract tremendous crowds. A Tuesday night throng of 72,434 watched him make his first start Aug. 3, 1948. He went seven innings in a 5-3 victory over Washington in the Stadium.

Ten days later, he pitched a five-hitter in a 5-0 victory in Chicago in front of a full house of 51,013. Chicago fans were so eager to see Paige that those who could not get tickets ripped out a turnstile and occupied every inch of space in Comiskey Park. Veeck, who confessed he became frightened when the fans poured in, guessed there were about 70,000 on hand.

On Aug. 20, a Friday, Paige drew 78,332 into the Stadium, the largest night-game crowd in baseball history to that time and still the league record. Paige shut out Chicago, 1-0, on a three-hitter. The Plain Dealer bannered the story in 84-point type across Page One: "78,332 SEE PAIGE WHIP WHITE SOX, 1-0."

Afterward, a writer suggested Paige might become rookie of the year. "You may be right, man," Paige said. "But 22 years is a long time to be a rookie."

After each victory, Veeck sent Spink a telegram, telling him how well the pitcher was doing.

Paige quickly became the most talked-about man in baseball. Time and Life magazines carried stories on him. The apologetic Sporting News called him the biggest gate attraction in the game. His rules for living, including, "Don't look back, something might be gaining on you," and "Avoid running at all times," became part of the nation's sports lexicon.

Paige got along well with his Indians teammates. "As a character, he was in a class by himself," said Steve Gromek, 78. "He didn't know many players' names. He called everybody 'Keed.' He was a clever pitcher. He had so much experience and control. His fastball was good enough. That's what made him great.'"

"I used to get a big kick out of him," said Eddie Robinson, 77. "I was amazed at his pitching. His stuff was not really that good, but with his tricks and change of speeds, he really helped us. Everybody liked him."

The youthful Doby was Paige's roommate. "He was part roommate, part gone," said Doby, referring to Paige's social life. "He was a very experienced person. Every town we played in Satch had been there before. He had a lot of friends." Doby denied the Veeck story that he asked for a new roommate because Paige carried a gun.

Paige would leave a ticket for a "Mrs. Paige" at every game. Each day, a different woman showed up. Veeck finally asked him, "Satch, are you married?"

"No, but I'm in great demand," he replied.

After a lifetime of free-lance traveling, Paige found it hard to adjust to the discipline of a big-league schedule. Boudreau became increasingly irritated as he missed trains. Once, Paige did not come to the ballpark, but the game was rained out. The next day, Boudreau asked him why he had not come to the park. "I knew it was going to rain," Paige said. "How did you know that?" Boudreau asked. "My toe hurt," Paige said.

"Everybody had to laugh," said teammate Bob Feller, 79. "Even Boudreau."

Paige had a 6-1 record through Aug. 30, his four winning starts coming against Washington and Chicago, the worst two teams in the league. After he was knocked out of a game against sixth-place St. Louis on Sept. 4, Boudreau dropped him from the starting rotation, going mostly with Feller, Bob Lemon and Gene Bearden down the stretch.

He became the first black pitcher to work in a World Series when he relieved in Game 5 that October.

Paige stayed with the Indians one more season, then drifted to the St. Louis Browns, where he had a 12-10 record in 1952, when he was 46. In his 50s, he was still pitching in the Class AAA International League. At age 59, he hurled three scoreless innings for Kansas City.

After retiring, he lived in Kansas City, Mo. He and his second wife, Lahoma, had eight children. He made a movie, "The Wonderful Country," with Robert Mitchum. Paige was inducted into baseball's Hall of Fame in 1971.

As he aged, Paige suffered from emphysema and needed a respirator to breathe. He died at 75 on June 8, 1982.

Jersey No. 21 Retired

BOB LEMON *May 10, 1998*

The old-timer sits quietly outside the quaint Long Beach Airport, enjoying the California sun as he waits for a visitor. Nobody recognizes him, but he seems completely at peace, watching the travelers. The bustling people do not know that he is Hall of Fame pitcher Bob Lemon, who won two World Series games for the 1948 Indians.

Lemon, once the most agile of pitchers, walks with a cane. His hands are big, with thick fingers. He has a strong grip. He smiles warmly and cracks a joke, just as he did in the days when he set a club record by winning 20 games seven times for the Indians.

"I'm not doing anything these days, and I do it very well," he said.

He is on the payroll of the New York Yankees, whom he managed to two pennants and one world championship. "[Yankees owner] George Steinbrenner always treated me very well," Lemon said. Steinbrenner, a Rocky River native, was an Indians fan when Lemon was in his heyday.

Lemon, 77, tries to ignore his health. "I'm so-so," he says. "I'm getting older. It's just a lot of little things. Walking is the main problem." He is a diabetic. He has had a slight stroke. He is not afraid of the future, saying he could have 10 minutes or 10 years left. "If they call me tomorrow, I'm ready," he said.

Lemon has something to look forward to. The Indians are retiring his No. 21 and will honor him at the reunion of the 1948 team in Jacobs Field the weekend of June 20. He is looking forward to the festivities. He will be the sixth Cleveland player to have his number retired, joining Bob Feller, Lou Boudreau, Earl Averill, Larry Doby and Mel Harder.

Lemon attends all the baseball reunions. Every year he goes to Cooperstown, N.Y., for the Hall of Fame inductions. He recently was honored at the annual banquet of the Southern California professional baseball players association. He was given a tremendous ovation. Lemon stood and was quiet for a long moment as the audience waited. Finally, he said: "Golden age, my butt" and sat down. He received another ovation from the teary-eyed colleagues who remember him as one of the most fun-loving ballplayers.

Lemon was a perfect fit on the '48 Indians. "That club had more camaraderie than any club I was ever on," he said. "Ten guys would go out to dinner together. It was the happiest team I was ever on." His best friend was his catcher and roommate, Jim Hegan. He fondly recalled utility infielder Johnny Berardino's clubhouse comedy speeches in which he imitated Charles Laughton's performance as Captain Bligh in the movie "Mutiny on the Bounty." Berardino later starred for years on the TV soap opera "General Hospital," playing Dr. Steve Hardy.

Lemon has lived in Long Beach since he was 2. He and Jane, his wife of 54 years, live in the house they bought when they were married. They have two sons, six grandchildren and one great-grandchild. One son is a school principal in Arizona. The other is a railroad employee. A third son died in a traffic accident at age 28. It still hurts Lemon to talk about it, but he merely said: "It was no day at the beach."

Lemon might have difficulty walking, but he has no trouble driving his Dodge Intrepid. He swings into Blair Field, where he played as a boy. "I lived only a block away," he recalled. "I was here all day long. I'd help put lime on the field before we'd play." Lemon peers at the empty, manicured field on the balmy afternoon, perhaps seeing the ghosts of long-lost teammates. A groundskeeper runs out and yells: "It's an honor to have you here, Mr. Lemon." A young photographer begins taking pictures. He orders Lemon into various postures and poses, making him walk too much. Lemon, who has discarded his cane, obeys the photographer's directions without complaint.

Lemon talks about the state of modern baseball. "The fans deserve a better break," he said. "With free agency, the fan does not get to know the players and root for the players of his choice. The players have all the money and all the rights. It's just the opposite of when we played. Hopefully, the pendulum will right itself some day." Lemon's top salary was $55,000. In 1948, he was paid $12,500 for going 20-14.

The Hall of Famer recalls his two 1948 World Series victories, which came after a tough September. The pressure of the pennant race had worn him down.

"My weight fell from 178 pounds to 148," said Lemon, puffing on a filtered cigarette. "It was my first full year, and I just didn't know how to handle it. I wasn't eating right. I won two World Series games weighing 148."

On June 30, he pitched a no-hitter against Detroit, one of his 10 shutouts that year. Dale Mitchell, the speedy left fielder, saved the no-hitter for Lemon, making a running catch of George Kell's line drive down the foul line.

"He was able to stretch his glove out to get it. If he was right-handed he never would have caught it," Lemon said. It was a splendid season for Lemon, who didn't start pitching until he was 25. Lemon had opened the 1946 season as a center fielder with the Indians and saved Bob Feller's 1-0 Opening Day victory with a fine catch. But his hitting was weak.

He said that player-manager Lou Boudreau suggested he try pitching midway through 1946. It had been noticed that Lemon had a live arm. Lemon began relieving in the final months of 1946, going 4-5 for a sixth-place team.

He was still in the bullpen in 1947, then was switched to starting and won 10 in a row to finish at 11-5. "Mel Harder taught me just about all I know," said Lemon, referring to the Indians' legendary pitching coach. "He taught me to throw the curve. He was the best. He also told me to junk my knuckler. Mel said he'd never seen a guy with a knuckler who could throw a good curve."

After he became a successful pitcher, his hitting improved. He went from being a sure out to one of the finest hitting pitchers, getting 36 home runs as a pinch hitter and pitcher. In '48, there was talk that Lemon might play the outfield between pitching starts.

Lemon, who had a tendency to be loose on the field, recalls how his veteran teammates taught him to stay focused. "[Third baseman] Kenny Keltner was on me all the time," Lemon said with a smile. "He'd yell, 'Get over there. Cover first.' If I was talking or laughing at the other team's bench he'd say, 'Let's quit dillydallying.' He'd throw the ball hard at me.'"

The Indians had one of the best infields in history in 1948. Veterans Boudreau, Keltner and second baseman Joe Gordon all batted in more than 100 runs and fielded brilliantly. They were All-Star Game starters. First baseman Eddie Robinson hit 16 homers and had 83 RBI.

"I never had an infield behind me that could play like that," Lemon said.

Six years later, Lemon was at his peak, winning 23 games as the 1954 Indians set the American League record with 111 victories in 154 games.

But his warmest memories are still with the '48 club. "It's hard to forget your first pennant, your first World Series," he said. "It sticks with you longer. I'd say the '48 team was better. It was just the way the team was made up."

Baseball's Ultimate Showman

BILL VEECK

Jun. 30, 1998

Bill Veeck never hit a home run, struck out a batter or caught a fly ball.

Nevertheless, he was the major reason the Indians became world champions in 1948.

Veeck was the flamboyant owner of the Indians. Most Cleveland fans alive then have no doubts that he was the best sports magnate the city has had.

In two years, Veeck took the town on a dizzying spree in which he transformed a dozing team into one that won the World Series, broke baseball's attendance records and became the darlings of the national media.

He was the classic example of how an enterprise can succeed when the man at the top knows what he is doing.

When the 32-year-old Veeck bought the Indians on June 21, 1946, they had drawn about 200,000 people that year. Almost before fans learned that Veeck's name rhymed with heck, or that he never wore a tie, they sensed he was a new Pied Piper who was going to bring excitement to the city.

By the end of that first season, Indians attendance exceeded one million for the first time, even though they finished in sixth place.

Veeck was largely responsible for that. He was a promotional genius, a man of the people. He sat in the stands with the fans, talking baseball. "If somebody else tried it, it wouldn't come off," recalled Rudie Schaffer, 86, of San Jose, Calif., Veeck's right-hand man and business chief with the Indians. "But with Veeck it worked, because he really enjoyed talking to fans." Veeck visited nearly every town and club in Ohio, making up to 1,000 speeches a year, sometimes five in a day. Trains full of baseball fans began coming to Indians games from all over the state. At night, Veeck pushed his message in Cleveland saloons and restaurants.

"I couldn't keep up with him," recalled Schaffer. "He could stay up all night, take a shower and then go through the whole day." Veeck's credo was, "Let's have fun at the ballpark." It was a revolutionary idea at a time when many considered baseball to be a religion.

He gave away hard-to-get nylon stockings to all the women at one game. The promotion was a big hit. "To this day, I don't know where he got the nylons," Schaffer said. Another time, he passed out orchids to the first 20,000 women in attendance. He hired a talented circus performer, Jackie Price, who would hang by the heels and hit baseballs, and catch balls while driving a Jeep. He used clowns, bands and balloons, all standard stuff now, but unheard of then. Once, when the umpires called for a rain delay, Veeck jumped onto the field and helped the grounds crew roll out the tarpaulin. It was quite a feat considering that Veeck walked with a crutch because he had an ailing leg that eventually needed amputation. The fans loved his act.

Veeck hated to postpone games because of rain. According to

Marsh Samuel, 85, the Indians' publicist in 1948, Veeck said, "A guy who drives 150 miles deserves to see a game." In '48, no home game was postponed. "There were several games we could have called," said Samuel, who lives in Delray Beach, Fla. One of Veeck's most famous promotions was Joe Early Night in September 1948. Veeck had thrown a night for veteran third baseman Kenny Keltner, giving him numerous gifts. Early, a night watchman, wrote a letter to the Cleveland Press saying that Keltner did not need a night, that he was making good money. Early suggested that the Indians throw a night for him, a fan. Veeck pounced on the idea and honored Early in front of more than 70,000 in late September. With Early standing at home plate, Veeck announced the Indians were giving him a house. An outhouse was rolled onto the field. Then he was given a car, an ancient Model T Ford that had flat tires and backfired. Early also received a swaybacked horse.

Finally, Early was given a new convertible, refrigerator, washing machine, luggage, watch and clothes. "It didn't cost us a dime," recalled Schaffer. "Everything was donated by merchants." Early became a local celebrity.

Between the fun, Veeck made a series of practical moves. The Indians had been splitting their games between pastoral League Park, which held 29,000, and the Stadium, which held 80,000. He moved them to the Stadium for good, then installed a fence on the huge Stadium field in 1947 to make it more hitter-friendly. The son of a former major-league executive, Veeck knew baseball talent. Acting as his own general manager, he built the '48 club with a succession of good deals. Most important was his acquisition of second baseman Joe Gordon from New York for pitcher Allie Reynolds. Gordon led the Indians in homers (32) and runs batted in (124) in 1948.

Veeck also traded for knuckleballer Gene Bearden, who won 20 games in '48; outfielder Allie Clark, who hit .310; and lefty Sam Zoldak, who won nine games. He purchased Larry Doby, who hit .301 and took over the center-field job as the first black player in American League history; Satchel Paige, who went 6-1; and Russ Christopher, who led the league in saves.

He almost made one unpopular move, when he tried to trade shortstop-manager Lou Boudreau, the fans' hero, at the end of 1947. Veeck did not like Boudreau's managing. When the story broke, Veeck found himself the target of furious fan criticism. Startled by the outburst, Veeck walked down Euclid Ave. and promised fans Boudreau would stay.

Boudreau hit .355 and won the MVP award as the Indians won the 1948 pennant, drawing a record 2.6 million. "Lou wanted to prove I was a jerk," Veeck later wrote. "He did."

His players loved Veeck because of his generosity. He relished giving them bonuses, cars and furniture for work well done. For Christmas, he gave television sets to his pals, the top baseball writers and columnists in town.

"Money had no value to Veeck," said Schaffer. "It was meant to be spent. He didn't save much. He always figured he could make more." When Claire Hegan, wife of catcher Jim Hegan, suffered a miscarriage, Veeck sat outside her door in the hospital until her husband arrived from the road. "Bill ordered nurses around the clock for me," said Mrs. Hegan. "He was wonderful."

"I loved Bill Veeck," said 1948 first baseman Eddie Robinson. "If you had a problem, all you had to do was talk to him. He was a man's man. You felt he really was your friend."

Nothing could take the smile off Veeck's face. His leg, which had been wounded in World War II, got worse. It was amputated in small stages. "They'd take a piece off it, and the next day he'd be at the game," recalled Clark.

"He could endure tremendous pain," Schaffer said. After one operation, Veeck threw a party in the Vogue Room of the Hollenden Hotel. "He hired an orchestra," said Samuel. "He was on the dance floor all night. The blood soaked his leg and got on the floor. It was not one of his better moves."

When the 1949 Indians were eliminated from pennant contention, Veeck conducted a funeral ceremony, complete with a hearse, and buried the 1948 pennant behind the fence in center field. Schaffer led the funeral parade as the mortician, wearing a tall hat and frock coat. At the end of the '49 season, Veeck had to sell the team as part of his divorce settlement. That ended his remarkable 3-year stay in Cleveland.

Veeck later bought the St. Louis Browns and Chicago White Sox, winning another pennant in Chicago. He died in 1986 at age 71 and was inducted into the Hall of Fame five years later.

Boudreau Had Mystique

LOU BOUDREAU

Aug. 12, 2001

It is difficult to explain the mystique of Lou Boudreau to people who never saw him play shortstop for the Indians. I saw him in his greatest years, and my overwhelming impression was that he looked as though he were in charge of everybody, from the players to the umpires to the groundskeepers and ushers. The former baseball and basketball captain at the University of Illinois was a natural leader.

Ed McAuley, the fine baseball writer for the Cleveland News, struggled to capture his genius. "I know it sounds trite, but there will never be another like him," he wrote. Hall of Fame manager Connie Mack, who had seen them all, said, "He's the greatest shortstop the American League has ever seen."

Boudreau, who died Friday at age 84, was the idol of Cleveland in the 1940s. He was clever, resourceful, never in a controversy off the field.

Almost every good amateur ballplayer in town wanted to play short because Boudreau did. "I used a glove without a pocket so I could get rid of the ball fast," Boudreau said. He was not fast, but he had lightning-quick reactions and was usually moving when the ball was hit. I saw him go to the right of second base to grab a grounder. He regularly fielded more chances than the great Omar Vizquel does today. He was matchless on double plays and still holds the team record for most twin kills by a shortstop in a season.

His batting stance, in which he held the bat high and crouched with his rear end protruding, was imitated by countless schoolboys. "He looked like he was getting ready to dance the rumba," wrote McAuley. Although it might not be correct to say in today's world, women fans loved him because of his skill, clean-cut good looks and gentlemanly demeanor.

He was the hero of heroes as Cleveland went crazy over the Indians in the miraculous 1948 season, setting a major-league attendance record that stood for a decade. When the Indians went to Boston to meet the Red Sox in the playoff game for the pennant on Oct. 4, 1948, Cleveland shut down.

In my school, East High, principal P.M. Watson, usually a stern, dour man, announced that the radio broadcast of the game would be piped into the study halls. I recall listening to the voices of broadcasters Jimmy Dudley and Jack Graney in one of the classrooms. The teacher was a fan, too, just like everybody in Cleveland at that time.

We cheered all afternoon as Boudreau went 4-for-4 with two home runs, giving Cleveland its first pennant in 28 years. The following week, the Indians defeated the Boston Braves in the World Series, setting up what might be the largest parade in Cleveland history.

I was in French class that morning, the first class of the day. Our teacher was Miss McMahon, who always planned meticulous lessons. We were all chattering about the Indians before the bell rang when good old Mr. Watson again came through. He announced over the intercom that all students would be excused from classes to attend the parade if they so desired.

Miss McMahon looked crestfallen. She had the day's program planned. We looked at her. She looked dolefully at us. I finally cried out, "Does that mean we can go to the parade right now?" "Yes," she said sadly.

"Let's go," I yelled. Everybody in the classroom charged out and headed for downtown on the streetcars.

The scene at Public Square was unbelievable. I have never, before or since, seen that many people there. I remember only fleeting glimpses of the Indians players as they rode through the square, sitting on the back seats of open convertibles. Boudreau, his late wife, Della, and late team owner Bill Veeck were in the first car. The width of Euclid Ave. was squeezed into half its normal size as the players rode through, absorbing the cheers. The parade continued all the way to University Circle, with people lining the streets on both sides. Police estimated the crowd anywhere from 200,000 to 500,000.

Why not? You don't win a World Series every day. We haven't won one since.

Fifteen years later, Boudreau and the 1948 team returned to Cleveland for a reunion. He was still the leader, making a graceful speech at the party. He was in Cleveland for the last time about 15 years ago, for another reunion. There were a lot of fine old ballplayers there, including some other Hall of Famers. But Boudreau was, as always, the center of attention, the media crowding around. By that time, his legs were bothering him a lot. As a player, he had always had his ankles taped before each game because of an arthritic condition. Now it was getting worse. He was barely able to climb the dugout steps. When he went to the mound to hear the cheers, he limped badly, reminding us that time waits for no man.

Three years ago, on the 50th anniversary of the '48 championship, I telephoned and asked if I could visit him. He suggested we meet at Balmoral Park racetrack, where he was a daily visitor. Like many retirees, he enjoyed making small wagers on the horses.

Boudreau drove himself to the track, then was met by a security guard who took him to the clubhouse in a wheelchair. Balmoral had given the Hall of Famer a private, six-seat booth. A plaque, decorated by two crossed bats and a ball, with the words, "Lou's Dugout," hung on a wall by the booth.

He was joined by various cronies. Boudreau's bets were clicking. He connected on a $43 daily double and a $73 trifecta.

He said that his legs were hurting and that he was planning to see a doctor. "Feel this leg," he said, lifting the trouser over his right calf. The leg was blue and hard.

Between the races, he talked baseball. He said being a playing manager was a tough job but that it appealed to his competitive nature. He said it gave him extra incentive to have a big year after Veeck almost traded him in 1947.

"He wanted to show everybody I was a jerk," Veeck wrote in his autobiography. "I was. He did."

Boudreau remained faithful to his '48 club, probably the most fondly remembered team in Cleveland sports history. "We had clutch players," he said. "We were smart. We'd win the World Series today."

"Thin Man" to the Rescue

Russ Christopher *Aug. 16, 1998*

One of the most important pitchers on the 1948 Indians had a bad heart.

He was lanky relief man Russ Christopher, who led the American League in saves despite his illness.

The story of Christopher is one of the more amazing tales in an amazing season.

"He was a medical freak," said Bill Veeck, owner of the '48 Indians, in his autobiography. "He was a blue baby grown up. His heart leaked blood instead of sending it to his lungs for oxygen." As a result, Christopher was almost always breathing hard and feeling tired.

Nevertheless, Veeck took a chance and bought the 30-year-old from the Philadelphia Athletics for $25,000 during spring training in 1948. The Indians needed a relief pitcher to team with Ed Klieman, the Euclid milkman.

Christopher had shown talent in his previous five years in the majors. He won 27 and lost 27 for the A's in the wartime seasons of 1944 and 1945, throwing 30 complete games. But by 1947 the ailing right-hander was restricted to relief work, winning 10 games and saving 12.

He threw a mean-looking submarine pitch, delivered from his cadaverous 6-3, 160-pound frame.

Veeck asked Connie Mack, the owner-manager of the A's, if he could buy Christopher. The gentlemanly Mack refused, saying the pitcher was in such poor health the deal would not be fair to the Indians. Veeck persisted and asked Mack to at least allow him to talk to Christopher.

He found the pitcher in bed in his hotel room, the covers up to his chin. He was freezing cold despite the warm weather. Veeck asked him if he could pitch.

"I don't know," Christopher said in a weak voice. "Look at me. I'm sick."

Veeck said: "I'm going to take a gamble on you." "I think you're crazy," Christopher whispered. "But I'll do the best I can for you."

The tall man pitched effectively from the start, but his health never changed. Shortly after the season began, he told Plain Dealer baseball writer Harry Jones: "When you feel so tired that you just want to lie down I think it's time to quit. It used to be that I could run across the field a dozen times. Now I can make it just about once."

Christopher went on to pitch in 45 games, working 59 innings. His illness turned him into the first modern reliever, often pitching to only one man, seldom more than one inning. Christopher saved 17 games, a lot in a season when the Indians had 66 complete games. He finished the season 3-2 with a 2.90 earned run average.

Jones called him a calm, cool and collected rally-stopper who represented one of Veeck's best deals.

His old Indians teammates have vivid memories of Christopher.

"Sometimes you didn't know if he was going to make it," said Hall of Fame pitcher Bob Lemon, 78. "His lips were ashen. When he warmed up in the bullpen he'd throw three pitches and say he was ready. He'd say, 'I don't want to leave it down here.' His body could take only so much."

"He looked blue," recalled Gene Bearden, 78. "Everyone felt so sorry for him. He'd get to the point where he couldn't breathe. Everybody said he was going to die. It was bad. He threw underhand but he'd get you out."

Former outfielder Bob Kennedy, 77, said: "He'd come in to relieve looking real pale and skinny. You'd feel so bad for him and here he's getting you out. He threw that sinker, zip. Boy, what a good competitor he was."

"He was a wonderful guy," said ex-first baseman Eddie Robinson. "He was emaciated-looking and had a very awkward underhand delivery that was hard to hit. He took his job very seriously." Christopher's teammates nicknamed him "the Thin Man" and "John Carradine" after the gaunt movie actor.

Christopher told Jones that doctors had warned him to quit playing baseball several times. "What else can I do?" he said. "Playing baseball is the only way I know how to make a living." In 1944, when he was still with Philadelphia, Christopher's heart rate suddenly jumped to 130 beats a minute, and he had to spend 10 days in bed.

According to Kevin O'Connell's new book, "City of Champions," on the '48 Indians, Browns and Barons, Christopher was hit in the stomach by a line drive in one game.

Shortstop-manager Lou Boudreau helped him up and asked if he wanted to throw some pitches to see if he was all right. "No," said Christopher. "A few pitches are all I have left. Why waste them?" He threw one pitch and got a double-play grounder. No matter how badly he felt, Christopher refused to give up. The worried Veeck said to him in mid-season: "You've done your share. Maybe you'd like to go home."

Christopher replied: "No, the doctors know what's wrong. They say it doesn't matter what I'm doing. I'm a pitcher. If I'm going to die, I might as well die pitching."

After each game, Christopher would take a hot shower to stimulate the blood flow to his lungs.

The low point in Christopher's season came late in August, when he gave up a two-run, two-out, ninth-inning homer to Vernon Stephens in Boston that rallied the Red Sox to a 9-8 victory. After the Indians won the pennant with an 8-3 victory over Boston in the historic playoff game, Christopher and 15-year-old batboy Billy Sheridan avoided the wild team party. They went to see a movie. In the World Series against the Boston Braves, Christopher pitched one scoreless inning.

It was the last time he pitched in organized baseball. Christopher retired to his hometown of Richmond, Calif., with his wife and two young children.

Veeck helped him out financially from time to time. Christopher had open-heart surgery in 1950 and died on Dec. 5, 1954, at age 37.

A Storied Life of Bittersweet Baseball Experiences

LARRY DOBY *May 31, 1998*

This is an exciting time for Larry Doby, the first black player in American League history. He was voted into baseball's Hall of Fame last winter and will be inducted in August. He is in constant demand for interviews and appearances. He was introduced in Jacobs Field for the Indians' opener and a couple of days later he was honored at halftime of a New Jersey Nets NBA game.

"People are coming out of the woodwork," he said with resignation. "I thought it would slow down after last year [the 50th anniversary of the arrival of Doby and Jackie Robinson as the first black players in the majors]. But it's even worse now. But I'm happy to go along with it."

Doby looks good, tall and straight. You would never guess he had a serious illness recently.

Doby, 73, had his left kidney removed because of a cancerous tumor last Oct. 24.

"I feel fine," said the former center fielder, one of nine surviving players who had major roles on the 1948 Indians. "I didn't need radiation. Just the operation."

Doby's wife of 52 years, Helen, suspects the cancer was caused by Radon, a soil contaminant that was ordered removed from around their house by a government environmental agency. The Dobys have lived in the bi-level home in Montclair, N.J., for 39 years.

"I have no idea if the Radon caused it or not," Doby said. "My wife and five children lived here too and they're all healthy."

Doby, an assistant to American League President Gene Budig, has been thinking about his Cooperstown speech. "It won't be long," he said. "I want to thank a lot of people. That will take care of most of it."

Larry Jr., one of his children, will be his presenter at the ceremony. "He wasn't hard to discipline and he's doing well," Doby said. "He deserves it." The son is a stagehand who just returned from a two-month tour with entertainer Billy Joel.

One of the people that Doby is sure to mention in his Hall of Fame speech is the late Bill Veeck, the dynamic Indians owner who brought him to the majors. "He was one of the greatest people I ever met," said Doby. "I lost my father when I was 8 and I certainly would have liked him to be the same kind of man Bill Veeck was." Veeck helped Doby through the rough spots as he endured racial torment in 1948.

"It was great to have someone like that to back you up," Doby said. "When he signed me I called him, 'Mr. Veeck,' He said, 'You call me Bill and I'll call you Lawrence.' We remained friends until the day he died. He personified the word 'human being.'"

Doby sits in the family room in his bedroom slippers, a leg draped comfortably over the edge of the sofa. The walls of the room are adorned with baseball memorabilia, including Doby's old jersey with the number 14, a photo of the old Stadium, another of Doby making a great catch over the Stadium fence, another of the Rev. Dr. Martin Luther King Jr. A team picture of the 1954 Indians is on prominent display.

"We won 111 games out of 154 in 1954," explains Doby. "No other team did that in the American League. We might have lost the World Series that year, but we know how good we were." There is no picture of the 1948 team. "I have one somewhere in the house, but I don't know where," he said. Doby's feelings might be affected by the fact he had his greatest season in 1954, leading the league in home runs (32) and runs batted in (126). By then he was an established star. In 1948, he was playing his first full season.

"Both were great teams," he said. "But if you ask me which was better, I'd have to say it was the '48 team. They won the whole thing."

He would not admit it, but perhaps the racism he went through in '48 has something to do with the team's absence from his family room wall. "I try to think about pleasant things in baseball," he said. There are plenty of good 1948 memories for Doby. He hit

.301 with 14 home runs, mostly in the second spot in the lineup. He rapped two doubles as Gene Bearden beat Boston, 8-3, in the playoff game for the pennant. In the World Series, he hit a home run off Johnny Sain to win the fourth game for Steve Gromek, 2-1. Asked to name his personal season highlight, he simply says, "Gromek." That is a reference not only to the homer but to the famous picture taken after the game, in which Doby and Gromek embraced in the joy of victory. It was the first time in baseball history, if not sports history, that black and white athletes were shown hugging.

"It was an emotional time," Doby said. "We had won and we showed respect for each other. The picture showed that black and white people could get along and work together. I don't think too many people were ready for that type of picture in '48."

At the start of the season, Doby was fighting for a job. Coming up as a second baseman in July 1947, he had sat on the bench most of the season behind the brilliant Joe Gordon. At the end of the '47 season coach Bill McKechnie, who had won four pennants as a National League manager and was shortstop-manager Lou Boudreau's top aide, approached Doby. "He was one of the good guys in baseball," said Doby.

The fatherly McKechnie told Doby, "We've got a second baseman in Gordon. I suggest you get a book and learn to play the outfield, because when you come to spring training that's where they're going to put you."

"It was no big deal to me," said Doby. "I had played every position in the Negro Leagues and high school. I just wanted to play regularly."

He read Yankee star Tommy Henrich's book on playing the outfield. At the beginning of spring training, he received instruction from Hall of Famer Tris Speaker, one of the greatest center fielders ever. Speaker had led the Indians to the 1920 world title as player-manager.

"Speaker talked to me about charging balls and throwing to the right base, that sort of thing," Doby said. "Speaker and McKechnie were the guys I talked to the most."

At the beginning of the year, he started in right field. When center fielder Thurman Tucker was injured, Doby moved over to center. "I stayed there for 10 years," he recalled. "The Cleveland fans were great. They never booed me even when I made a mistake." The biggest error came in a 1948 daytime game in the Stadium, when Doby was hit in the head by a fly ball after losing it in the sun. The muff cost the Tribe a game.

Another time Detroit's Hal Newhouser struck him out five times in a game.

But the pluses far outweighed the minuses for Doby, who was paid $5,000 in 1948 and whose top career salary was $36,000. He provided one of the most stunning moments of the season when he crushed a long home run in Washington off Sid Hudson. The Plain Dealer story said it would have gone 500 feet had it not hit a light tower above the field and bounced back on the field.

Doby, not knowing the ball had gone out, raced around the bases and slid into home, where he was mobbed by awed teammates. "I remember people said Babe Ruth had hit one there too," said Doby.

There are bad memories too. In spring training that season, the fans threw bottles at him in Texarkana, Texas, driving him out of the game. In an exhibition in Columbia, Ga., ushers refused to let him enter the front gate even though he was in full uniform. "You have to go in through the center-field gate where the colored folks go in," he was told. So Doby entered through center field. During the season, he was the target of vicious taunts from opposing teams. "You had more bench jockeys in those days," he recalled. "They would yell everything you can think of. But that's all right. Life has been good to me. I'm still here and a lot of those guys are gone."

He singled out McKechnie, Gordon and catcher Jim Hegan as the men he felt closest to on the '48 Indians. "I didn't have too many people to talk to," he said. As the conversation continued, however, Doby named several of his white '48 teammates as being good guys. The Indians are holding a reunion of the 1948 team June 19–21, and Doby is looking forward to it. "It will be a chance to see players you haven't seen for a long time," he said. "Even if you were a kid in 1948, you're old now."

Ironman Catcher Was a Leader in the Clubhouse

JIM HEGAN *Jul. 26, 1998*

If there was such a thing as a Hall of Fame for defense in baseball, the late Jim Hegan would be in it.

"He was the best defensive catcher I ever had," said Hall of Famer Bob Feller. "He had a great arm and great mechanics. You couldn't throw a ball past him."

Hegan, a five-time All Star, was the aristocrat of catchers, exhibiting perfect fundamentals in the most demanding of positions. He stalked pop fouls with the relish of a lion tracking down a zebra.

A tall, strong man, he must have had some iron in his system, for he frequently caught both ends of doubleheaders. The popular catcher was behind the plate in 142 of the 154 games in 1948. The next year, he pushed his workload to 152 games. By comparison, Sandy Alomar Jr., the current Indians All-Star catcher, was in 125 of 162 games last season.

Hegan had the confidence of his pitchers.

"When I first started pitching, I used to shake him off sometimes," said Bob Lemon, another Hall of Famer. "Invariably, they'd get a hit. So, I stopped shaking him off."

Hegan's weakness was hitting. Usually, he was the eighth hitter in the lineup, just above the pitcher. But he was far from a sure out. He hit 14 home runs, drove in 60 runs and hit .248 in '48. He often had a facility for hitting in the clutch. In the fifth game of the World Series, in front of 86,288, then the largest crowd in baseball history, he hit a three-run homer.

"He loved baseball," said Hegan's widow, Claire, from her home in Lynn, Mass. "He couldn't believe people were paying him to play." Hegan's top salary as a player was $20,000, the going rate for a star in those days.

For more than a decade, Hegan was a bulwark of stability in the Indians' clubhouse. He was the best singer on the team, leading the barbershop quartets. He acquired the talent from his father, who was a policeman in Lynn. "You would go into their house and they'd go, 'Boom, boom, boom,' and start singing," recalled Claire, who knew Hegan since she was 15. "His mother played the piano. Jim had a wonderful voice."

Claire remembered that Hegan was actually better in basketball than baseball. "He was wonderful at rebounding," she said. "He played semi-pro basketball in the off-season with top college players until he broke a bone in his hand. Then, [Indians owner] Bill Veeck made him quit."

First baseman Eddie Robinson remembered that Hegan was an avid socializer, even though he was one of the few players on the team who did not drink. "He'd go out with us and drink pop and have as much fun as anybody," Robinson said.

Hegan and Lemon had a legendary friendship, rooming together for 17 years, starting when they were 18 and in the minors. Yet, they were completely different.

"I drank and he didn't," Lemon said. "Once, Joe Gordon spiked his coke with a drink while we were barnstorming. Jim said, 'What's this,' and spit it out. He told Joe, 'Do that once more and we're going to meet.'

Claire said the Hegans shared an apartment with Jane and Bob Lemon when they first came up to the Indians.

"Lem was always so full of fun," she said. "He'd wear a fake arm and shake somebody's hand and the arm would come off. Jim was quiet. He was dignified, even when he was young. He was almost embarrassed when people recognized him as being a major-leaguer. Sometimes, people took it the wrong way and thought he was aloof."

Claire attended the historic 1948 playoff game in Boston, in which the Indians won the pennant, 8-3. She sat in the stands with Jane Lemon, Virginia Feller and Sandy Harder. She recalls that the Boston crowd was in a frenzy. The four women did not want to cheer as the Indians gained control of the game for fear the fans might get angry.

"We were all so happy, but we had to keep quiet," Claire said. At the end of the game, Sandy Harder [wife of coach Mel Harder] broke into tears of happiness. Thinking she was broken-hearted, a Boston fan sitting nearby consoled her.

"Don't worry, lady, we'll get them next year," he said.

Mike Hegan, veteran Indians TV and radio announcer, was Jim's son. He said his father was a disciplinarian, but fair. "He didn't yell or scream, but when he gave you that look, you didn't go any further."

Mike Hegan was attending John Carroll University when he signed with the Yankees to begin a professional career that eventually wound up with 12 years in the big leagues. He was still living at home in Lakewood and came home at 2:30 one morning. "When I pulled into the driveway, I saw a light on in the kitchen," Mike said. "My father was sitting at the table." The father was not happy and let Mike know it. "You've got a whole career in front of you, and I don't want to see you start screwing up," he said. "I don't want you coming home this late again." Mike got the message.

Jim Hegan's 16-year career with the Indians ended in 1959, and he thought his playing days were over. But Lou Boudreau, his old Cleveland manager who was then running the Chicago Cubs, called in June 1960 and asked Hegan, 39, to rejoin him as a player to handle his young pitching staff.

"We had a family meeting around the kitchen table," Claire said. "Jim didn't know if he wanted to play again or not. Jim said, 'What do you think?' Mike said, 'I wish somebody would ask me. I'd give my right arm to play in the majors.'"

That settled it. Hegan decided to give it a final shot with the Cubs, but he wanted to work out a bit first. "I pitched batting practice to him at Lakewood Park," said Mike, a standout athlete at St. Ignatius. "Two months later, he hit a home run off Sandy Koufax."

In 1961, the New York Yankees offered Jim Hegan a job as bullpen coach. "That was one of the biggest breaks of his life," Claire said. He was a Yankees coach under manager Ralph Houk until 1972, working on teams that won four pennants and two World Series. Mike Hegan joined the Yankees when his father was a coach. "I felt I had to be better to justify being the coach's kid," Mike said. "But dad treated me just like any other player." When Houk became Detroit manager in 1973, Hegan went with him. He had his first heart attack while pitching batting practice for the Tigers.

Six years later, on June 17, 1984, Jim was being interviewed in his backyard in Swampscott, Mass. "He stood up to have his picture taken and collapsed and died," Claire said. He was 64. They had been married 43 years.

"Baseball was very good to us, but I miss him terribly," Claire said.

"Fat Pat" Gave All or Nothing at the Plate

PAT SEEREY *May 15, 2001*

If Pat Seerey had been a gambler, he would either have broken the bank at Monte Carlo or gone home wearing a barrel. "He was an all-or-nothing ballplayer," recalled Lou Boudreau, 83, his manager on the Indians from 1943 to 1948. "He never held anything back. He went up there swinging." Seerey was the spiritual ancestor of many of today's strikeout artists. He would either fan or hit the long ball. He led the American League in strikeouts three straight seasons with the Indians. Although his strikeout totals of

99, 97 and 101 were modest by today's standards, they were accomplished in comparatively few at-bats. Seerey never had more than 414 trips to the plate in a season.

The fans loved the stout Irishman, who stood 5-9 and weighed about 230 pounds. They called him "The People's Choice" or, more to the point, "Fat Pat."

They were mesmerized by his outbursts of power. He and teammate Jeff Heath were among the first players to hit the ball into the upper deck of the old Stadium. The customers loved the way Seerey strode to the batter's box, full of optimism. He stepped into the ball with a picture swing, looking great. He simply lacked the hand-eye coordination to make contact regularly.

Sometimes the fans would turn on Seerey. One day, when he struck out three times and popped to the pitcher, the fans shook the Stadium with their boos.

He never complained. He just kept swinging and missing much of the time. But when he hit the ball it stayed lost. "He was the most fascinating, frustrating character ever to wear the Tribe uniform," wrote Ed McAuley of the old Cleveland News. "He could hit a ball with more sheer line-drive force than anyone in the history of the game. His friends numbered in the thousands and his critics in the tens of thousands, but you couldn't stay mad at him." Gordon Cobbledick of The Plain Dealer said Seerey would have been the most popular player in Cleveland history if he had been able to hit 30 homers a year. He had that kind of charisma. "I will never look at Seerey without thinking of what might have been," Cobbledick wrote.

Franklin Lewis of the Cleveland Press commented: "I saw Seerey and I wouldn't have missed him for anything in the world." In the long run, he was an average player, performing in the big leagues for a mere seven years. He was finished at 26.

Yet, in one of those quirks that always occur in sports, Seerey did something that surpassed all the great sluggers in history, from Babe Ruth to Mark McGwire.

He came closer than anybody to hitting four home runs in a game twice.

On July 13, 1945, he pounded three homers and a triple in Yankee Stadium as a member of the Indians.

Then, after he was traded to the Chicago White Sox, he hit four home runs in a game against Philadelphia.

The record books do not carry the statistic, but he and Hall of Famer Willie Mays are believed to be the only players in modern history to total 31 bases in two games. Mays also hit four homers in a contest, but in the other game he had two homers, two triples and a single.

Seerey had been benched by Boudreau for weak hitting before his New York performance. There was more of a stigma attached to striking out in the old days than there is now. But when right fielder Paul O'Dea incurred an injury, Boudreau installed Fat Pat in his position, batting third in the lineup.

In the first inning, Seerey smashed a triple to deep left-center off fastballer Atley Donald. It might have been a homer in most parks, but Yankee Stadium's alley was 457 feet deep. In the third, Seerey hit the first of his three homers to left, again off Donald. In the fourth, he hit a grand slam off Walt Dubiel. In the seventh, he victimized Steve Rozer. He had eight runs batted in during the 16-4 victory.

When he came up in the ninth against Rozer, Plain Dealer reporter Alex Zirin wrote that the Yankee Stadium crowd of 10,283 cheered wildly for Seerey, hoping he would hit No. 4. But he lined out weakly to third baseman Oscar Grimes. Seerey finished the season with 14 homers, 56 RBI and a .237 batting average. He had his best year in 1946, hitting .225 with 26 homers and 62 RBI.

But Boudreau tired of watching Seerey cut and miss. On June 4, 1948, with the Indians headed toward a world championship, Seerey and pitcher Al Gettel were traded to the White Sox for right fielder Bob Kennedy, who had the strongest outfield arm in the league.

Six weeks after the trade, on July 18, 1948, Seerey unleashed again, blasting four homers in Philadelphia's Shibe Park. The shots came against Carl Scheib, Bob Savage, Charley Harris and Lou Brissie. The last came in the 11th inning, giving the White Sox a 12-11 victory. The first three homers cleared the left-field roof. The fourth was into the upper deck. Seerey had seven RBI. At the time, he was the fifth player in modern history to hit four homers in a game. Even today, only 10 have done it since 1900. Seerey, Gehrig and Rocky Colavito are the only American League players.

Seerey made extra money with the homers. A Shibe Park scorecard advertisement had a standing offer of $300 for any player who hit three in one game. After Seerey hit his third, the advertiser phoned the Athletics and said he would make it $500 if he hit his fourth. Seerey did it and collected.

Pitcher Steve Gromek, Seerey's teammate on the Indians, was not surprised by the exhibition. "I pitched against him once in

Comiskey Park and he hit four long balls to left field," Gromek, 82, recalled. "All of them should have been homers, but the wind held them up."

The tremendous show could not save Seerey. He was released by the White Sox in 1949 after playing only four games. He wound up with 86 homers and 485 strikeouts for his career, with a .224 batting mark. He died in Jennings, Mo., in 1986, at the age of 63, a legend forever.

Batboy of '48

BILLY SHERIDAN *Oct. 2, 1993*

Billy Sheridan is probably the best-known batboy in Indians history. Before he came along, batboys were chosen in haphazard fashion. A groundskeeper or front-office person might ask a gang of urchins outside the ball park, "Which one of you kids wants to be the batboy today?" Then he would select a boy who had a wide smile and a lot of enthusiasm.

Sometimes several boys worked the job in the same year. But when Sheridan was chosen in 1948 it was a big deal. Bill Veeck, owner of the Indians at the time, asked The Plain Dealer to sponsor a batboy contest in 1947. Thousands of baseball-crazy kids entered. The paper would put a huge picture of the winner on the front page, accompanied by a long story.

Sheridan, the second winner of the contest, had the luck to be picked in the greatest season in Indians history—1948—when they won the pennant in an unprecedented playoff and then took the World Series.

"I'll never forget how I was picked," Sheridan recalled. "They brought 25 kids (finalists) to the Wigwam and interviewed us one by one. The next day Gordon Cobbledick (PD sports editor) and Harry Jones (baseball writer) came to my house near E. 105th and St. Clair and told me I won."

Sheridan was the envy of every teenager in town. His schoolmates at Patrick Henry Junior High asked him to get autographs, baseballs and tickets. "How do you think I passed English?" Sheridan joked. "My English teacher was a big Indians fan."

He remembers the 1948 season fondly. "It was a wonderful

year," Sheridan said. "I was the greenest kid you ever saw, but the players all treated me great."

He recalls the barbershop quartet singing by Jim Hegan, Joe Gordon, Kenny Keltner and trainer Lefty Weisman before and after games and clubhouse comedians such as Hank Edwards, Sam Zoldak and Hal Peck. When the Indians went to Boston for the playoff game, they took Sheridan along. Groundskeeper Marshall Bossard and his wife, Mayme, chaperoned 16-year-old Billy. After the 8-3 victory in the afternoon the Indians had a party in the Kenmore Hotel, but Billy skipped it and went to a movie with pitcher Russ Christopher, a non-drinker. The next morning Sheridan had breakfast with pitching hero Gene Bearden, who had won the playoff game. "I had scrambled eggs," he recalled. "Gene had a scotch and soda."

After the Indians won the World Series, Sheridan rode with the team in the massive parade through the city that was witnessed by 200,000 people.

The Indians voted Sheridan a half-share of their World Series money, about $2,000. "I bought my mother a washer with part of it," Sheridan said.

The batboy job was the springboard that catapulted Sheridan to a career in baseball. Except for four years in the Navy, he has been with the Indians ever since. He was a groundskeeper for about 20 years and then became the chief of the visiting teams' clubhouse in the early 1970s, a position he still holds. The popular Sheridan, like Indians clubhouse boss Cy Buynak, is as much a part of the Stadium as the foul lines. He was a member of the grounds crew when he helped carry pitcher Herb Score off the field the night he was hit in the eye by a batted ball in 1957. He has pitched to players such as Jackie Jensen, Mickey Mantle and Yogi Berra. He has known players from the time they were rookies to when they became coaches and managers.

But he rarely consents to be interviewed, preferring a low profile. "If you quote me, I'll deny I said it," is one of his favorite lines.

If Sheridan is sentimental about leaving the Stadium after 45 years and going to Gateway, he isn't revealing it. "I won't have to cross that bridge anymore," Sheridan said, a reference to the fact he rides a bus to work from his Lakewood home, getting off at W. 3rd St. and walking north.

He is happy to be leaving the Stadium because the visitors' clubhouse is so small. "Baseball teams have so much more equipment now," he said. "They all carry videotapes and cameras. It's hard to find room for all of it. In the old days, they had nothing but balls, bats and gloves."

But, like many people of his generation, Sheridan finds nothing wrong with the Stadium as a place to watch games. "I used to watch a lot of games in the bleachers," he said. "I loved it out there."

Era Ends as Last of the Bossards Retires

MARSHALL BOSSARD *Dec. 29, 1985*

It was a day long ago when the young Ted Williams was playing left field for the Boston Red Sox at the Stadium.

Marshall Bossard was sitting near the bullpen and heard a gorgeous young woman shout to Williams: "Ted, I'm leaving now. I'll see you by the clubhouse."

Williams, in the giddy blush of romance, turned from his position and shouted, "OK, darling, I'll be right there." It was the ninth inning and the Red Sox were leading.

Just as Williams turned his head and talked to her, a line drive went sailing by him and the Indians scored two runs and won the game," recalls the jovial Bossard. "Boy, did Joe Cronin (Red Sox manager) give it to Ted when he ran into the dugout."

Bossard, who will retire Jan. 1 after 48 years with the Indians' grounds crew, has a thousand stories like that. He should. Since 1937, he has seen every game the Indians have played.

It has been a wonderful life, spent in a healthy, outdoor job, watching ball games instead of being chained to a desk or a piece of machinery. Bossard enjoyed every bit of it. He was a friend to one and all.

Now, with his retirement, an era ends. He is the last of the famous Bossard family that for many years made the Stadium diamond, in the opinion of every ballplayer, the best in the American League. His father, Emil, was the chief groundskeeper for many years. His brother, Harold, succeeded him, with Marshall as chief henchman.

He is a walking page of history, for his career spans baseball from the time when it was a kind of charming, bucolic sport to today, when it is big business.

"I remember that Lou Boudreau (manager of the Indians in the 1940s) had a liquor cabinet in his office," Bossard said. "The writers would come in after a game and they'd all have a drink or two and talk about the game.

"In 1948, when we won the World Series, Lou would bring in some of the players after a tough loss. Guys like Joe Gordon, Ken Keltner and Dale Mitchell would sit around, have a drink or two and talk about what went wrong, plan strategy for the next game."

That kind of scene is incomprehensible now. With night ball, everything is rush, rush, rush.

A player on that rollicking 1948 team said, in confidence, that the Indians couldn't have won the pennant without Bossard. He was stationed in the scoreboard with binoculars, flashing the opposing team's catcher's signals to the batters.

Standing inside the old scoreboard and wearing a white shirt, he would stick an arm out of the hole in the scoreboard when a fastball was coming. If he kept his arms inside, the batter knew a breaking ball was on its way,

Bossard downplays it. "We tried it out," he said. "We rehearsed it and I think Boudreau was the only guy who did good with it. But a lot of teams were doing it then, and if you'd score three runs in one inning, they'd change the signs in the next. It was too dangerous."

Boudreau and Bossard were close friends. When the Indians went to Boston for the one-game playoff in 1948, Boudreau asked Marshall and his wife, Mayme, to come along. "Mayme can sit with my wife at the hall game and you'll sit in the dugout," Boudreau said.

The day of the game, however, the Indians could not get cabs to Fenway Park. They had to walk from the Kenmore Hotel. Boudreau suspected a plot on the part of the Red Sox. "In the pep talk before the game, he told the team that and said, 'Let's show them what we're made of,'" Bossard recalled.

He remembers Johnny Berardino, then a Tribe utilityman and now a television star on "General Hospital," riding the Red Sox starting pitcher, Denny Galehouse. "Throw up that slop, you broken-down batting practice pitcher," Berardino shouted. The Indians, with Boudreau hitting two home runs, won, 8-3, in the most important game in Cleveland baseball history.

After the victory Bill Veeck, flamboyant owner of the Indians, organized a spectacular train trip home from Boston. The Indians and their wives traveled like conquering royalty. "When you had a drink, the whole bottle was given to you," Bossard said. "Veeck sent all the wives fresh flowers and a corsage. It was first class all the way."

Bobby Avila, batting champ of the 1954 Indians who won a modern-day record 111 games, credited the Bossards with being the "10th men" in winning the pennant that season.

They knew all the tricks of doctoring a field to the Indians' advantage. Despite Avila's compliment, Bossard thinks the '48 club would have beaten even the magnificent '54 team.

"It seemed like when a hit had to be made or a ball had to be caught, they were there," he said of the '48 collection of clutch players. He probably is right

"I don't think we'll ever have a season like that here again," Bossard said. "We'd draw 35,000 even when last-place Washington was here." The Tribe gate was 2.6 million that year.

The forever-young Bossard is not one of those people who looks down on today's players. Despite their gargantuan salaries, he says today's heroes are pretty much the same as the old guys. George Brett, the Kansas City slugger, gives him a friendly bear hug every time he sees him.

It's been a big year for Bossard, the grandfather of 11. He and Mayme celebrated their 50th wedding anniversary a few months ago, renewing their vows at St. Felicitas Church. Now comes this pivotal move.

"I'm going to miss it" Bossard said. "Everybody has been so good to me, the ball club, the players, the media. I'll still drop in a couple of times a week."

Rookie Stunned Everyone but Himself

GENE BEARDEN *Jun. 14, 1998*

Of all the wild and wonderful occurrences in the 1948 Cleveland baseball season, the most astounding was the emergence of pitcher Gene Bearden.

The left-handed rookie knuckleballer, who was almost killed in World War II, was merely trying to make the team at the beginning of the season.

By the end of the year, he was the Indians' best pitcher, a 20-

game winner. In September and October, he had a sensational streak under pressure that has not been exceeded by any Cleveland pitcher. Then, like a comet that was too hot to sustain its brilliance, Bearden faded. He never won more than eight games in another season and finished his seven-year major-league career with a 45-38 mark. But he will always have 1948. He was the surprise package. Without him, the Indians would not have won the pennant.

Today, Bearden works in West Helena, a town of 10,137 about 10 miles west of the Mississippi River. Bearden grew up in the area and seems to know everybody. He chats with the stream of customers that enter his office, where he rents storage units. "Eight or nine of us get together every morning for coffee," said Bearden, 77. "We fight and argue and fuss. I'm usually here in the office by 7 or 8. I'm not planning to retire. It keeps my mind busy and keeps me out of trouble."

Bearden had a hip replaced 21 years ago and is blind in his left eye. Otherwise, he is in good health. He is as lean and tall as he was 50 years ago.

He and Lois, his wife of 54 years, have two children and two grandchildren. They suffered a devastating blow two months ago, when their youngest son, Shea, 51, died of leukemia. Bearden said his son had been ill a long time, the result of an encounter with Agent Orange while serving in the Vietnam War. "It turned into cancer," said Bearden. "You never think it can happen to you. You remember the things you should have done, and it's always too late. But slow but sure the family is getting over it. All you can do is keep plugging."

Bearden had his own near-fatal experience in the South Pacific during World War II. On July 6, 1943, when he was a machinist's mate on the USS Helena, the light cruiser was hit by Japanese torpedoes and sank near the Solomon Islands. Six hundred people died. Bearden's knee was crushed and he suffered a head wound when the second torpedo hit. Unconscious, he was placed on a rubber raft with shipmates and floated in the boiling Pacific sun for three days. Bearden remembers hardly anything about the ordeal. "I was in and out," he said. "I knew I was hurt. On the third day, we were picked up by a tin can [U.S. destroyer]."

The war was over for Bearden. Doctors inserted 2-by-3-inch aluminum plates in his knee and head. "It took a lot of time for me to learn to walk and talk again," he said. "Sometimes I talked but didn't make much sense."

In 1945, he resumed his minor-league career in the New York

Yankees chain, winning 15 and losing 5. In 1946, he was 15-4 for Oakland of the Pacific Coast League. In December 1946, the Yankees traded him, Al Gettel and Hal Peck to Cleveland for Sherman Lollar and Ray Mack. He played in Oakland in 1947, going 16-7. When he came to spring training with the Indians in 1948, Bearden knew it was his big chance. The Indians had the best pitcher in baseball, Bob Feller, and Bob Lemon looked promising. After them, there were some jobs open.

"I played winter ball in Mexico, and I was ready from day one that spring," Bearden recalled. "I went full tilt. I pitched batting practice the first day and the second day. When they wanted somebody to pitch to Pat Seerey [a frustrating hitter], I'd pitch to him after practice. The more I threw, the better I felt. I'm a firm believer that the more you pitch the stronger your arm gets."

Bearden impressed playing manager Lou Boudreau enough to win a job, but he didn't get his first start until May 8 in Washington. "I was more nervous for my first start than I was in the playoff game," Bearden recalled, referring to the pennant-winning game he pitched.

His roommate, veteran third baseman Kenny Keltner, tried to settle Bearden, reminding him that Washington's Griffith Stadium had a huge field. "Let them hit it," Keltner advised. "It's a 10-minute cab ride to left field."

Bearden won, 6-1, throwing his dipping knuckleball about 50 percent of the time. "They accused me of throwing a spitball," he recalled. Bearden kept improving. By Sept. 10, he was 13-7. Then he really turned it on, knuckling his way to a 7-0 mark the rest of the way. He won four of the last eight games the Indians played.

"I felt I could always go home and rest during the winter," Bearden said. "In those days we didn't need four or five days' rest like they do today. You didn't look over your shoulder to see who was warming up. You'd figure to go nine. We didn't count pitches. We counted outs."

He had 15 complete games in '48, 11 more than the Indians had last season.

Confident Indians fans thought Bearden's regular-season work was done when he shut out Detroit, 8-0, to clinch a tie for the pennant on the second-last day of the season. But on the last day, the Tribe lost to Detroit and Boston beat New York to tie for first.

The only one-game, winner-take-all playoff game for the American League championship was scheduled for the next day in Boston. Boudreau called a team meeting after the loss. He told the club he had decided to pitch Bearden on one day's rest in the franchise's biggest game.

Utility infielder Johnny Berardino strenuously objected. But second baseman Joe Gordon said: "Lou, you've been picking them right all year. Let's not change now."

Bearden was 1-1 in two games in Fenway Park during the season, pitching a 2-0 shutout on June 8 and being pounded in an 8-4 loss on Aug. 26.

Bearden, who was brimming with confidence, was not surprised that Boudreau had chosen him to work against a potent Red Sox lineup that included future Hall of Famers Ted Williams and Bobby Doerr. He had a good night's sleep on the train ride to Boston. "My goal was to get the first man out in each inning," Bearden remembered. "If you can do that, it makes your job a whole lot easier. And I pitched inside-out, throwing the ball on the inside corners instead of outside. The Red Sox were so used to looking away because of the short foul lines that I got away with it." With Feller and Lemon warming up throughout the game, Bearden went the distance and won, 8-3. Boudreau hit two homers, and Keltner hit the big blow, a three-run homer.

Bearden was carried off the field by his jubilant teammates. In Cleveland, delirious fans celebrated the city's first American League pennant in 28 years.

But Bearden was not through. Four days later he shut out the Boston Braves, 2-0, in the third game of the World Series. He saved the sixth game, entering in the eighth inning of a 4-3 victory that gave the Indians the world championship. Again, Bearden was carried off. He still has the baseball that left fielder Bob Kennedy caught off Tommy Holmes' bat to end the Series. "It's in a bank vault," he said, a souvenir of his dizzying spree.

From the Series to the Soaps

JOHN BERARDINO *Aug. 23, 1998*

Johnny Berardino, the charismatic utility infielder on the 1948 Indians, was half ballplayer, half actor. Berardino had bit parts in the movies since boyhood and made no secret of his desire to become a full-time actor after his baseball career ended.

In salary negotiations, Berardino sometimes threatened to quit baseball and go into show business immediately. Indians owner Bill Veeck, never one to miss a publicity gambit, inserted an insurance clause into Berardino's 1948 contract. If the infielder's face was damaged by a bad-hop grounder, thus jeopardizing his movie career, Berardino would collect $1 million.

Berardino became one of the '48 club's most successful and famed alumni after his departure from the ball fields. For almost 35 years, he starred as Dr. Steve Hardy in the ABC television daytime soap opera, "General Hospital." He changed his last name to "Beradino" for marquee purposes. As the reserved and fatherly Dr. Hardy, Beradino submerged the noisy personality he displayed with the Indians, where he was known as the club's best bench jockey.

But he was still a lively person off the screen. "Everybody adored him," said actress Rachel Ames, who starred with Beradino for three decades in the role of Audrey Hardy on the soap opera. "John was like a father confessor to everybody in the cast. He always had a cheery word and liked to tell funny stories. He was a great dancer and loved to ride horses. On breaks between acting, he would play catch."

According to Ames, who is still on "General Hospital," Beradino had a picture of the '48 Indians prominently displayed on his dressing room wall. "He wore his championship ring all the time," she said. "It was gorgeous. His wife made it even more beautiful, putting in a giant stone. He was so proud of it. He was always talking about his baseball days. He was wonderful in reciting 'Casey at the Bat' at cast parties."

The streetwise Beradino enjoyed trips to Las Vegas and racetracks. He liked Jack Daniel's whisky. "But only after work was over," Ames said. "He was very strict about that."

Beradino took his acting work seriously. "He always knew his lines and everybody else's lines," the actress said. "He watched the show very diligently, where some of us didn't. He followed the ratings very closely. He wanted us to beat 'Guiding Light.' He was very competitive."

The former ballplayer would offer story ideas to the show's director and writers. "They were always good ideas," Ames recalled. "He always wished Dr. Hardy wasn't so square. He loved playing gangsters."

In one story line, Beradino suffered a head injury, lost his memory and became a Mafia don. Dr. Hardy and Audrey were married to each other three times in the course of the long-running program. Beradino looked amazingly youthful well into his 70s, before he was stricken with cancer. "He had been such a healthy man," said Ames. "It was sad to see. He was sick for about eight months before he died. His wife encouraged him to keep working and he needed that. He appeared in his last show a month before he died. He had become so gaunt.

"The last time I saw him he tried to be cheerful. We had two or three lines together. He just walked off and said, 'I'll see you.'" Beradino died on May 19, 1996, at age 79.

Born in Los Angeles, he had acted in "Our Gang" comedies in the movies since he was 7 years old. Beradino usually played the tough kid in the short films that were shown between double features. He took time out from acting when he became a major-league ballplayer with the St. Louis Browns in 1939. He had a couple of good years, hitting .258 with 16 homers and 85 runs batted in 1940. The next season, he hit .271 and had a career-high 89 RBI. Beradino's baseball career was interrupted by World War II, when he served in the U.S. armed forces for more than three years. On Nov. 22, 1947, the Browns traded him to Washington for infielder Gerry Priddy, but the deal was canceled when Beradino refused to report. He threatened to quit and go into the movies rather than be moved to another losing team.

"A fellow never gets to know how good he really is playing with second division clubs," Beradino told The Plain Dealer after he was traded to the Indians. "Remember Harland Clift, our third baseman on the Browns? He hit 34 homers one year and what did it get him. People were saying, 'What's his name?'"

Beradino told Browns General Manager Bill DeWitt that he wanted to be with a winner and asked to be traded to the Indians, who had finished fourth in 1947. "I thought they were better than a fourth-place club," he said.

On Dec. 9, 1947, the Indians acquired him from St. Louis for George "Catfish" Metkovich and $50,000. Metkovich was returned to Cleveland because his finger was broken and Veeck completed the deal by sending the Browns an extra $15,000.

Beradino played in 66 games for the Indians in '48, filling in at all four infield positions. He hit .190 in 116 at-bats. His highlight came on Aug. 8, when he hit a first-game home run to start a rally that ended with a doubleheader sweep of the New York Yankees in front of 73,484 in the Stadium.

Beradino was playing in place of injured shortstop Lou Boudreau that day. It was the same day that playing manager

Boudreau lashed his storied pinch hit that drove in two runs. Beradino also played capably when second baseman Joe Gordon was injured for a week. Beradino was in 20 games at first base, playing against left-handed pitchers.

Despite his meager playing time, Beradino was no shrinking violet. He objected loudly in the clubhouse when Boudreau revealed he was going to pitch Gene Bearden on one day of rest in the pennant playoff game in Boston.

"You can't pitch a lefty in Fenway Park," Beradino yelled. Bearden won anyway.

Beradino functioned as both a bench jockey and jester in '48. He was noted for his Captain Bligh speech, in which he imitated actor Charles Laughton's performance in the movie "Mutiny on the Bounty." "It was funny," said Hall of Fame pitcher Bob Lemon, 77. "He'd say, 'I'll fight the sea and I'll be back, Fletcher Christian.' [Beradino] was one of the comrades on the team. He did it all.'"

"He was a thespian," said Al Rosen, 74, a rookie in '48. "He would jump on a table in the clubhouse and sprinkle water on everybody while giving his Captain Bligh speech."

"On train rides he would invent a show," said Allie Clark, 75, the former outfielder. "He'd get a tape recorder and each guy got a part and had to say something."

"He was always very theatrical," team publicist Marsh Samuel, 86, remembered. "He'd make up these plays on the spur of the moment and they were funny . . . He and Joe Gordon were the best actors. They were always going to the movies."

Beradino had attended the Pasadena Playhouse, where Victor Mature and Robert Preston, who later became movie stars, were his classmates.

During the 1948 season, Beradino said he would return to Hollywood to learn more about movie production after the Indians won the pennant.

"Production is a marvelous field," he told Plain Dealer baseball writer Harry Jones. "If you get the right script and right financial backing, you can do all right. In a few years I think I'll be on my own."

Beradino played baseball through 1952, winding up with a .249 batting average and 36 homers in 912 games. His production plans never materialized, but he co-starred with Leslie Nielsen in a TV police series, "The New Breed," in 1961–62 before becoming Dr. Hardy, the role for which he will always be remembered.

Who's On First? Outfielder Was Shocked to Discover That He Was

ALLIE CLARK *May 3, 1998*

Allie Clark was spending his usual sleepless night as the Indians traveled to Boston for their historic playoff game for the 1948 American League pennant.

Clark never could sleep on trains. He kept thinking about the next day's game as the hours and miles slowly passed.

"The Red Sox were playing in their own yard and they could hit," Clark, 74, reminisced. "But we thought we could still win. We had just as many good hitters as they did."

The hard-hitting outfielder was unprepared for the shock he received when he walked into the Indians' clubhouse on that Oct. 4 morning. Clark, who had never played first base, found a first baseman's glove in his locker.

He looked at manager Lou Boudreau and asked: "What's this?" "You're playing first base today," Boudreau said. That was it. There was no pep talk, no encouragement, no visit to a team psychiatrist.

"Lou didn't give me any directions," Clark said. "He just told me to go out and play."

Clark was being asked to perform at an unfamiliar position in the biggest game in franchise history.

Sitting in the living room of his upstairs apartment in South Amboy, N.J., the white-haired Clark chuckles at Boudreau's audacity. The shortstop-manager played Clark at first over Eddie Robinson, a left-handed hitter, because he wanted to fill the lineup with right-handed batters to attack Fenway Park's cozy left-field wall. Clark had hit .310 with nine homers in 271 at-bats that year. Clark appreciated Boudreau's gesture of confidence, but he still was worried.

"I was scared with guys like Ted Williams hitting," he said. Williams, a murderous left-handed hitter, pulled everything toward first base and right field.

"What it boiled down to, it wouldn't have been my fault if something went wrong," Clark said. "Lou would have taken the blame."

Clark did well, handling five putouts without an error. Batting in the second spot, he grounded out twice in two at-bats. The clutch-playing Boudreau took care of any potential second-guessers by going 4-for-4 with two homers as the Indians won the pennant with a 8-3 victory.

Clark's day ended in the fourth inning after third baseman Kenny Keltner hit a three-run homer to put the Indians ahead, 4-1. Boudreau then sent Robinson to first for defensive purposes. "I was the happiest guy in the world when Eddie came in," said Clark.

Clark played four more games at first in his seven-year major-league career, which ended in 1953. Hampered by a sore arm, he never duplicated his hitting success of '48.

After retiring, Clark returned to his native South Amboy, a small town on the Atlantic Ocean shore. He has lived there his entire life. For 20 years, he was an ironworker. "It was a lot of hard work," Clark said. "But I didn't mind it. I was an ironworker in the off-season even when I was playing ball. We didn't have enough money to take the winters off." Clark was paid $9,000 by the Indians in 1948. His top baseball salary was $12,000.

Like other old-timers, he does not begrudge the current players' enormous salaries. "More power to 'em," he said. "We just came along 50 years too soon."

In recent years, Clark has had health problems. In 1990, he underwent a quintuple heart bypass.

Four years ago, he had cancer of the jaw and throat, undergoing an operation and 36 radiation treatments. The scar on the left side of his jaw has faded.

"I blame the cancer on cigars and chewing tobacco," said Clark, who used to smoke 12 cigars and chew a pack of tobacco a day. "I did that for 50 years," he said. "That ain't bad. I miss the cigars very much." His voice remains strong despite the operation, although he sometimes takes a break if he talks too long. His doctor told Clark to stop his long habit of drinking beer, which he has refused to do.

"I drink about four glasses of draft beer a day," he said. "I used to drink more, but I can't do it anymore. I feel great. My knees hurt, but I'm almost 75. What do you expect?" Every afternoon, he meets a group of four or five old friends in a neighborhood tavern. They stay about two hours, talking about sports and the state of the world.

A local baseball field is being named in his honor. Clark and his wife, Frances, a friendly, lively woman, have been married for 54 years. They have known each other since their days at St. Mary's

High School and were wed a few days before he left for World War II Army service in Europe. They have six children and 13 grandchildren.

The old ballplayer is proud of St. Mary's. "Five guys from that school made it to the majors," he said, naming himself, Eddie and John O'Brien, and managers Jack McKeon and Tom Kelly. Clark's apartment is decorated with baseball memorabilia, including team pictures of the '48 Indians and the 1947 New York Yankees, with whom Clark played as a rookie. Both teams won world championships. He is full of happy recollections about his baseball career, including his association with the late Indians second baseman Joe Gordon.

"When I was in school, my idol was Joe Gordon," said Clark. "Then when the Yankees traded me to Cleveland, my roommate was Gordon. That was amazing."

Gordon, who had been the American League's most valuable player with the Yankees in 1942, was the Tribe's cleanup hitter in '48. He led the club with 32 homers and 124 runs batted in and played acrobatically in the field.

Clark recalls the camaraderie of the Indians in '48. "We had a great bunch of guys," he said. "We'd sit around the clubhouse after games, then go out someplace and have a couple beers. We all stuck together."

Clark's nickname on the team was "Eddie Bracken," because of his slight resemblance to the actor.

He fondly recalls the clubhouse singing, with barbershop quartets led by catcher Jim Hegan, pitcher Bob Lemon, Gordon and utility infielder Johnny Berardino.

He remembers poker games on trains with Keltner, backup catcher Joe Tipton, pitcher Sam Zoldak and outfielder Hank Edwards. Stakes were 10 and 25 cents.

All of those poker players have died. Only nine players who contributed substantially to the 1948 team are still alive. Aside from Clark, the others are Boudreau, Robinson, Larry Doby, Steve Gromek, Lemon, Gene Bearden, Bob Kennedy and Bob Feller. Three others, rookies Al Rosen, Ray Murray and Ray Boone, spent most of the year in the minors and totaled 14 at-bats.

Clark praised Boudreau's managing style. "He never hollered at anybody or hurt anybody," said Clark. "If you made a mistake, he wouldn't bawl you out in front of everybody. He'd call you into his office. He was a great manager."

Clark has no doubts that the '48 Indians were special. "I don't think any team today could compare with that club," he said. The Indians led the league in hitting, fielding, home runs and pitching in that memorable year. It is something for Clark to talk about with his old pals at the tavern.

Remembered for a Hug

STEVE GROMEK *Apr. 26, 1998*

Steve Gromek was a good major-league pitcher. He won a World Series game for the 1948 Indians and had 123 victories in 17 years in the big leagues.

But he always will be remembered most for a hug.

It occurred after Gromek beat the Boston Braves, 2-1, in the fourth game of the '48 Series. Rookie center fielder Larry Doby hit a home run off Johnny Sain to provide the margin of victory. It was a vital game, giving the Indians a 3-1 Series lead, but it was a newspaper photo taken of Gromek and Doby after the game that gave it added significance.

The picture showed Gromek, who is white, and Doby, who is black, hugging in jubilation.

It was the first time in baseball history that a white and black man were photographed embracing in the spirit of friendship. The picture, considered a civil rights milestone, was carried by newspapers all over the country.

It was no big deal to the affable Gromek. "Color was never an issue with me," said the pitcher, who played with and against many black youths while growing up in Detroit. "Doby won the game for me. I was happy. I always got along well with him. He won a lot of games for me with his bat and glove."

Gromek has another distinction. He was Hall of Famer Bob Feller's last roommate.

The two split amicably after Feller threw a no-hitter against the Yankees in New York on April 30, 1946.

Feller, the most famed pitcher in baseball even before the game, was in demand all over the Big Apple after his sensational performance. Gromek felt like the absent Feller's secretary as he fielded a continuous succession of phone calls to their room. Never afraid to speak his mind, the next day Gromek told Feller he did not like the situation, which did not figure to change. Feller agreed that it was not right that a fellow ballplayer should be put in the position of being his caddie. So Gromek got another roomie, and Feller roomed solo for the rest of his career.

Gromek, 78, still enjoys privacy in his roomy condominium in Shelby Township, Mich., north of Detroit, where he lives with his wife of 52 years, Jeannette.

The condo has pickled hardwood flooring and several cathedral ceilings. A huge team picture of the 1948 Indians hangs on a wall, next to a plaque that Gromek received when he was named to the National Polish-American Sports Hall of Fame. Gromek looks fine despite some health problems. Seven years ago, he was playing golf when he suddenly felt weak. He left his foursome, drove to the clubhouse and phoned Jeannette. She called a doctor, who told her to get him to a hospital immediately. "That's all I remember," Gromek said.

He woke up in a hospital, where a pacemaker for his heart was installed. The doctors also found he was diabetic and put him on medication.

"I'm on and off," he said, referring to his health. It is a change from the days when he was the fun-loving fellow who delighted his Indians teammates by tap dancing in his spikes in the clubhouse, rapping out a rhythmic beat. Second baseman Joe Gordon would say to him, "Steve, give us some of that old soft shoe."

Gromek still plays golf. He used to be a seven-handicapper but now comes in at 24. He likes to watch sports on television. He and Jeannette have two sons, Carl and Greg, who are successful attorneys in the Detroit area, and five grandchildren.

It has been a happy life, but tragedy shook the household when their youngest son, Brian, died of a cerebral hemorrhage at 16 when he was practicing high school baseball 29 years ago. The hurt look still is in Steve and Jeannette's eyes when they talk about it. Gromek retired from baseball in 1957, having posted a 123-108 record. He managed the Detroit Tigers' Class A farm team in Erie, Pa., but gave it up after one year.

"I didn't like it," he said. "I was with a bunch of little kids, 17 years of age. The parents would come to me and say: 'Please watch my boy. It's his first time away from home.' I was a father and nursemaid combined. The Tigers wanted me to continue, but I said no.'"

Gromek then took a sales job with the American Automobile Association, where he stayed for 20 years until retiring. He marvels at today's high salaries. Gromek was paid $3,000 in his first season and climbed to $15,000 after winning 19 games in 1945. He bought his first house when he received his $6,800 World Series share in 1948.

As a poor, young player, Gromek wore casual clothes. That was in an era when ballplayers were expected to dress well. Early in his career, Gromek pitched fine ball in a long relief stint. After the game, Indians shortstop/manager Lou Boudreau said to him, "Wear a shirt and tie from now on because you're one of my starters." He was a key figure in the Indians' drive to the 1948 title, going 9-3 as a spot starter and adding the Series victory.

At the start of the season, however, he just was worried about staying in baseball. Just before spring training, the Indians changed his number from 25 to 27, an ominous note for the Gromeks. He had had a bad year in 1947, going 3-5 and suffering a knee injury. "When they changed his number, he thought that might be the end of his career," said Jeannette. The Tribe gave his No. 25 to a hot prospect.

"I was in my fifth year in the big leagues," said Gromek. "At that time, you needed five years for a pension. I just wanted to get that fifth year in. I knew my knee was bad."

The Gromeks soon began to think of No. 27 as a good luck charm when their first son was born on Feb. 27.

Boudreau wanted to send Gromek to the minors because the knee kept him from pitching. But veteran Tribe coach Bill McKechnie, who had won four pennants as a National League manager, advised Boudreau to keep him.

"Don't get rid of the kid," he said. "He's going to help us." Gromek finally worked out his knee problems, getting his first victory on June 6, when he beat the Philadelphia Athletics, 11-1. He was used almost exclusively to start the second games of the doubleheaders that took place each Sunday and kept rolling up victories in the hectic pennant race.

Boudreau would approach Gromek after a victory in the first game and say, "This first game doesn't mean anything unless you win."

"I would go out there shaking," Gromek said. Boudreau never had much confidence in Gromek, probably because he had only one pitch.

"I had a good rising fastball but not much of a curve," Gromek said. "Boudreau told me he'd fine me $250 if I ever threw a curve. And he told [catcher] Jim Hegan he'd fine him $500 if he ever called for one with me pitching."

But Gromek's rising fastball could be so effective that he once went through an entire game without giving up a ground ball. All the outs were on popups.

One of Gromek's biggest 1948 victories came on Aug. 8, when he beat the Yankees, 2-1, in front of 73,484 fans in the Stadium. Boudreau, one of the great clutch players of all time who had won the first game with a memorable pinch single, shook his hand and said: "You came through for us, Steve. It was a big game."

With the Indians leading Boston two games to one in the World Series and everybody expecting Feller to pitch the fourth game against Braves ace Sain, Boudreau shocked everybody in a clubhouse speech. He told the team: "Gentlemen, I'm not pitching Feller tomorrow. I have decided to pitch Steve Gromek."

"I almost fell off my chair," said Gromek. "Feller was Feller in those days."

According to Gromek, Boudreau added a disclaimer to his speech, saying, "I'm willing to sacrifice this game." The manager reasoned that if Gromek lost, the series would be tied, the Braves would have used up their best pitcher—Sain—and Feller would have an extra day of rest going into the fifth game.

"I was a bundle of nerves before the game," Gromek said. "I couldn't wait to get started. After that, I was fine. I had great stuff." Gromek's 2-1, complete-game victory gave the Indians a comfortable feeling about winning the Series.

"It was the highlight of my career," Gromek said.

"Nobody hustled more"

KEN KELTNER *Jul. 5, 1998*

Ask any longtime Indians fans what they remember most about Kenny Keltner and it is even money the answer will be: "He always looked at the ball before he threw it to first." That was the third baseman's signature move. Whenever he had the time, he would study the baseball as though it was a jewel before firing it to first base. He always seemed to time it so he got the runner by a step.

You see third basemen doing the same on occasion now, but with Keltner, it was a constant.

The habit exasperated some Indians pitchers. "I'd say, 'Don't read it, throw it,' said Gene Bearden, 77, who won 20 games in 1948. Steve Gromek, 78, who won a World Series game that year, said: "I'd yell at him, 'Throw it, throw it.' But he could grab anything he reached.'"

"He looked at the ball because he wanted to grip it right," said Keltner's son, Randy, 58, of Milwaukee. "He didn't want to hold it on the seam so it would sail."

Shortstop-manager Lou Boudreau, who played alongside Keltner for a decade, never interfered with his third baseman's style. For one thing, Keltner had been with the Indians longer than Boudreau. Also, everybody knew Keltner was an outstanding fielder. If there had been such a thing as the Gold Glove Award then, Keltner would have won it.

The same goes for Boudreau. For 10 years, he and Keltner formed a seemingly impregnable wall on the left side of the infield. They knew each other's moves so well that a couple of times Boudreau flipped Keltner the ball after making a stop at deep short. Then Keltner threw to first to get the runner. Keltner's most famous fielding accomplishment came in 1941, when he made two brilliant stops in the Stadium to stop Joe DiMaggio's 56-game hitting streak.

In these days of free agency, it is hard to find ballplayers like Keltner. He held the Indians' hot-corner position for 12 straight seasons, except for one year when he was in the Navy during World War II.

He was a big fan favorite, even though he caught flak when he unsuccessfully applied for unemployment insurance one winter early in his career.

The fans knew all his mannerisms. At the plate, he stood upright, his feet about 18 inches apart, his hands low and the bat held in a vertical position.

Always a good hitter, Keltner was chosen an American League All-Star seven times. In his rookie year in 1938, he drove in 113 runs. He was a right-handed hitter, but he learned to bang the ball off League Park's right-field wall, which was 290 feet away. The next year, he hit .325, getting three home runs in one game in Boston. Keltner had his best year in 1948, when he hit .297, with career highs of 31 home runs and 119 runs batted in as the Indians won the world championship. His three-run homer was the decisive blow as the Indians won the playoff game for the pennant against the Boston Red Sox.

It was a season in which the breaks evened out for Keltner. The previous year, Indians owner Bill Veeck promised him a $5,000 bonus if he hit .280 and drove in 80 runs.

The third baseman hit .257 with 76 RBI, but Veeck gave him the bonus anyway because he suffered some tough luck, constantly lining balls directly at outfielders.

Keltner died in 1991 at the age of 75, but he is alive in the memories of his teammates and family.

"Nobody hustled more than Keltner," said Boudreau, 80. "If he hit the ball back to the pitcher, he would run as hard as he could to first base even though he was a sure out. He was a fine player with good power."

"He was a very no-nonsense guy," said Eddie Robinson, 77, the first baseman in 1948. "He kind of kept to himself, but he had a dry sense of humor. I really liked him. As a hitter, he had great wrists." Bearden, 78, was Keltner's roommate in 1948. He gave him his nickname of "Benny Beltner."

"I started calling him that because after he hit a home run he would always come into the dugout and say, 'I really belted that one,'" Bearden said. "He was a wonderful person. He was tough."

Randy Keltner, a father of three who works as an export manager in Milwaukee, was a young boy in 1948, but he remembers that magical season.

"It was extremely exciting," he said. "The town was crazy, with all those huge crowds. I remember the time the Indians gave dad a night [Sept. 9]. I went onto the Stadium field with my grandparents for the ceremony. Dad got a station wagon with true wood panels on it, and a beautiful collie, which we kept for years. We have pictures of that night."

The emotional Keltner choked up when Veeck presented him with the station wagon.

Randy Keltner said his businesslike father was always nice to the fans. "After a game, he would be surrounded by a hundred people asking for autographs," Randy said. "I wanted to go home, but he would sign every one. At times, the younger kids would ask for my autograph, too. That was neat."

Kenny Keltner was a typical veteran of the era in that he was a drinker. In those days, it was almost expected. "Keltner liked to drink," Boudreau said. "But I let him go on because he always produced. I drank with him a lot, too. When we went to Philadelphia, I knew he had a spot there that he liked. So, I always had the hotel security man look for him and take him to his room. Kenny never did anything wrong. He would just be talking baseball. The whole team was like that."

Former outfielder Bob Kennedy, 77, recalled that Keltner drank on the train ride to Boston for the unprecedented playoff game. "He ran into a couple of writers and called them every name in the book," Kennedy said. "They had been on him. The next morning, we got to the park and Kenny was hurting. Boudreau walked up to him and said, 'I hope you have a good day.' Keltner said, 'So do I.'"

Keltner then laced three hits, including a three-run homer off Denny Galehouse in the fourth inning that gave the Indians a 4-1 lead on the way to an 8-3 victory.

Keltner retired after the 1950 season, then worked as a salesman of industrial products throughout Milwaukee. "Fame never went to his head," Randy Keltner said. "He was very generous and had a lot of friends. If he liked you, he would give you the shirt off his back."

As a father, Keltner would play catch with his two sons. Both were good high school players, but he never tried to push them toward a career in baseball. Apparently, he was an easygoing father. "My mother was the taskmaster," Randy Keltner said.

Kenny Keltner's life did not end happily. His wife suffered a stroke and had to be put into a nursing home. "Dad was with her every day for three years in the nursing home," Randy Keltner said. "It was very tough on him."

Keltner would burst into tears discussing his wife's stroke. Keltner, who seemed to be in good health, died before his wife, suffering a heart attack. He passed away Dec. 12, 1991. "It was a shock for all of us," Randy Keltner said. "My mother died of a broken heart 11 months later."

Fan Favorite Combined Bat Control and Blazing Speed

Dale Mitchell — *Aug. 2, 1998*

The late Dale Mitchell, Indians leadoff man in 1948, had two exceptional baseball talents. He could hit line drives, and he could run as fast as a jackrabbit.

Those traits made Mitchell a huge favorite with baseball-crazy Indians fans in '48.

The left-hander hit .336 in that magic season, third-best in the American League. His 204 hits were second in the AL, three behind St. Louis' Bob Dillinger.

Mitchell's teammates on the '48 team remember his combination of hitting skill and speed.

"He could go to first as fast as anybody I ever saw," said Bob Kennedy, 77.

Gene Bearden, 78, said: "I saw him get on base nine times in a doubleheader by hitting the ball on the ground. Only one or two balls went out of the infield. He could really motor."

Mitchell was one of the most difficult men in baseball history to strike out. In '48, he fanned 13 times in 608 at-bats. His career ratio of 2.9 whiffs per 100 at-bats is ninth-best. Unfortunately, he fell 16 at-bats short of the 4,000 required to make the list in most reference books.

Indians playing manager Lou Boudreau was a big Mitchell booster, predicting in a 1948 interview that he would hit .340 to .350 every year.

Mitchell did not achieve Boudreau's expectations, but he was still an extremely capable performer. His 23 triples in 1949 are the most in a season since Kiki Cuyler had 26 in 1925. (Adam Comorowky also had 23 in 1930.)

Mitchell had five hitting streaks of 20 or more games, with a high of 27. He led the American League in hits once. He made two All-Star teams and hit better than .300 six times with the Indians. It was all the more astounding because he had been in a severe accident as a boy. According to "City of Champions," a book by Kevin O'Connell on the 1948 Indians, Browns and Barons, Mitchell was hit by a truck when he was 10 and suffered a broken knee, kneecap and collarbone.

Mitchell did not have the base-running ability to make full use of his speed. His 13 steals in '48 were his career high. He usually averaged about 82 runs scored.

In left field, he was adequate, although his arm was not strong. He saved Bob Lemon's no-hitter in '48 by making a running, leaping catch of George Kell's drive. "Don't talk to me," Lemon told writers after the game. "Talk to Mitchell. It wouldn't have been a no-hitter without him."

Although he was a big man at 6-1 and 195 pounds, Mitchell hit 41 homers in a 10-year career. But when he hit them, they went a long way.

Mitchell, who died in 1987 at age 65, was extremely successful in business after his baseball career, operating a cement company in Tulsa, Okla., and Denver.

"When he left baseball, he got a job for $600 a month, selling oilfield rental tools," said his oldest son, Dale Jr., 55, of Washington, D.C. "He worked himself up to president of the cement company. He did better in business than baseball."

Mitchell is remembered most nationally for taking the called third strike that finished Don Larsen's perfect World Series game for the New York Yankees in 1956. Mitchell was a pinch-hitter with the Brooklyn Dodgers.

Mitchell's first wife, Margaret, watched the game in Yankee Stadium with the other Dodgers wives. "If Dale gets a hit, we better get out of here quick," she said. "Otherwise, we're dead." Umpire Babe Pinelli, who was working his last game, ended any potential problems by calling Mitchell out on a pitch that most observers said was a foot outside. Mitchell turned to argue, but bedlam had broken loose as the Yankees swarmed Larsen, celebrating the only perfect game in Series history. Mitchell returned to the Dodgers bench, where he was greeted by teammate Pee Wee Reese. "Don't worry, Dale," Reese said. "Now you'll be in the history books forever."

It was Mitchell's final at-bat. He had joined the Dodgers that season, after a decade in Cleveland. Several years later, when he was running the cement company, the strikeout paid off for Mitchell. According to Dale Jr., he wanted to get the cement contract on a shopping center being put up by Del Webb, co-owner of the Yankees. But the manager of the project would not even allow him to make a bid. He was giving the job to a friend. Mitchell telephoned Webb. "We've never met, Mr. Webb," he said. "But my name's Dale Mitchell, and I'd like to at least be able to make a bid on your project."

Webb said: "I know you. You made me a lot of money when you struck out against Don Larsen. You've got the job."

Dale Jr. recalled that his father would always take an extra $1,000 with him when he played in old-timers' games. "He would give money to his old friends who were down and out or couldn't pay their hotel bills," he said. "He would come back from those games feeling angry about the high salaries in baseball today. He said nobody was worth that much."

Chad Caldwell, University of Oklahoma publicist, called

Mitchell the greatest baseball player in Sooner history. He holds the university's season (.507) and career (.467) batting records. The university's baseball stadium is named after him.

Andy Mitchell, 24, of Denver, remembers Mitchell as a warm-hearted grandfather. "He liked the simple life," Andy said. "He'd sit in his big red chair and talk to me about baseball. If he had his scotch to drink and his pipe, he was happy. He loved watching baseball on TV." Mitchell's second son, Dudley, 48, of Denver, said: "Everywhere he went in Oklahoma people knew who he was. Up to the day he died he was getting cards."

Dudley said his father loved to talk about the '48 Indians. "He always wore his championship ring and told us how great that team was," he said.

His sons said Mitchell enjoyed his time in baseball so much he couldn't believe he was being paid to play. "He never haggled over salary or asked for a raise," said Dudley, who was named after Jimmy Dudley, who broadcast the Indians games with Jack Graney in '48. "His top salary was $24,000." Dale Jr. recalls the happy boyhood days when he would play in the Indians clubhouse with Mike Hegan, son of catcher Jim Hegan, and other players' sons.

"Dad always told us to stay away from Bob Feller and Early Wynn on days they were pitching," he said. "They were a couple of tough guys. Once I squirted my water pistol and the water accidentally hit Feller right between the eyes. I'll never forget the look he gave me. I ran. They were all rough-and-tumble guys on that team, including dad."

Mitchell suffered his first of four heart attacks in 1975, when he was 54. His first wife, Margaret, died of cancer. In 1979, he married his second wife, June, whose husband also had died of cancer.

He lived a comfortable, happy retirement in Tulsa. Mitchell belonged to Southern Hills Country Club, where he liked to play cards and golf.

"He still looked great," Dudley said. "He was a Hall of Fame dad." "He was a wonderful man, a giving person," June Mitchell said from Tulsa. "He could sit down with truck drivers and talk to them, and he could talk to presidents of corporations."

In 1987, Mitchell made a New Year's resolution to stop drinking. Five days later, he had a heart attack and died. A crowd of about 500 attended the funeral. He was buried in Cloud Chief, Okla., the tiny town where he was born.

Browns

One of the Best Linemen in Browns History

BILL WILLIS

Feb. 23, 2003

Nobody ever had a more spectacular debut with the Browns than Big Bill Willis.

When he arrived in training camp in early August 1946, coach Paul Brown installed him at middle guard for a scrimmage. Willis opposed Mike Scarry, a fine blocker who was the Browns' first center and who had held the post for the Cleveland Rams 1945 National Football League champions.

Scarry, 83, speaking from his home in Fort Myers, Fla., gave a graphic description of what happened when he tried to snap the football to quarterback Otto Graham.

"Bill crouched and got me under the arm and knocked me back on top of Otto," Scarry said.

"I tried again and he knocked me into Otto again. I asked Fritz Heisler [assistant coach who was monitoring the line play] if he was offside. Heisler said he was not.

"He was under me, driving like a madman on every play. I couldn't get a snap off. Otto said, 'What the hell's going on?'" Willis was the immediate sensation of camp.

Scarry delighted in watching centers on other teams play against Willis for the first time. "I used to think, 'Poor guy, you don't know what you're in for,'" he said. "We played some teams that had trouble getting the snap off the whole game. Defensively, he was the greatest."

Willis was one of the best linemen in Browns history, maybe the best. He was also the team's first black player. It is appropriate to review his career during Black History Month.

People spoke of him only in superlatives during his playing days. He is in both the Pro Football Hall of Fame and College Hall of

Fame, having been a two-time All-American at Ohio State. He played under coach Brown as the Buckeyes won the 1942 national championship. As the brilliant middle guard in the days of the Cleveland dynasty, he dominated centers and harassed quarterbacks from 1946–53, playing on teams that won five league championships in the old All-America Football Conference and the NFL.

"Lenny Ford [another Hall of Famer] and I used to compete to see who could get to the quarterback first," recalled Willis, 81, from his Columbus home.

Willis' most legendary play came in 1950, the team's first season in the NFL. He saved a 8-3 playoff victory against the New York Giants with a diving tackle of Gene "Choo Choo" Roberts on the 4-yard line in the last quarter. Roberts had gone 32 yards when Willis caught him.

"Roberts was zigzagging and I had an angle on him and went straight at him," Willis recalled.

Coach Brown called Willis the "greatest lineman in American football" after the game.

The Browns beat the Los Angeles Rams for the NFL title the next week.

Paul Brown liked to hold footraces in training camp, matching players of similar speed. He always had Willis, a track sprinter at Ohio State, race against a running back. "He was a super athlete, super quick, and a great guy besides," said Scarry. "He had skinny legs, but from the waist up, he looked like he weighed 300 pounds, with no fat."

The 6-2 Willis had a 32-inch waist in his heyday. He also played offensive guard and linebacker in the days before unlimited substitution.

He fondly recalls the way Bob Neal, the Browns' first play-by-play man, would introduce him. Neal would go through the lineup, calling out the names of the bigger players, such as, "Chubby Grigg, 280 pounds," or "Lou Rymkus, 250 pounds." Saving Willis for last, he would say with emphasis, "Big Bill Willis, 215 pounds." Even though he was comparatively light, Big Bill was his standard nickname. Actually, he weighed less than 210.

Willis was the first black player in the AAFC. Fullback Marion Motley joined the Browns about 10 days later. They were the only black men in the league. The NFL's Rams employed two other African-Americans that year, halfback Kenny Washington and lineman Woody Strode, the first in the league since 1933. Willis credits Paul Brown for easing the integration of the Cleveland club. "Football players take their lead from the coach," he said. "Paul didn't put up with that kind of foolishness." Nevertheless, Willis and Motley had to suffer many of the same torments that were later inflicted on baseball pioneers Jackie Robinson and Larry Doby, who came into the major leagues a year later.

Some opposing players told Willis to his face that they were racists. Others called him the usual derogatory names. He always took care to protect himself from physical shots from dirty players, especially after the whistle.

Browns teammates told him not to retaliate to the point he would get thrown out of games. "Just tell us who did something to you and we'll unload on him," he was told.

It was tougher for Motley, who also became a Hall of Famer. He would get kicked and piled on when carrying the ball. Willis would pull opponents off him, saying: "Let's play ball." Scarry says Willis' talent and demeanor made life easier for him on the field. "Guys who were calling him names at the start of a game would be saying, 'Yes sir,' to him after they saw him in action," Scarry said. "He'd knock guys down and then help them up with a big smile."

In the Browns' first season, Willis and Motley did not make a trip to a game in Miami after they received death threats, according to the Football Encyclopedia. "Paul just told us we were playing a weak team and that we could win without us," Willis recalled. Willis and Motley were never excluded from a team hotel, as many black baseball players were. That was because Brown notified hotel owners they had to have rooms for all of his players if they wanted the team's business.

"Bill trusted and admired Paul Brown," said Odessa Willis, his wife of 56 years, with whom he has three children and four grandchildren. "In later years, Paul would ask him to help keep certain players in line."

Brown was his presenter when Willis was inducted into the Pro Football Hall of Fame in 1977.

When Brown became the boss of the Cincinnati Bengals, he extended a standing invitation to the Willises to all their games. "Bill sat next to Paul Brown in his suite," said Odessa. Mike Brown, Paul's son, has continued the open invitation.

After leaving football, Willis worked for the Cleveland Recreation Department and then served for 20 years as a director of the Ohio Department of Youth Services. He retired in 1983. In 1989, he suffered a stroke and had to learn to talk and walk all over again. He is fine now and remains loyal to his great old team. "If we were playing today I really think we'd do as well now as we did then," he said. "We had tremendously talented players whose execution was flawless."

He Was the Best

OTTO GRAHAM *Dec. 26, 1983*

Unbelievable. What a holiday gift. There was the greatest quarterback of them all right here in the office fracturing the routine of an otherwise normal day.

Otto Graham, 62, sat down on the desk top and protested, "No, I wasn't the best." He said, "Today's players are better than any of us were. A quarterback today has to read defenses better and he has to throw harder because the openings are so small."

But it doesn't matter what he says. He was the best. What other quarterback played in ten straight title games and won seven of them?

A few weeks ago, The Sporting News, using the current National Football League rating system, listed the most effective passer ever. Graham came out No. 1.

We worshipped Graham as children, sitting in the Stadium bleachers, watching the Browns play for 25 cents. He could throw short and he could throw 70 yards, his passes flying light as feathers. This is forgotten, but in his first year he played 60 minutes in every game.

Can you imagine Brian Sipe playing safety today and returning kicks?

Oh, it was fun to be a Browns fan then. There was no frustration, no defeat. They simply won and won and won. Under Coach Paul Brown and a squadron of other geniuses, they were one of the great sports organizations of all time.

And now Graham was sitting on the desk. It was the first time I ever met him. The current sports stars we know are just people, for we have grown up. Here was a god. The heroes of youth are the ones who mean the most.

Having had a colostomy a few years ago, Graham was in town to make tapes on behalf of the American Cancer Society. He looks good, still has that easy carriage of the natural athlete. He has only a little gray at the temples. He wisecracks a lot.

We could have gotten into a philosophical discussion about sports today, but that would be like talking about the rate of inflation with Leonardo da Vinci. When you have Graham you talk football and his unforgettable career with the Browns from 1946 to 1955.

He always had fine receivers. "Mac Speedie was the smoothest, but Dante Lavelli had the best hands," said Graham. "If you threw the ball near him he would do anything to get it, bite, scratch and kick. He'd come into the huddle and tell you he could get open on the guy who was guarding him. That meant he was open by three inches. That was all he needed.

"Now when Dub Jones told you he could get open, you knew nobody would be even close to him."

The magnificence of those old Browns was symbolized in a series against Buffalo in 1947. The Bills had a first down on the one-yard line. They failed to score in four downs. On the next play, Graham let the furious Buffalo defenders pour through and then threw a screen pass to Speedie on a goal line. It went for a 99-yard TD.

Graham talked of Paul Brown's cold toughness. "If you did something wrong, he would just look at you," he said. "Or he would say something to another coach so you could hear it."

Once Brown took Graham out of a game and put in George Ratterman. "At least we'll have a quarterback with the guts to stay in the pocket," Brown said.

"If I'd had a gun, I'd have shot him," laughed Graham.

He recalled an inter-team scrimmage when Moe Scarry was the center. Big Bill Willis, probably the finest lineman the Browns have ever had, was bedeviling Scarry, going over him and under him. Once Graham fell down after taking the snap.

"Why did you fall?" Brown asked Graham.

"Scarry stepped on my toe," replied Graham.

Brown stopped the scrimmage. He called the whole team around him and said, "Okay, everybody. I don't want anyone to step on Otto's toe."

"He knew who to needle," said Graham. "He was a master at getting a team ready for a game."

But Graham also told the story of the famous 1950 National Football League title game against Los Angeles which the Browns won 30-28.

With about eight minutes left and the Rams leading, 28-20, Graham fumbled. "I wanted to crawl into a hole and die," he said.

"But Brown said, 'Don't worry about it. We'll get 'em.'"

And they did. I was in the bleachers. Greatest game I've ever seen.

Graham has been the athletic director of the Coast Guard Academy in New London, Conn. since 1959, except for a four-year stint of coaching the Washington Redskins.

He said his old Bay Village neighbor, George Steinbrenner, got him the job through his shipping connections.

"Where the hell is the Coast Guard Academy?" Graham said when Steinbrenner, now boss of the New York Yankees, told him about it.

Graham and his wife went there to look around. When they left, she said, "Thank God we'll never see that place again."

"I like it," said Graham. Now she does too.

"Sports there are the way they should be," said Graham. "You try hard and you do your best, but the world doesn't come to an end if you lose."

Happy Holidays, Otto.

Memories of a True-Blue Brown

LOU GROZA *Dec. 1, 2000*

What a perfect nickname. The Toe.

It fit Lou Groza just right. He liked it so much he used it on his auto license plates for the rest of his life.

Merely booting footballs was not all he did, however. For 10 years, in the great days of the Browns' football dynasty, he both kicked and played offensive tackle.

Groza made his most famous kick, the 16-yard field goal against Los Angeles that won the 1950 NFL championship, at the end of a long day of battle on the frozen Stadium turf.

"You have to remember that he almost always had to kick after playing the line and blocking on a long drive," said former teammate Bob Gain. "He didn't have a chance to get a rest, the way the kicking specialists do today."

In Groza's time, there were only 33 or 35 players on a team. Few clubs could carry a player just to kick field goals and extra points. Groza earned his keep, at first, as a backup tackle. He became a regular when coach Paul Brown saw how he destroyed opposing ball carriers after he kicked off. Groza enjoyed contact and became an excellent blocker.

Edgar "Special Delivery" Jones, 82, one of the Browns' early running stars, recalled from his home in Scranton, Pa.: "Groza was one of the best. We had an arrangement on our 25 play, where I would take a handoff and go straight up the middle. Lou would wiggle his right foot or left foot when he lined up, so I knew which way he was going to block. Then I'd go inside of him or outside. That's all I needed. I depended on him. If he didn't make the block, I'd get killed. But he always did it."

"I don't think he hardly missed any block," said Otto Graham, 78, the Browns' Hall of Fame quarterback.

As much as Groza enjoyed the job in the trenches, offensive linemen are consigned to anonymity. It was as a kicker that Groza will always be remembered. At the time of his retirement in 1968, he had all the kicking records, most field goals, extra points and total points.

"Pressure didn't bother him," said Graham, of Sarasota, Fla. "He was so good with the fundamentals and he'd practice and practice." Tommy James, 77, of Massillon, held the ball for Groza for eight seasons. After the team's practices at old League Park, Groza and James would go out and start their drills. "We were good buddies," recalled James. "But some days it would be so cold and he'd kick and kick. He'd stay out there as long as somebody would hold the ball. We'd be out there for half an hour and I'd be freezing, but I couldn't get him to stop." Maybe that was why Groza was able to kick the field goal that won the 1950 title on a bitterly cold day. He wore a black high-topped cleated shoe on his right foot and a tennis shoe on his left that day.

Frank "Gunner" Gatski, who centered the ball for Groza's kicks for a decade, recalled Groza's conscientiousness and attention to detail. "I'd snap him 100 balls a day," said Gatski, 78, of Grafton, W.Va. "He'd put a chalk mark on one shoe for every one he made and another chalk mark on the other shoe for each one he missed."

Groza was the sensation of the Browns' first home game in 1946. He used a 10-foot tape as a guideline, placing it behind the football when he kicked. Nobody had ever seen that before and nobody has seen it since.

The next day's newspapers stories reported at length on the tape, which he used for four years, as long as the Browns were in the All-American Football Conference.

James would put one end of the tape on the ground, then Groza would stretch it out in line with the goalposts. "He kept his head down through the follow-through, almost like a golfer," said Bob Yonkers, 86, of Rocky River, who covered the Browns for the Cleveland Press in the first nine years of the franchise. "He was a technician."

When the Browns entered the NFL in 1950, the tape was outlawed. "I'd try to scratch a line in the ground instead," James said. "But the officials would always rub it out."

Still, Groza was accurate. As the years went by, Groza turned back many challengers for his job, including future NFL kickers Errol Mann, Dave Lee, Fred Cox, Sam Baker and Dick Van Raaphorst. He had his best year percentage-wise in 1959, when he connected on 16 of 21 field-goal attempts. At age 41, when he was the oldest player in the NFL, he made 22 of 32 tries as the Browns won the 1964 league championship.

Quarterback Frank Ryan, 64, of Grafton, Vt., remembered that it was Groza's field goal in the second half that gave the Browns a 3-0 lead and started them to their 27-0 win over Baltimore in the title game. "He broke the ice," Ryan said. "It was a hefty kick too." Chuck Heaton, 83, of Bay Village, who covered the Browns for The Plain Dealer for many years, said opposing teams often targeted Groza, but he never complained.

Gain, 71, of Eastlake, agreed. "They would take some cheap shots at him," he said. "But he was strong, about 250 pounds when opposing guards were about 230. And he was durable." Groza was the Cleveland kicker until Don Cockroft came along. Cockroft, 55, of Canton, recalls his first look at the legend in training camp. "His legs looked bigger than my waist," Cockroft said. "He could still kick. I could tell he wasn't ready to give up the job. It was kind of amazing.

"When I was in high school we watched a Browns game on television and my dad pointed to Groza and said, 'If you had a player like him to show you how to kick it would be great.' Now I was competing with him."

Groza won the kicking job again in 1967 when the rookie Cockroft injured his back in a car crash. The next year Cockroft became the kicker and Groza became an assistant coach. "The year I was out was a blessing in disguise," Cockroft said. "I learned a lot just by watching Lou. After he retired, he worked with me for a couple of years. I owe a lot of my success to him." Cockroft was the Cleveland kicker through 1980 and became the team's second-leading scorer. "If I missed a kick, he would tell me to forget it and remember that I'd get another chance, the usual stuff," Cockroft said. "But coming from him, it meant more."

Groza was always an outstanding athlete. A big rebounder and scorer, he led his Martins Ferry High School team to the Ohio state title in basketball. His brother, Alex, became the star center on the University of Kentucky's national champion basketball team. James said the 6-3 Lou was the shortest of the Groza brothers. Groza's parents owned a restaurant and bar in Martins Ferry, which is about 20 miles south of Steubenville.

An amazing twist in the Groza legend is that he never played varsity college football. He was limited to a couple of freshman games at Ohio State. But the freshmen would scrimmage against the varsity, which was coached by Paul Brown. Groza once recalled that when he was practicing kicking he could see Brown in a window in a nearby building, watching him.

Groza was called into the service when World War II began. While serving as a medic on Okinawa, he received a contract offer from Brown, who was starting the professional team, the Browns, in 1946. Groza immediately accepted and was paid while the war was still on. He stepped in as the Cleveland kicker when the war ended. "He was a special favorite of my father," said Mike Brown, Cincinnati Bengals president and the son of the great Cleveland coach. "He called him 'My Louie.' He was a clutch player who won a lot of games for the Browns. My father insisted Lou had to go back to Ohio State in the off-season and graduate, which he did." After football, Groza had a thriving insurance company. He and his wife, Jackie, had four children, Jud, Jon, Jeff and Jill. He was constantly involved in civic causes.

Former colleagues heaped praise on Groza after the news of his death. "It's a sad day," said former receiver Dante Lavelli, 77, of Westlake. "Everybody liked him. I don't ever remember him missing a field goal with the game on the line."

"It's always tough when a real good friend passes on," Graham said. "You could count on him for anything. He was really a nice guy."

"He almost never complained about anything that was written about him," said Heaton. "The only thing he didn't like was when somebody wrote he was hurt. He never wanted to talk about that. I wrote once that he was injured and he called me over and we talked about it. Once he got it off his chest, he forgot about it. He was one of the best people I ever met in football."

"It's a terrible loss," Yonkers said. "I feel so sad. As Paul Brown said, 'He's good people.'"

"Four Times More Valuable Than Jim Brown"

MARION MOTLEY *Jun. 28, 1999*

Every once in a while, a film clip of Marion Motley at his powerful best pops up on TV sports shows.

Motley, the former Browns fullback, is shown running over several tacklers in a game that took place about 50 years ago. He is hit at least five times. He almost falls. His helmet is knocked off by the force of the collisions.

But he somehow keeps his balance and staggers into the end zone for a touchdown, with the bodies of the failed tacklers strewn across the field behind him.

"It's one of the great plays in Browns history," said Tommy James, a former teammate of Motley.

Motley, who was inducted into the Pro Football Hall of Fame in 1968, died yesterday in Cleveland at age 79. He had been suffering from prostate cancer and diabetes.

A 240-pounder who ran with sprinter's speed, Motley was the leading rusher in the All-America Football Conference, which the Browns dominated from 1946 to 1949, when the league went out of business. He continued punishing tacklers when the Browns won the NFL championship in 1950, leading the league in rushing. Motley's running was a study in efficiency and economy. In a game against Pittsburgh, he gained 188 yards in 11 carries, an average of 17.1 yards per effort, still an NFL record.

For his career in both the AAFC and the NFL, he averaged an amazing 5.7 yards each time he ran the football.

Another Cleveland fullback, Jim Brown, who is generally considered the best runner in football history, averaged 5.2 in his career, all in the NFL. "Marion was a great player," said Otto Graham, the former quarterback who was Motley's partner in the old Browns' pass-and-trap offense. "I would take him over Jim Brown.

Marion was a great blocker. He saved my life many a time. Nobody ever knocked him over.

"He was a great guy who always gave 100 percent. I'm really sorry to hear he died. He was a wonderful man."

Graham, speaking from his home in Sarasota, Fla., recalled that he and Motley teamed up on football's first draw play by accident. "I was going back to pass and I bumped into Marion," Graham said. "We had some kind of mix-up. I didn't know what to do, so I gave him the ball. He started running and made a good gain. That started it." The Browns won five league championships while Motley was on the team.

Motley would terrorize smaller backs, who would shy away from him when he broke into the open. "Not many would try to tackle him head-on," said James. "I hit him in practice. It was like running into a stump."

Edgar "Special Delivery" Jones, another former teammate, recalled the AAFC game in which Motley trampled Elroy "Crazy Legs" Hirsch, who later became a Hall of Fame wide receiver. "The next time Motley came at him, Hirsch got out of the way and Marion ran 60 yards for a touchdown," said Jones from his home in Scranton, Pa. "That's when they changed Hirsch to receiver." Motley was ahead of his time. He was bigger than most linemen of that era.

Lou "The Toe" Groza, another Browns teammate, recalled the first time he tackled Motley in a 1946 scrimmage when both were trying to make the team. "I ran into him head-on and I saw a big flash in my eyes," said Groza, of Berea. "From then on I tried to tackle him from the side."

Groza, an offensive tackle in addition to being the Browns' greatest kicker, said it was easy to block for Motley. "He didn't need much of a hole," The Toe said. "He was a real load coming through. He was a real competitor."

Motley and middle guard Bill Willis were two of the early black players in pro football and the first on the Browns. Both had to endure some bad treatment from opposing players. Willis, of Columbus, remembered some of the racism. "They'd call you names and give you the elbow," said Willis. "They would try to gang tackle Marion. One guy would hold him and the others would drive into him. Marion wasn't the type to mouth off, but he would make it his business to run over them and give them an elbow in return."

Former receiver Dante Lavelli, of Rocky River, visited Motley last week and the two reminisced about those days. "Marion said he got bit sometimes," said Lavelli. "But he never made an issue out of it. He waited until the next play to get even."

"Paul Brown would remind us to just tend to business," Willis recalled. "He would say, 'The worst thing that can happen to those guys is for us to beat them, give them a thrashing.'"

Motley and Willis suffered the humiliation of not going to Miami to play an early Browns game. A law in Florida prevented blacks from playing against whites.

His old teammates remember Motley as being a congenial person. "He was a good buddy," said James, of Massillon, who knew Motley from the time they were rivals at Canton McKinley and Massillon High. "He always called me Little Red. He could mix well." Lavelli and Motley often golfed together in retirement. "He won $10,000 for a hole-in-one once," said Lavelli.

"Motley was a very dedicated, very sharp football player," said Jones. "I think he was the greatest fullback I ever saw. He was four times more valuable than Jim Brown. He was a runner, blocker, receiver, linebacker, a team man and a hell of a nice guy to boot."

Paul Brown would often insert Motley into a linebacking spot for goal-line stands. "Paul said he could have been an all-pro just as a linebacker," Willis said.

Bill Lund of Chagrin Falls, another early teammate, remembers Motley's speed.

"Paul would hold 50-yard races for the players," said Lund, who could run 100 yards in 9.6 seconds. "Me and Bob Cowan were the only guys who could beat Marion and he weighed about 50 pounds more than we did. And we only beat him by a foot. Besides that, he was just one of the most friendly guys I can remember. I really loved him."

After his retirement, Motley, whose highest football salary was $12,000, had a variety of jobs. He worked for the post office, coached a woman's football team, operated a tavern, and was a part-time scout for the Washington Redskins. "He was never really compensated for the contributions he made," said Lavelli.

The First to Grab 3 TD Passes in the NFL

MAC SPEEDIE *Dec. 2, 2001*

The late Mac Speedie's name sounded as if it belonged to a character on the comic pages. But it fit him perfectly. The great Browns receiver was one of the speediest men in football in his time.

Speedie led the All-America Football Conference in catching passes three times. In his last year, 1952, he led the NFL. "He could make defensive backs look bad," recalled Mike Scarry, 81, of Fort Myers, Fla., the Browns' first center who became a longtime assistant coach in the NFL. "He looked like a sack of potatoes coming at a defender, but then he'd turn on a burst of speed and leave 'em flat-footed."

Speedie had several other distinctions.

He was one of the few players to run out on coach Paul Brown, possibly costing him a chance at the Pro Football Hall of Fame. He was involved in a memorable police incident, reminiscent of the recent Browns affair with Mike Sellers and Lamar Chapman. He overcame a severe childhood disease to become a perennial all-pro.

Fifty years ago today, on Dec. 2, 1951, he became the first Browns player to catch three touchdown passes in an NFL game. He grabbed TD passes of 39, 22 and 6 yards from the legendary Otto Graham as the Browns won, 49-28, over the Chicago Cardinals after building up a 40-0 lead.

"He looked like he wasn't moving, but try to keep up with him," said ex-running back Edgar "Special Delivery" Jones, 84, of Scranton, Pa. As a boy, Speedie suffered from a bone ailment that kept one leg in an iron brace for four years. "The leg was thinner and shorter than the other," said former teammate Dante Lavelli, 78, of Westlake.

Speedie recovered to star at the University of Utah, becoming one of the fastest hurdlers in the country. When Fred Wolcott of Rice set a world hurdles record, Speedie was the runner-up in the race. "He had an unusual gait, with short steps," Lavelli said. "He limped slightly."

Speedie and Lavelli were the catchers and Graham the pitcher as the Browns developed one of football's most lethal passing combinations. Lavelli was extremely aggressive, fighting for the football.

The lanky 6-3 Speedie was the elegant aristocrat, using finesse to defeat power.

"We'd practice pass routes for 20 minutes after the regular practices," Graham, 79, recalled from his home in Sarasota, Fla. "I got so I knew exactly where Speedie and Lavelli were going from the way they wiggled their fannies."

Speedie got a late start in pro football, not joining the Browns until he was 26, following service in World War II. Despite playing only seven years in Cleveland, Speedie's 339 catches in both the AAFC and NFL rank third in Browns annals to Ozzie Newsome and Lavelli, who are both in the Hall of Fame. In yardage, he is fourth to Newsome, Lavelli and Ray Renfro.

Speedie's most spectacular play came in the 1948 AAFC title game. It happened seconds after the Browns stopped the Buffalo Bills on four shots from the 1-yard line. Graham called for a screen pass to Speedie.

"I had always wanted to throw a screen pass from my end zone," Graham recalled. "The Bills were really mad and came roaring in. They wanted to kill me."

Graham flipped the football over the heads of the onrushing linemen to Speedie, who went 99 yards for a TD, the longest pass play in team history. The Browns routed the Bills, 49-7. "Mac caught the ball on the goal line," said Graham. "It was actually a 100-yard play."

The police scrape occurred on Dec. 13, 1946, nine days before the Browns were to play the New York Yankees for the AAFC championship in their first season.

Speedie and starting tackles Jim Daniell and Lou Rymkus had attended a civic luncheon in the Browns' honor that day, then went out on the town.

That night Daniell, the team captain, was driving along Euclid Ave. around E. 79th St., with Speedie and Rymkus in his car. A police car cruised slowly in front of them. Daniell began honking his car horn, yelling to the police to speed up. When the police stopped for a light, Daniell pulled alongside and reportedly yelled, "Why don't you go sit on the bench?"

According to the Cleveland News, the police went to the players' car and asked them to step out. They declined. Another police car arrived with reinforcements and the players hiked into position and pretended to start a line plunge, to the amusement of a crowd of spectators.

The players were taken to the police station, where Daniell was charged with intoxication. Rymkus and Speedie were booked for disorderly conduct. All pleaded not guilty and were released from jail.

The story hit the front pages. It caused more of a sensation than the recent incident, for athletes seldom got into police trouble then. Brown fired Daniell, who was over the hill, but retained the talented Rymkus and Speedie.

As the years went on, Speedie began having salary disputes with Brown, whose basic idea of negotiations was to tell his players what he was going to pay them.

Jones claimed Speedie ended a salary hassle with Brown by tossing a dollar on the table and saying, "Here, buy yourself a coffee." Then he walked out the door, Jones said.

"Special Delivery" was a close friend of the receiver. "You couldn't get Mac mad," he said. "He was quiet, with a lot of humor. If you loved to drink beer, you'd love Mac."

"He was a good, good person," said Scarry. "When I was coaching at Western Reserve, he'd help me with the ends. He was very conscientious."

Despite his annoyance over salary, Speedie kept playing outstanding football. He caught 11 passes in a game twice, once in each league. He piled up 228 yards in one game. He was all-league in both the AAFC and NFL.

Speedie decided to leave the Browns after leading the NFL with 62 catches for 811 yards in 1952. At 33, he knew he didn't have much playing time left. He announced he was going to play in Canada for the Saskatchewan Roughriders. He signed for $20,000 a year, about $9,000 more than he had been getting from the Browns. "It was the toughest decision of my life," Speedie told Bob Yonkers of the Cleveland Press. "I feel I owe it to my family. I've enjoyed playing with the Browns and I hope I have Paul Brown's blessing. He and his assistants have been wonderful to me." Brown was angry.

"It's a bitter disappointment," he said. "I hate to see him end his fine career in such fashion. I held him out of the championship game last December because I didn't want to risk further injury to his knee and endanger his career. Then he pulls a stunt like this."

Speedie played for three years in Canada, two with Saskatchewan and a final season with British Columbia, then retired. After serving as an assistant for several years in the American

Football League, he became head coach of the Denver Broncos during the 1964 season. He resigned in 1966, compiling a 6-19-1 record with the Broncos.

Speedie died on March 12, 1993, at age 73. "He belongs in the Hall of Fame, without doubt," said Graham. Scarry agreed, saying, "He was a phenomenal receiver, one of the best I ever saw."

Graham feels Speedie has not been honored because Brown refused to endorse him, keeping hard feelings over his departure. "When the head coach doesn't back you, it's hard to make it," he said. Hall of Famer or not, he was one of the Browns' finest players.

Brown Defined Football in Cleveland, Cincinnati

PAUL BROWN *Dec. 10, 1999*

As the Browns prepare to play the Cincinnati Bengals Sunday, let us bow our heads in memory of the late Paul Brown, the founding coach of both teams.

Brown was the flinty genius who brought pro football into the modern age. He invented the playbook, the detailed study of game films and the face bar on helmets. He was the first to hire assistant coaches full time at each position and give mental tests to players.

Most of his former players regard him as the greatest football coach in history. "He doesn't get the credit he deserves because he never played up to the New York press," two of his Hall of Famers, Otto Graham and Dante Lavelli, said.

When he started the Browns in 1946, Brown said he wanted to make the team the New York Yankees of pro football. He came close to succeeding. In the 15-year period from 1946 to 1960, before Art Modell came along, his teams won seven league championships, lost four times in title games, and finished second in their conference three other times.

Brown, the small-town boy from Norwalk, ran the Browns like a dictator. "He didn't allow us to talk to reporters," said Edgar "Special Delivery" Jones, the former running back. "And he didn't talk much to us."

"When you win a game, say little," Brown ordered. "When you lose, say nothing."

Kenny Konz, the old defensive back, recalled the speech Brown would give at the start of each training camp. "If anybody here is playing just for the money, you can get up and leave right now," he would say.

The Monday meetings after games are what the old Browns remember most about the coach. The team would gather in a conference room, watching the game films.

"You didn't want to get your name mentioned too often," Lou "The Toe" Groza recalled. "If you did, you weren't going to be around long. He'd single out a guy for a bad play and say, 'Look at yourself. What were you thinking about?' Then the guys would kid you later on top of it.'"

"I made a mistake in a game and he kept running the film back and forth," Mike "Moe" Scarry, the Browns' first center, remembered. "He said, 'Is that you, Moe? Is that you?' I said, 'Yes, sir, that's me.' Nobody laughed in those sessions, no sir. But I never heard the man swear or raise his voice. He was very quiet, but when he got nose to nose with you with those piercing eyes, you got the message."

Brown never played favorites. Scarry, for example, was one of his early captains, a fine player. Even the great quarterback Graham was no stranger to his needle.

"One time, Otto was the last man at a meeting and Paul climbed all over his butt," Konz said. "He said, 'You're supposed to be our team leader.'"

At the start of each season, Brown would stare at a team full of future Hall of Famers—Graham, Lavelli, Groza, Marion Motley, Bill Willis—and say, "Don't any of you think you've got your position locked up. You've got to earn your job." According to Lavelli, the great fullback, Motley, fell asleep while sitting in a back row during a team meeting. Brown hit him in the face with a towel and brought him to the front row.

Brown had strict training rules. "If you have to smoke, don't smoke in public," he said. "If you drink, you're fired." Brown had his soft side too. Bob Gain, former tackle, was called into the service during the Korean War. "Paul would call my wife once a week and ask if she needed anything," Gain said. "He was very generous."

When guard Jim Ray Smith's father was dying, Brown talked quietly with him every day.

Brown was never a front-runner. Konz recalls the 1953 NFL title game in which Detroit's Jim Doran got behind Warren Lahr, the

Browns' all-pro defensive back, and caught the winning touchdown pass with two minutes left. Brown told the disconsolate Lahr on the ride home, "I'm giving you a $500 raise because I believe in you." Physically, Brown had the easiest and shortest workouts in pro football, about an hour and 15 minutes a day. "Guys who came to us from other teams couldn't believe it," said former center John Morrow. "Paul's theory was that you can't learn when you're physically tired. Everything was so well organized he didn't need any more time. He had it down to a science."

Milt Plum, the Browns quarterback who succeeded Graham, recalled that Brown called every play. "We could not audible," Plum said. "One time we were playing the Steelers, and he called for a run. At the line, I saw nobody was guarding Ray Renfro. The Steelers had only 10 men on the field. So I took a chance and passed to Renfro for a touchdown. Brown just looked at me. Good thing it worked."

As time went on, Brown became closer to the great players who had won so many titles for him. "You could come off the field and tell him a play would work, and he'd listen to you," Gain recalled. Proof of the affection many of the players had for Brown is that several asked him to be their presenter when they were inducted into the Hall of Fame years later.

Only once did the old Browns ever challenge Brown. That was before the 1954 NFL championship game against Detroit in the Stadium. The Lions had beaten the Browns in close title games the previous two years and there was talk that Brown's play-calling had become too conservative.

The night before the game, Lavelli, Graham and the other superstars gathered in the Carter Hotel, where the team was staying. They agreed to call their own plays if the score was going against them. The plan never came to fruition because the Browns came out of the gate fast under the coach's plays and destroyed the Lions, 56-10. Things began to change when Art Modell bought the Browns in 1961. "Modell was envious of Brown," said Galen Fiss, former linebacker and captain. "He looked at Brown as a threat to his position. He was resentful of the respect Paul had."

Brown chafed under Modell's presence. "Paul didn't like it when Art would come to practice," Plum said. "You could see he was ticked off. His face would get red. They'd go over to the side and talk."

Fiss recalled that Modell was always chatting with Browns players, much more so than previous owners ever did. "We went to the

West Coast on a train, and Art was cornering guys and trying to build a case against Paul," Fiss said.

"When an owner fraternizes with the players, it's a bad deal," Smith said. "He's undercutting the coaches."

"Those last two years Paul was losing his focus," Gain said. "His wife was going blind and he took her all over the world, trying to find a cure. And he had the infighting with Modell." After Brown went 8-5-1 and 7-6-1 in his two seasons under Modell, he was fired. The coach's record in Cleveland was 167-53-8 for a .759 percentage.

For five years, Brown brooded at his home, collecting the $90,000 a year Modell owed him. His first wife died and he remarried. In 1968 he emerged, becoming the coach, general manager and part owner of the new Cincinnati Bengals of the American Football League.

In 1970, Brown performed one of the most astounding coaching feats of his career, winning the Central Division title in his first year in the NFL. His 3-year-old team beat out the Browns, who had gone 11-3 the previous season. The 62-year-old Brown ran off the field like a schoolboy after the Bengals defeated the Browns, 14-10. At age 67, in his final coaching season, Brown led the Bengals to an 11-3 record. He continued to run the front office and the Bengals got into two Super Bowls.

The Browns are still trying to get into their first one.

A Stunning Show of Speed

BOBBY MITCHELL *Oct. 14, 1999*

One of the great but forgotten individual performances in Browns history occurred on Nov. 15, 1959, when Bobby Mitchell pranced and danced his way to 232 yards rushing in a 31-17 victory over the Redskins in Washington.

Mitchell, perhaps the fastest man ever to play for the Browns, carried the football only 14 times that day. He averaged an amazing 16.6 yards per carry and finished 5 yards short of the existing NFL record of 237 yards, held by teammate Jim Brown.

"It was one of those games," recalled Mitchell, 64. "I was hot. Every time I touched the ball it was plus yardage. Even on the short runs I was getting 7, 8 or 9 yards. Games like that don't come along too often.

"Today they'd be interviewing me on ESPN and all the Sunday football shows, but it didn't do much for me then."

Mitchell outshone the celebrated Brown, who ran 16 times for 40 yards that day. "They were keying up on Jim and left it open for me," said Mitchell, who is the Redskins' assistant general manager. Mitchell began his remarkable game with a 90-yard touchdown dash on the Browns' second play from scrimmage, taking a flip from quarterback Milt Plum and going around right end. He recalled that he got a fine crack-back block from teammate Ray Renfro to help spring him. "Then Willie Davis led me halfway down the field," he said. "Once I got past the first wave, the rest was easy."

Mitchell also scored on runs of 23 and 5 yards. "I had all those great blockers on the line," he said, naming Mike McCormack, Jim Ray Smith, Art Hunter, John Wooten and Gene Hickerson. The speedball from the University of Illinois was not given a chance to break Brown's record, however. Coach Paul Brown took him out of the game early.

Mitchell says he did not play the entire fourth quarter. A fan letter to The Plain Dealer at that time complained he was out for the last eight minutes.

Fans were upset about the exit. They felt Mitchell deserved a chance to break Brown's record. In the ensuing days, they wrote scathing letters criticizing the coach for keeping Mitchell out. The move has never been thoroughly explained.

"Everybody was telling Paul I was 5 yards short of the record," Mitchell said. "He said, 'Records don't mean anything to us.' I think so many people were saying I should go back in he got riled up and was going to be stubborn.

"I never approached him about it. It was only my second year in the league, and I was just happy to be there. I know he and I were not having problems. We got along great."

If anything, Mitchell thought Brown might put him back in as a way of keeping Jim Brown in hand. "Jim was so big that Paul loved to stick it to him," he said. "He always looked for little things to prod him. I could see him looking Jim in the eye and saying, 'Heh, heh, Bobby broke your record.'"

Mitchell is convinced he could have set a mark. "I would have had another 100 yards in the fourth quarter," he said. The current NFL record is 275 yards by Chicago's Walter Payton in a 1977 game.

Mitchell had come to the Browns as a Big Ten champion sprinter who could run 100 yards in 9.5 seconds. He loved track and thought about remaining an amateur so he could compete in the 1960 Olympics. "I wasn't that crazy about football anyway," he said. But Brown, always a worshipper of speed, drafted him in the eighth round in 1958. "I was married, so when Paul offered me some money I decided to play football," Mitchell said. His first contract offer was for $7,000.

"I was advised by Tommy O'Connell [former Browns quarterback and a fellow Illinois graduate] to send it back and ask for more," said Mitchell. "Paul then gave me $8,000. He told me, 'When you start working for a living, ask your boss for a $1,000 raise and see what happens.'" Mitchell was a success from the start, running, catching passes out of the backfield and returning kicks. In 1961, he was drafted into the Army but still played for the Browns on weekend leave. As Green Bay began to win championships, coach Brown decided to emulate the Packers offense, which used two big backs in Paul Hornung and Jim Taylor. He felt the 185-pound Mitchell was too small for the role and traded him to Washington for the draft rights to Heisman Trophy winner Ernie Davis.

"I was devastated," said Mitchell. "I loved playing in Cleveland. All my friends were there, Jim Brown and John Wooten and the others. I had just bought a house on the East Side." The trade turned out to be a disaster for Cleveland. Davis, the big back Brown had been yearning for, became ill with leukemia. He died and never played a down for the Browns.

In the meantime, Bill McPeak, the Washington coach, made the move that eventually put Mitchell into the Pro Football Hall of Fame. "He told me he had a good young quarterback in Norm Snead, but that his offensive line wasn't too good," Mitchell remembered. "He asked me what I thought of switching to the outside to become a receiver. I agreed before the words were out of his mouth. Paul Brown had originally wanted to put me at wide receiver, but he had Renfro there."

Renfro, who played for the Browns from 1952 to 1963, was another burner. He still holds the club record of most yards per catch, 19.6, for a career.

Mitchell and Snead had problems during their first exhibition season together. "He couldn't find me and I couldn't find him," Mitchell said. "Finally, in the last exhibition, everything started clicking."

Mitchell led the NFL in receiving yardage in each of his first two years. Any time he caught a pass, he was a threat to go all the way. He is tied with Tony Dorsett with 91 career touchdowns, 16th-best in NFL history. In a game against Cleveland on Sept. 15, 1963, he tied a NFL record by catching a 99-yard touchdown pass from George Izo. He was lethal on kicks, returning eight for touchdowns.

But he still has a mild regret that he didn't break the rushing record on Nov. 15, 1959. "When I played we didn't worry about stats, but now that's what they measure players by," he said. "If I had the record, it would have been proof I was a good runner."

"The Greatest Running Back Ever"

Jim Brown *Nov. 19, 1996*

This is the 35th anniversary of one of Jim Brown's finest days in football.

On Nov. 19, 1961, Brown rushed for 237 yards, tying his National Football League record, as the Browns defeated Philadelphia, 45-24, in front of a Stadium crowd of 68,399.

He was 25, at the peak of his strength and speed. He carried 34 times, with his longest run 18 yards as the desperate Eagles ganged up on him. He scored four touchdowns on short runs. "The blocking was tremendous," Brown said afterward. "I don't think I ran any better than usual. You always go all out and sometimes you gain and sometimes you don't."

"Hold this," an old photographer commanded, handing a football to Brown. "Give us a good smile now."

Jim obeyed, in the style of those times when athletes and journalists considered themselves friendly colleagues. "I wasn't tired," he continued. "I was for a while in the second half, but then I got my second wind. After that, I could have run all day. That was the best blocking of the year. I always had a chance to get to the line of scrimmage and there were places to go after that."

The 228-pound Brown worked with his usual combination of power and elusiveness. At one point he crashed into veteran Eagle back Bobby Freeman and knocked him flat on his back. "Jimmy tore us up," Freeman said. "There is no runner in the league to compare with him. When you think you have him stopped for a yard gain, he ends up with 5 or 6."

Rookie Eagle linebacker Glen Amerson said: "It isn't that he hits so hard, but the way he drags you along until you fall off. That's if you even get a chance to hit him."

Columnist Frank Gibbons of the Cleveland Press was reminded that Los Angeles Rams coach Sid Gillman had predicted disaster for Brown four years earlier because of overwork.

"If he carries the ball that much in many more games he's got to wind up punch drunk or a basket case," Gillman said. He was wrong. Brown repeatedly ran about 30 times a game throughout his nine-year career, which ended when he became a movie actor in 1966.

Gibbons wryly noted that the man in the cashmere topcoat (coach Paul Brown) had a good day calling plays. "The general feeling among those who have been building a scaffold for Brown was that he had his thinking hat on for this one," Gibbons wrote sarcastically.

It should be remembered that 1961 was the first year Art Modell owned the Browns. The new owner was already unhappy with Paul Brown, who considered Modell a football neophyte and felt he was necessary only to pay the bills.

"A couple of blocks and passes go right and you're a genius," Paul Brown said. "If they miss you're a bum." The Browns were 7-3, a game behind the New York Giants. It would be only a little more than a year before the great coach would be fired by Modell.

Former Browns tackle Bob Gain, who was selected to the Pro Bowl five times, played in the game. The Eastlake resident complimented Jim Brown for his ability to take punishment. "Everybody was always gunning for him," Gain said. "At first, the opponents thought he was a prima donna who would quit if they kept hitting him. Sometimes he'd get hit so hard you'd think he'd never get up. But on the next play he'd run like nothing happened. He was very durable and he had terrific balance. He got their respect."

"He'd get up after a tackle and walk real slow back to the huddle," recalled Hall of Famer Mike McCormack, president of the NFL's Carolina Panthers, who was an offensive tackle for the Browns. "Once, when it was real hot, Jim was walking back slower than ever to the huddle. I asked him why he was walking so slow. He said, 'They only pay me to run forward. They don't pay me to go to the huddle.'"

Nothing Brown did on a football field surprised McCormack.

"You expected Jim to do great things," he said. "It gave you a vicarious pleasure to block for him. He'd run in any direction. I liked it when he ran right and I'd pull out and get the linebacker, but the most fun was blocking for him on screen passes. He could take a little pass behind the line of scrimmage and turn it into a 80-yard TD."

Brown caught three passes from Milt Plum in that long-ago game, gaining 52 yards. He also returned a kickoff 24 yards after replacing injured Preston Powell and even made a key block, allowing Bobby Mitchell to race 91 yards for a touchdown on a kickoff.

For years, the critics said Brown never blocked. His old teammates dispute that. "You couldn't expect him to block a heck of a lot when he was carrying the ball 30 times a game," said Gain. "People are always eager to look for chinks in stars," said McCormack. "He could block when he had to block."

It is amazing to recall that the devastating Brown sometimes paired with Mitchell to give the Browns an unbeatable kickoff return duo. "I think they were the greatest kickoff combination ever," said McCormack. "I don't think you'll ever see anything like that again. Today the talent is too spread out, with 30 teams." Outstanding running backs do not perform on specialty teams today.

Gain and McCormack said the team quickly accepted Brown when he arrived as a rookie in 1957. McCormack recalled the sprint races Paul Brown put the players through on the first day of training camp. "He'd clock you and then pair you up for a 40-yard race with somebody of similar speed," said McCormack. "I'd usually race somebody like Lou Groza [Hall of Fame tackle] or Don Colo. Paul put Brown up against Mitchell, who had been the Big Ten sprint champion. Brown weighed about 40 pounds more than Bobby, but he beat him. Bobby couldn't get over it. Later on, he'd challenge Jim to more races and he'd win some and Jim would win some. The whole team would watch when they ran. It was something to see."

It didn't take Paul Brown long to understand he had a running genius in Jim Brown. After seeing him in his first scrimmage, he tersely told him, "You're my fullback."

In the intervening years, with the aid of rules changes designed to put more offense into the NFL, Brown's record of 237 rushing yards in a game has fallen. With the hash marks moved toward the middle of the field and blockers being allowed to use their hands, Walter Payton of Chicago increased the NFL mark to 275 yards in a game in 1977. O.J. Simpson of Buffalo also exceeded Brown's mark a couple of times.

But Gain and McCormack echo the sentiments of most veteran football followers: "Jim Brown was the greatest running back ever," they say.

In '62, Hope Became Heartbreak

ERNIE DAVIS *Aug. 17, 2002*

One of the most heartbreaking moments in Cleveland sports history took place 40 years ago tomorrow, on Aug. 18, 1962. The occasion was the first exhibition football doubleheader in Cleveland Stadium. After Detroit defeated Dallas, 35-24, in the opener, the Stadium was darkened for the introductions of the Browns, who were to meet Pittsburgh in the nightcap. The Browns ran out of the dugout, one by one, receiving applause under the focus of a spotlight.

When the last man came out, the 77,683 patrons stood and shook the ballpark with a thunder of cheers that Plain Dealer sportswriter Chuck Heaton said was the loudest he ever heard in his long career. The ovation was for Ernie Davis, the heralded Browns rookie. It was an open secret that he was a dying man. Davis, 22, trotted out in civilian clothes, wearing a sport coat and tie, then sat on the bench as the Browns routed the Steelers, 33-10. The Heisman Trophy winner of 1961 looked perfectly healthy. Nine months later he was dead from leukemia.

It was a sad end to a story that had begun when Cleveland coach Paul Brown traded future Hall of Famer Bobby Mitchell and a first-round draft pick to Washington for the rights to Davis. Davis had broken most of Jim Brown's records at Syracuse University. Coach Brown's dream was to have the two big runners in the same backfield, alternately hammering opposing lines. "Dad thought they would be an unmatched tandem," said Mike Brown, son of the great coach and now president of the Cincinnati Bengals. "They were both big and awfully fast. We played on a heavy field in Cleveland."

Paul Brown always said he liked a November team. He wanted a backfield that could push the football through the rain, snow and mud of the late season. The champion Green Bay Packers had done that with Jim Taylor and Paul Hornung.

The Browns outbid Buffalo of the American Football League to get Davis, signing him to a three-year contract for $65,000, plus a $15,000 bonus.

But Davis never played a down for the Browns. He soon became ill. Mike Brown recalled that his sickness was discovered at the College All-Star Game before the season.

"He started to bleed in his mouth," Mike Brown said. "At first they thought it was a dental problem."

Instead, it turned out to be the first symptom of his fatal illness. Paul Brown, concerned for Davis' health, restricted his activity to attending practices and meetings, standing on the sidelines and light conditioning.

The Cleveland newspapers, in deference to Davis' feelings, never reported that he had leukemia. They explained his absence by saying he had a "blood disorder." But somehow the word got around. It was common gossip around town that Davis had leukemia. The illness further damaged the already fragile relationship between Browns owner Art Modell and Paul Brown.

"Art wanted my father to play him in a game," said Mike Brown. "My father did not want to play him because he feared for his health. A Cleveland Clinic hematologist had told him he should not play. They had a confrontation over that.

"Art wanted him to return a kickoff. My dad told him that would be like charging a machine gun nest."

Another doctor had told Modell that Davis could play, according to the book "When All the World was Browns Town," by the Akron Beacon Journal's Terry Pluto.

"It would have been crazy to play him," said former Browns teammate Bob Gain. "Other teams wouldn't care if he was ill. They would hit him like anybody else. What if something broke and he started bleeding on the field?"

"We knew what was wrong with him," Gain continued. "It was a shame. He was a friendly, humble guy. All you could say was, 'Keep your chin up and hope for the best.' I think he knew how ill he was."

Gene Hickerson, another teammate, recalled Davis' appearance: "He looked as healthy as any other guy. It was amazing. That used to bug me. You look at someone like that and you know he's going to die, it's terrible."

"I think of Ernie a lot," said former Brown Dick Schafrath. "He always thought he'd beat it. I've had cancer three times and you have to feel that way. The Browns did the right thing in not letting him play, but he was on our basketball team during the winter. He was great in basketball. You wouldn't think there was anything wrong."

Gain and Hickerson both feel Davis would have been a tremendous addition to the Browns.

"If he'd been all right, we would have been better than Green Bay," said Gain. "There would have been no stopping us." Both running backs were about 6-2, with Brown weighing 230 and Davis 215, huge for backs at that time.

Hickerson said: "Ernie might have pushed Jim Brown a little. In appearance and size, he looked like a great running back. He had a body that was unstoppable, like Jim."

Former quarterback Frank Ryan, however, feels the duo would not have clicked. "Paul Brown would have had real difficulty having them in the same backfield," Ryan said. "It would have been a disaster. Jim was used to being a one-man show. Both were great, but both needed to be the focal point, not the bifocal."

It is a question that will never be answered. Davis, looking healthy to the end, except for a slightly swollen neck, entered Lakeside Hospital in May 1963. He died 36 hours later. Browns players and coaches attended his funeral in Elmira, N.Y. It was said to be the biggest funeral in the city's history. A thousand people crammed into the First Baptist Church for the services. Another 3,000 stood outside. President John F. Kennedy, who had invited Davis to the White House after he won the Heisman, sent a telegram of condolence.

The Browns retired his jersey, No. 45.

Jim Brown said: "He was a champion, a real champion. Just a wonderful fellow."

"Everyone was jolted," said Mike Brown. "It was a tragedy."

The Browns' Other Toe

DON COCKROFT *Oct. 21, 1999*

Life has changed for Don Cockroft. For 13 seasons he kicked footballs for the Browns in front of screaming, massive crowds at the old Stadium, performing splendidly under extreme pressure. Now he lives quietly in a cabin outside Lake George, Colo., a mile-and-a-half away from the nearest human.

"My neighbors are mountain lions, deer and bighorn elk," Cockroft said over the phone. "I watched a mountain lion for 10 minutes the other day and he watched me. He was about 200 yards from the cabin, where he just killed a deer."

Do not get the idea that Cockroft, 54, is a hermit. He drives 57 miles to Colorado Springs each day, where he works as a vice president with Alliance Petroleum.

His cabin is not the sort you would associate with a pioneer in the Old West either. It has 25-foot windows, three bedrooms and 1,400 square feet.

Cockroft's family lives around Colorado Springs. He is divorced from his wife, Dianna, whom he dated since the ninth grade. They were married more than 30 years.

"We have a cordial relationship," he said. The Cockrofts have two grown daughters, Michelle, a teacher, and Melinda, a consultant for Creative Memories, a photo service. Their son, Matt, 18, lives with Dianna and often goes hunting with Cockroft.

"He's a good basketball player on the high school team," Cockroft said with pride. "He has a vertical leap of 33 inches."

From time to time, Cockroft might tell his son stories of his exploits with the Browns. The kicker scored 1,080 points, second on the team only to Lou "The Toe" Groza, who had 1,345. Cockroft kicked 216 field goals, the longest coming from 57 yards against Denver in 1972.

His most notable kick came on Nov. 19, 1972, when he booted a 26-yard field goal with 13 seconds left to defeat the Pittsburgh Steelers, 26-24, in the rain and cold in front of 83,009 at the Stadium. "It was the most memorable game of my entire career," Cockroft said. Cockroft was the goat only two minutes earlier, when he missed from 27 yards after Steelers rookie Franco Harris ran 75 yards for a touchdown and a 24-23 Pittsburgh lead.

"When I missed, life ended for me right there," he said. "I had been making almost every kick all year but then I missed the most important kick of my career."

Linebacker Billy Andrews told the downcast Cockroft: "Keep your chin up. We'll get the ball back."

Andrews' words were prophetic. The Browns forced the Steelers to punt. Quarterback Mike Phipps drove the team downfield and Cockroft was called on again.

"I was praying like never before," he recalled. "The ball was in almost the exact spot where I had just missed. The field was terrible, a good old Cleveland mud bath. Other kickers used to say to me, 'How can you kick in that place week after week? It's horrendous.'"

Cockroft knew he missed the previous kick because he was overanxious. Center Fred Hoaglin snapped the ball to holder Phipps and this time Cockroft kept his head down and followed through. "The ball was dead center," said Cockroft. "I looked up at the sky and said, 'Thank you, Lord.' I was never so thankful. The guys surrounded me after the kick. I never got hit so hard.'" The victory put the Browns in a tie with Pittsburgh at 7-3 with four games to go. Cleveland wound up 10-4, a game behind the Steelers.

Cockroft credited Al Tabor, Browns assistant coach from 1972 to 1977, for making the key contribution to his kicking career. After a fine rookie season in '68, Cockroft struggled the next three years, and the Browns drafted kicker George Hunt in the fifth round in '72. "I think Art Modell wanted to keep Hunt, but Tabor said, 'Who do you want, the best kicker or George Hunt? Cockroft is the best kicker.' Al gave me tremendous support mentally. He helped me believe in myself. It gets lonely out there.'"

Once Cockroft kicked a 35-yard field goal in horrible weather, with no grass under the ball. Tabor said to him: "If you can make that kick, you can make any kick."

Cockroft was also the team's punter for nine years. "I was the last double-duty kicker in the NFL," he said. "In those days, the roster limit was 40 players, so if you could both kick and punt you gave the team another position player. I took great pride in my punting."

Cockroft, who still holds the club career record for most punts (651), said punting was more demanding than place-kicking. "When you punt, you have to catch the ball, drop it, and the steps have to be right there," he said. "In place-kicking the ball is sitting there." He said the techniques in punting are entirely different from place-kicking. "But I don't think it affected me," he said.

When Cockroft entered the NFL, the only soccer-style kickers were Pete and Charlie Gogolak. When he departed in 1981, he and Mark Moseley were the only straight-on kickers left. "The soccer style makes sense," Cockroft said. "You have more room on your foot to kick and you see the ball a little longer."

The kick Cockroft did not get to take has a vital role in Browns history. That was when quarterback Brian Sipe threw an interception in the end zone on the infamous Red Right 88 play with 49 seconds remaining in a playoff game after the 1980 season. A field goal by Cockroft would have meant almost certain victory for the Browns, who lost 14-12.

"I was disappointed when I didn't get the chance to kick it," said Cockroft, who had missed two field-goal attempts and an extra point on the cold, windy day. "It was the end of my career, even though I wasn't ready to retire."

Cockroft, who had surgeries for torn knee cartilage and a herniated disk during the off-season, came to camp in 1981 to compete for the kicking job with rookie Dave Jacobs. During the preseason, Browns coach Sam Rutigliano told him: "You've had a great career, but we've decided to go with Jacobs."

"I told Sam he had hired a flaky kicker," Cockroft recalled. "If this kid makes a few field goals, he'll be OK. But if he misses a few, you're in trouble."

Cockroft proved to be right. Jacobs was released after a few games. Cockroft, in the meantime, has a secure place in the Browns' record book.

Twenty Years Ago, It Was Sam's Town

SAM RUTIGLIANO *Nov. 18, 1999*

Time gallops onward. Sam Rutigliano, probably the most likable coach in Browns history, is already in his 11th season of coaching football at Liberty University in Lynchburg, Va. Fifteen years have passed since Browns owner Art Modell fired him.

Rutigliano, 67, sounds happy to be at Division I-AA Liberty, where he has a career 63-46 record.

His health is excellent. He and his wife, Barbara, who have been married 44 years, have three grandchildren. Two of his three children have jobs with the Liberty football program. The Rutiglianos still maintain their home in Kirtland Hills, spending several months here every year.

When he is in town, Rutigliano attends Indians and Cavaliers games. He has not seen the Browns yet, but plans to do so. "Cleveland is an unbelievable city," he said. "Everywhere I go, the fans tell me how they appreciated the fun of the Kardiac Kids and the way I handled the job."

Like all coaches, Rutigliano had his second-guessers when he was with the Browns. But nobody could criticize his personal style. He was the opposite of the grim coach of football cliché. He enjoyed talking to the media, players and fans.

"He should have been a philosopher," said former receiver Reggie Rucker, 52, who credits him with saving his career with a stern lecture when he was in the dumps. "He knew how to reach people." Even Modell once said of Rutigliano, "He relates better to players than any coach I've ever seen."

When the Browns lost a tough game, Rutigliano offered solace to his team with the immortal line, "Eight hundred million Chinese don't even know you played."

When a quarterback made a poor decision and threw an interception, he said dryly, "He should have thrown it to the blonde in the first row of the bleachers."

Rucker recalled Rutigliano's swarthy complexion and the way he was picked up in limousines wherever the Browns played. "I was convinced he was in the Mafia," Rucker laughs. "He looked like a Mafia guy and so did the guys in the limos. He got a kick when I told him that. But they were just his friends. Sam had friends everywhere."

Rutigliano led the Browns to one of their most exciting seasons, the Kardiac Kids year of 1980, and was twice voted United Press International Coach of the Year during his tenure with Cleveland from 1978 to 1984.

Asked to name the highlight of his time in Cleveland, Rutigliano selected the Browns' 27-24 victory in Cincinnati in the final game of the 1980 season, which put the team into the playoffs for the first time in eight years.

"We were tied at the half, 10-10, and then Cincinnati intercepted a pass by Brian Sipe and the Bengals went ahead, 17-10," Rutigliano recalled. "Brian came back to the bench and said, with that supreme confidence he always had, 'Don't worry, we're going to beat these guys.'

"I said to him, 'Yeah, Brian, but you've got to start throwing the ball to our guys.'"

Sipe responded by hurling for more than 300 yards for the sixth time of the season and the Browns rallied to win on Don Cockroft's 22-yard field goal with 1:25 left. The players carried Rutigliano off the field. Every coach and player was given a game ball. "I'll never forget the reception at the airport after the game," Rutigliano said. "There were about 20,000 people there. We couldn't land the jet."

"Mayor [George] Voinovich erected a stage on the tarmac," said Rucker, who caught a touchdown pass in the game. "It was the most spectacular thing I ever saw." The players went onstage at the Brook Park Tank Plant to wild applause from the fans. It was the fifth time in the season that the Browns had won by three or fewer points and the town decided to celebrate that Christmas week.

"It was amazing," Rutigliano said. "Just going Christmas shopping was great. I knew it could be a once-in-a-lifetime thing, so I savored it."

"Sam was the king of Cleveland," said Rucker, who is still close to Rutigliano.

It all came apart two weeks later as the Browns lost to Oakland, 14-12, when Sipe's second-down pass toward Ozzie Newsome was intercepted by Mike Davis, who made a diving catch in the end zone on the infamous Red Right 88 play.

When the broken-hearted Sipe came off the field, Rutigliano said to him, "I love you, Brian." Never a front-runner, it was the coach's way of reminding the quarterback of the great season he had. Sipe was the NFL MVP that year.

Rutigliano maintains that he made the correct decision in having Sipe pass with the ball deep in Oakland territory, instead of having Cockroft go for a field goal. It was a windy day with a temperature of zero. Cockroft had already missed two field goals and one extra point. "I would have had Cockroft kick on fourth down," he said.

"Davis made one of the greatest plays I've ever seen," Rucker said.

The Browns slipped off the precipice after that game, going 5-11 in 1981. Rutigliano blames injuries, along with the cycle of luck. "We lost the close games we had won the year before," he said. After the 4-5 strike year of 1982, plus a playoff loss, Rutigliano coached the team to a 9-7 season in 1983 before being fired with the Browns at 1-7 in 1984.

Before his departure, Rutigliano created the Browns' Inner Circle program, to help players who had drug problems. The players, whose identities were kept secret, met several times a week with psychiatrists, counselors and Rutigliano. They were given urine tests every couple of days.

"We learned that some players were snorting drugs at halftime," Rutigliano said.

Some observers thought Rutigliano became more interested in saving souls than winning football games. Rucker disagrees. "Sam was way ahead of his time," Rucker said. "He was doing what corporations do today, providing help instead of throwing good employees into the trash bin."

Rutigliano was only 53 when he was fired. Surprisingly, he never coached in the NFL again.

"I could have coached Buffalo," Rutigliano recalled. "I was contacted by other teams. But I made up my mind I didn't want to do it anymore. When I left the NFL after 18 years, we had moved 19 times, sold 12 houses and our kids had gone to 23 schools."

"He was disillusioned," said Rucker. "He was the toast of the town one moment, and then got fired the next. I knew the Browns were letting a good man go. It was a tough day for me."

Rutigliano had another incentive for getting out of the big-time grind. Modell had to pay him for the remaining five years of his contract. "It was better than being on welfare," Rutigliano joked. "If I took another NFL job he would only have had to pay me the difference in salaries. It would have been like working for nothing."

Rutigliano makes no effort to disguise his feelings about Modell, who transferred the old Browns out of Cleveland to Baltimore in 1995.

"That was a betrayal of the city," Rutigliano said. "He lies through his teeth when he talks about what he gave the city. The city gave him far more than he gave the city."

Rutigliano derisively speaks of "that whole gang" on Modell's staff. "He is surrounded by phonies who tell him what he wants to hear," Rutigliano said. "They're only interested in themselves.

"He fired coach Paul Brown, the greatest of the greatest. If he hadn't done that he would have gone to five or six Super Bowls." Rutigliano said he knew he was going to have trouble with Modell in his first season.

"I told my wife I was not going to grow old gracefully in this job," Rutigliano recalled. "He had too many people involved, criticizing personnel decisions. Art didn't interfere, but he interfered."

Rutigliano's major regret is that he let Sipe escape to the United States Football League after the 1983 season. He thought young Paul McDonald was the quarterback who would pick up where Sipe left off. "That was my mistake," he said. McDonald never made it. "I think we could have kept Sipe if we sweetened the [financial] pot," Rutigliano said. "I think we could have got into the Super Bowl once or twice."

Notorious Interception No Longer Haunts Former Browns Quarterback

BRIAN SIPE *Dec. 3, 1999*

That old surfer and matinee idol, Brian Sipe, is enjoying the sunshine and warm waters of the Pacific these days. "As we speak, I'm staring out the window at the ocean," said Sipe, 50, whose house is on the beach in Del Mar, Calif. "I go surfing nearly every day with my son, Nolan, who's 14. He wants to become a professional surfer. It's a great workout, just like swimming. I feel like a kid. I've been a surfer since junior high school."

Sipe, who holds most of the Browns' career-passing records, is a house designer. His current project is a 7,000-square-foot Spanish colonial home that will be built near a golf course. His clients are primarily people who want dream homes.

Many fans were disappointed Sipe did not attend last week's reunion of 120 former Browns in Cleveland.

"I was there for the new stadium opener," Sipe explained. "That was my one shot for the year. I'm trying to raise a family and make a buck."

Sipe is an expert on the kind of physical pounding rookie quarterback Tim Couch has been taking this season. Couch was knocked into a daze last Sunday, but continued to play and led a touchdown drive.

Sipe's problems were more serious than Couch's. He suffered from concussions going back to his high school days and while playing at San Diego State.

"I had at least nine concussions with the Browns," recalled Sipe. "I just figured it was part of the game. Eventually, they had a lot to do with my decision to retire."

Like Couch, it was tough to get Sipe out of the game. He played through a lot of the concussions. "I didn't want anybody to find out I didn't belong in there," he joked.

After some concussions, Sipe could not remember the game the next day. "A concussion is a bruise of the brain," he said. "It causes disorientation and confusion. It's like a computer being erased. You feel like you're looking through a tunnel. You lose your short-term memory and can't call plays. That's when you have to leave." In an effort to end the concussions, Sipe experimented with various medicines and even tried breathing through a bag on the sidelines. Nothing helped.

Sipe gave the opposition a continual headache in 1980, when he was voted the NFL's Most Valuable Player, throwing for 4,132 yards and 30 touchdowns. He has fond memories of the Browns' division-clinching victory in Cincinnati in the final game of the regular season.

"There was a plane delay and we had to spend two hours in the Cincinnati airport after the game," Sipe recalled. "It was the most fun I ever had with the team. Everybody was buying us beer, even the Cincinnati fans. Then we had that great reception when we got back to Cleveland."

Two weeks later, the season ended when Sipe threw the infamous interception on the Red Right 88 play in a first-round playoff game against Oakland. The Browns were deep in Raiders territory when Mike Davis stole the pass intended for Ozzie Newsome. "I was hit right after I threw the ball," Sipe remembered. "I was down on the ground and didn't see Davis intercept. But the crowd got completely quiet. That's how I knew what happened. I was numbed. It was a long time before I sorted it out." Sipe said the second-down pass from the Oakland 12 was originally intended to be a crossing slant to Dave Logan. "If he was not open I was supposed to throw it away," he said. "But they showed blitz and I saw Ozzie one-on-one with Davis. Ozzie was open. I threw a good pass and thought it would be a touchdown, but it was an icy, windy day and the ball didn't go where I intended. In September I'm going to hit that pass every time."

In the aftermath of the 14-12 loss, Sipe was angry with coach Sam Rutigliano for calling the play. "I assumed we'd run a play and then kick the field goal," Sipe said. "But now I realize Sam gave me the biggest compliment you can give a player when he made the call. He felt I could make the play. But I let him down. I regret it very much. It was hard for me to reconcile with that."

Sipe has come to terms with the disappointment. "I don't think we ever had a Super Bowl quality team," he said. "In 1980, we almost got there by sheer tenacity."

He consoles himself with the thought that the Browns, who had a porous pass defense, probably would have lost their next game anyway. They would have met San Diego and Dan Fouts, an outstanding quarterback.

"It was better we went out with a bang instead of a whimper," he said. "The way we lost people will always remember us."

Sipe never even thought he would have an NFL career when he was drafted in the 13th round in 1972. "I thought my chances were zero to none," he said. "I was hoping I'd be able to spend a year or two in the NFL. It was like a kid visiting the circus for the first time."

But once he came to training camp, Sipe realized the quarterbacks, led by Mike Phipps, were not that far out of his range. Strangely, Sipe was casual about the opportunity.

"I wasn't real serious," he said. "I just didn't have a good work ethic. It was the 1970s and I had a surfer's mentality." Coach Nick Skorich, who often yelled at Sipe, put him on the taxi squad. Sipe fully expected to be cut coming into camp in the second season, after the Browns acquired a couple of backup quarterbacks. "But one guy couldn't bench press 150 pounds and was let go," he recalled. "He was the most important guy in my career." When he began playing in exhibitions, it became obvious Sipe was a leader who could move the football. He kept his taxi squad job. By 1974, Skorich had him start some games and he moved on from there.

Sipe, who holds the Browns' NFL career records in touchdown passes (154), completions (1,944) and yards (23,713), had many memorable games. One came when he sparked a 26-7 defeat of the powerful Dallas Cowboys in a Monday night game at the Stadium in 1979. "My father was dying from cancer," he recalled. "I knew this might be the last time I'd see him. Sam let him come to all the practices." A week later, his father died.

With the Browns playing in San Diego this week, it is worth remembering that Sipe hit Harry Holt for a 48-yard touchdown pass to beat the Chargers in overtime, 30-24, in 1983. That was Sipe's last season in Cleveland. His time with the Browns did not end happily.

"I knew I was no longer wanted that year," he said. "I was playing without a contract and they weren't answering calls from my agent." It was clear to Sipe the Browns were favoring Paul McDonald, the quarterback they had just drafted.

"Finally, with four games left, [owner] Art Modell gave me an offer at the airport. It was less than the offer to McDonald. Here I'm trying to take my team to the playoffs and he's offering my backup more than me."

Sipe knew it was time to leave. After the Browns finished 9-7, he signed with the New Jersey Generals of the United States Football League, getting a guaranteed $2.2 million for three years. "The Browns played poker with me and they lost," he said. "It was too bad. We had the makings of a very good team in Cleveland, a lot of talent."

McDonald did not make it with the Browns. Sipe played two years in the USFL, then retired because of injuries. "My biggest regret is that we never played in a Super Bowl," Sipe said. "But I don't know anybody who played in the NFL who felt he got 100 percent out of his career. It's always a bittersweet experience."

Don't Get the Rocking Chair Yet for Durable Dieken

DOUG DIEKEN *Aug. 16, 1984*

The Browns have been trying to have the venerable Doug Dieken stuffed, mounted and placed over the mantel for years. Every summer they produce a candidate who might be able to send him to a rest home for the happy retirement his efforts so rightly deserve.

Several years ago it was Cody Risien. Dieken withstood the challenge and Risien had to find employment on the other side of the Browns' offensive line, where he labors with extreme effectiveness.

Last year it was Bill Contz who is big and strong and possesses all the necessary instincts. Dieken survived again. Contz is now a utility man, playing center, tackle and guard.

This year the Browns have summoned Paul Farren, a 6-5, 260-pounder who was in the fifth grade when Dieken began playing left offensive tackle for the Browns in 1971. Farren played the whole game Monday as the Browns beat the Los Angeles Rams. His name wasn't mentioned once, suggesting he did a good job. Anonymous offensive linemen get a call only when they are caught holding or when they let a defender slip by them for a sack of the quarterback.

"Farren's good," said Dieken yesterday. "He's gonna be real good. He might be Groza's great-grandson. I thought Contz might be. But he was only an illegitimate child last year."

The reference was to Lou Groza, who started the amazing dynasty of left offensive tackles with the Browns. In the 34 years the team has been in the National Football League, it has had only three men at the position. There was Groza, from 1950 to 1959; Dick Schafrath, from 1959 to 1971, and Dieken.

In Dieken's humorous turn of mind, they represent the great-grandfather, the grandfather and the father.

To appreciate how long Dieken has been on the job, consider that gasoline cost 34 cents a gallon when he arrived, and that Richard Nixon was making tricks in the White House.

"Hopefully, I'll be around long enough to get a Super Bowl ring," said Dieken, 35.

Don't laugh at Dieken's optimism. With the NFL suffering from the disease of parity, it could happen any autumn.

Farren willing, Dieken will play in his 188th consecutive game for the Browns when they open the season in Seattle Sept. 3. That will equal the club record held by kicker Don Cockroft.

Perhaps it would be fitting and proper if Dieken moved Cockroft off the honor roll. Having a kicker hold an endurance mark in a rough game like football is like giving a medal for gallantry to an army sergeant who spends the war behind a desk.

But Dieken's record is a bit of a phony too. In 1980, he suffered sprained knee ligaments in a Monday night football game. The next Sunday against Baltimore, coach Sam Rutigliano sent him in for the first play and then pulled him, keeping the streak breathing.

"If I had to play I could have," said Dieken, defending his iron man reputation. "But at that time Baltimore was no challenge and we were playing Pittsburgh the next week. Sam put me in because he respected the fact I had the streak going and that it meant a lot to me. As an offensive lineman, there's not many rewards you can get."

One thing Dieken has always received a lot of is the attention of the officials. In the old days, he was always being called for holding, sometimes three times in a game. Lately, he seems to have cut down on that vice, perhaps because of the liberalized rules which allow offensive linemen to push opponents with their hands.

"Everybody was doing it anyway," he said. "So they legalized it."

Dieken has few regrets about his holding calls. "I was just trying to make sure some quarterback didn't get carried off the field," he said.

He rates Elvin Bethea, who retired from the Houston Oilers this year, as the best all-around end he ever faced, with Lee Roy Selmon of Tampa Bay next and Joe Klecko of the New York Jets in the third spot. For pure pass rushing, he picks Lyle Alzado of the Los Angeles Raiders.

"But we don't only go one-on-one the way we used to," he said. "That was a real street fight. Now I don't always block the end. I might go for the linebacker and somebody else might take the end. The blocking schemes are all different."

It could be that Dieken has lasted as long as he has because he came up the hard way. He was a lowly sixth-round draft choice. "I didn't even take my suitcase out of the car when I came to camp the first time," he said.

"I was just going to wing it. I actually got waived and Miami claimed me. But somehow they withdrew the claim and I went on the Browns' cab squad."

He's had a job ever since, even though a lot of guys have tried to take it away from him.

Postscript: Dieken's streak of 203 consecutive games, a Browns team record, ended in 1984.

Byner Plays It Tough on the Field

EARNEST BYNER *Dec. 24, 1985*

With all the talk about reading defenses, memorizing playbooks and absorbing terminology, it is easy to forget that football is a game for very, very tough people.

The more brutes you have on your side in this form of legalized mugging, the better off you are.

That is why Browns coach Marty Schottenheimer likes Earnest Byner. Pound-for-pound the fullback is one of the most violent players in the National Football League. He plays mad.

He was always like that. When he was a young child in Louisville, Ga., he was always getting into fights.

"I was really a bully," the NFL's newest 1,000-yard rusher said yesterday. "I had a bad attitude, a bad temper. I was always starting fights. I looked for fights. I probably would have been in serious trouble if I hadn't gone into sports."

Like many extremely rough men, Byner has a jovial, extroverted personality. Maybe it is because he gets all of his hostilities out on the field. He is still getting into battles. Hardly a game goes by that he isn't in a scuffle.

"When I'm on the field, I won't let anybody take advantage of me or the Browns," he said, referring to cheap shots.

Last Sunday, in the loss to the New York Jets, Byner scrimmaged with Harry Hamilton, Jet safetyman. "He blocked me in the back," said Byner. "So I blocked him in the back."

The two scuffled briefly, but were separated. For the rest of the game, Hamilton kept yelling to his teammates, "Dog him out," in reference to Byner.

"I said, 'I'll dog you out.'" Byner recollected. "After the game was over, he said, 'Nice game.'"

Byner's worst imbroglio took place against New England this season when he threw punches at Ray Clayborn, Patriot cornerback, in a fight that involved many players.

It isn't that Byner is a stark, raving madman. He goes into a game trying to maintain an attitude of businesslike calm. But all kinds of sins, unseen to the fans, take place amid the pileups.

Byner said he endured numerous fouls from nose tackle Jerry Boyarsky in the last Cincinnati game. "I took it and I took it," Byner said. "I told him, 'You gotta stay away from me, you're hurting me.' He was hitting the back of my legs and twisting my legs when we were on the ground."

It did not matter to the 5-10, 215-pound Byner that Boyarsky weights 290 pounds and is built like a bison. He stuck up for his rights.

Schottenheimer always tries to pacify Byner in such situations. He doesn't want one of his best players thrown out of the game. According to Byner, Schottenheimer tells him, "Get his number and we'll get him fair later."

That means the Browns will attack an offender with extra, but legal, vigor.

Byner, a 10th-round draft pick from East Carolina, was sitting on the bench as a rookie last year until Schottenheimer took over the coaching job in mid-season. One of his first moves was to give Byner the fullback job ahead of veteran Mike Pruitt.

The move has worked out well, even though the released Pruitt showed he still has life by running for more than 100 yards in a game for Kansas City this season.

Byner went over the 1,000-yard rushing mark Sunday. In these days of the 16-game season, that is not an accomplishment on the level of MacArthur storming Inchon, but it is still pretty good.

Byner and comrade Kevin Mack form only the third tandem in pro football history in which each partner has run for at least 1,000 yards.

They are in fast company with Franco Harris and Rocky Bleier and Larry Csonka and Mercury Morris.

Schottenheimer is a nice, gentle man, but he admires nothing more than a player who relishes collisions with full force.

In the 1984 training camp, when Schottenheimer was still defensive coordinator, he told the lightly regarded Byner that he liked the way he played and had confidence in him.

"He probably liked the way I blocked Chip Banks (Pro Bowl linebacker) a couple of times in scrimmages," said Byner. "I hurt all over after I hit him, but I made the block."

The pro scouts obviously blew it when they ranked Byner as a lowly 10th-round choice. "I think I got lost in the crowd that year because East Carolina had so many other talented players," he said. "Terry Long, Steve Hamilton and Chet Harris were all drafted before me."

It figures that Byner's favorite running maneuver is the Mash 'Em Play, labeled the 26 Power O, in which he goes between guard and tackle. Byner gave each member of the offensive line a bottle of champagne after he cracked the 1,000-yard figure Sunday. "A small token of my appreciation," he said.

A Nice Guy Who Finishes First

KEVIN MACK *Oct. 13, 1985*

It has been a long time since the Browns' clubhouse has been adorned with a fellow as friendly and humble as Kevin Mack, the rookie running star.

The burly 23-year-old, whose thighs are as wide as a chorus girl's waist, is respectful to elders. He answers questions with a shy smile. There is never a hint of braggadocio in his voice. Reporters seeking colorful quotes are advised to go elsewhere.

He behaves more like a guy trying to make the team than the player who is leading the Browns in rushing and pass yardage and is tied for the lead in scoring with running mate Earnest Byner.

Maybe that is why he hasn't received more attention. As some extroverts claim, "If you don't tell the world about yourself, nobody else will."

"He's such a nice kid," said center Mike Baab, who has the locker next to Mack's in the Browns' clubhouse, "He just sits in a corner and doesn't talk to anybody. I have to poke him with a stick to make him talk to me."

"I talk to him now and then," protested Mack, smiling. He was always that way, even back in his hometown of Kings Mountain, N.C. "I stayed pretty much to myself," he said.

Mack makes all his noise on the field. It is beginning to look as though the Browns made a great move when they signed him out of the United States Football League.

Mack ran for 130 yards against San Diego two weeks ago and came back with 115 more in the New England game last week. He also mixed in 12 catches for 134 yards in the two games.

Even though he hardly played in the opener, after five games he ranks fourth in the National Football League in total yardage on runs and passes.

"Right now Kevin is one of the best backs in the NFL," said linebacker Eddie Johnson. "Before it's over, he might be the best. He reminds me of Herschel Walker. He picks holes extremely well. Some backs just run straight ahead, but he waits to see what the line is doing."

"When you first see him run you might think he's timid," said safety Al Gross. "But he reads, takes small steps and bursts through. Not too many guys can grab him by the shirt and pull him down."

These are pretty good accolades for a player who signed with Los Angeles of the USFL because he wasn't sure if he had the ability to make it in the NFL.

"I didn't want to start out in the NFL and have a big letdown, maybe get cut," Mack said.

Now that he is in the major league, Mack says there isn't that much difference between the two. "The guys in the NFL are more serious, more competitive," he said. "Maybe they're a little bigger and stronger, too. But there's not really that much difference physically."

Coach Marty Schottenheimer gave him the encouraging words he needed when he came here. After watching him in an exhibition game against Buffalo last August, he told the new man, "You're better than 90% of the guys out there."

So far it looks as though Schottenheimer is correct.

Nevertheless, Mack is surprised at his immediate success. "I've been thinking this week if this is really happening," he said.

If he rushes for 100 yards today he will become the first Browns rookie to have three straight games over the century mark. (No, Jim Brown didn't do it in 1957, according to the Browns' publicity department.)

"Houston's pretty tough, all I want to do is help the team win," said Mack, in the team-man tones you would expect from such a nice fellow.

He and Byner have a friendly competition during the week. "We kid each other about who is going to gain more yards on Sunday," Mack said.

Byner began as the chief enforcer in the Browns' ground game. Schottenheimer loves his fire. But fumbles have troubled him and now it seems Mack is taking over.

"Give the credit to the line," said Mack. "They're knocking people over."

After each game, Mack phones his parents in Kings Mountain. "They heard the news before I called last week," he said. "They're happy I'm doing so well and hope I can keep it up. My dad's not really into sports. He's an industrial worker. But he tells me to keep my head screwed on straight."

His mother wasn't crazy about Kevin playing a rough game like football when he began. But she went along with it when she saw it might give her son a chance for a higher education. Mack majored in industrial education at Clemson University.

"He has a knack of punishing tacklers and protecting himself by dropping his shoulder," said Johnson. "He's our Mack Truck."

Drug Death Doesn't Deserve Tribute

Don Rogers *Jul. 8, 1986*

This may sound heartless, but the Browns should not do anything more to honor the memory of Don Rogers.

They have done enough for their late defensive back, who died of a cocaine overdose. They paid for his funeral and sent a front-office delegation to the sad affair. They held a local service. They inserted a one-page memorial to Rogers, complete with black border and his picture, in their new news media guide.

That is plenty. Even the tribute to Rogers in the media guide should have been omitted. Drugs are such a big problem in this country that pains must be taken not to portray any user in a sentimental way, as a hero. It is more apropos to make the addicts look like the fools they are.

Yet, the Browns are thinking of doing even more in Rogers'

memory. There is talk that they will play this season with Rogers' number, 20, emblazoned on their helmets, or they will wear black armbands all season. A moment of silent tribute to Rogers at a game also is being discussed.

"We haven't decided yet," said Kevin Byrne, Browns public relations chief, yesterday. "We're talking to the players. The first eight or 10 we talked to would like to do something."

What nonsense. What bad taste. Rogers committed a crime when he used cocaine. A black armband is supposed to honor a man of distinction, not a loser. If the Browns ask 80,000 people to stand up at the opener to honor this felon, there will be at least one person who will remain sitting.

It is understandable that the players want to remember their late comrade. He was a likable, friendly man. But their outlook is not objective. They were too close to him. The mother of John Dillinger, Public Enemy No. 1, insisted he was a fine boy. The nation would smirk if the Browns went out of their way to glorify a drug user.

If the players want to pay homage to Rogers, they should do it with a moment of prayer in the clubhouse on the day of the first practice, and again on the day of the first game, in private. That is probably the way Rogers would want it. Let the poor guy rest in dignity.

Byrne gave assurance, at least, that the Browns would not retire Rogers' number, which is what the misguided zealots at the University of Maryland did for basketball player Lenny Bias, who died of a cocaine overdose a couple of weeks back.

It was amazing to see how Bias and Rogers were eulogized after their tawdry deaths. There was all this talk about these wonderful young men who "touched our lives." Baloney. They were lucky they weren't in jail.

With television showing beautiful young women crying at the funeral services, it is easy to see how impressionable youths could be led to believe that guys such as Bias and Rogers were people to be emulated. It recalled the old saying that many used to believe in, "Live fast, die young and have a good-looking corpse."

The funerals of Bias and Rogers were almost reminiscent of those old Chicago gangster funerals, in which the crooks were made to seem like mischievous darlings rather than the scum they were.

George Deukmejian, governor of California, called Rogers and Bias champions who were murdered by the same killer—drugs.

Can you believe it? The cocaine did not jump into their system. Rogers and Bias took it.

Deukmejian would have served his constituents better had he pointed out that Rogers had a confused sense of values, from which trouble was almost certain to erupt. He fathered an illegitimate child when he was still in college, yet was about to wed another woman when he died. Was he thinking about his child? He bought his younger brother a $30,000 BMW auto with part of his Browns bonus money. Wouldn't the gift of a $7,000 car have been generous enough for a kid still going to college?

The deaths of Rogers and Bias have brought renewed force to the call for mandatory drug testing of athletes. All but the most persistent Pollyannas must, by now, see the need for this. Sure, a urine test is an invasion of privacy, but so is a policeman's search of a suspected bank robber.

But it is possible that not even testing can stop the drug plague. Despite all the warnings, all the deaths, the odious epidemic continues to grow like a poisonous vine around the nation's neck.

Maybe it is our sick society that is at fault. A people who say it is all right to peddle pornography in milk stores, who spend billions on bombs rather than feed the starving and revel in war over a pipsqueak country like Grenada, can expect more trouble.

Perhaps the most effective deterrent among professional athletes would be to reveal the names of drug addicts. They do it at the racetracks, where horses who are on drugs such as Lasix or Butazolidin are listed in the program. This is a help to the bettors. The many Americans who gamble legally on games every week deserve the same kind of service. Listing the users also would remove the stigma from athletes who are clean.

It is impossible to be surprised anymore when it comes to drugs. We wouldn't be shocked if it was announced that Betty Crocker and Santa Claus are hooked. Because of what happened to nice-guy Rogers, all the Browns are suspect. That is Rogers' legacy. Let's not build a statue to him.

A Prototype NFL Lineman

CODY RISIEN *Dec. 13, 1986*

Football's offensive linemen are good guys. I never met one I didn't like.

Maybe it is because of the nature of the position. You cannot be a temperamental prima donna and play on the offensive line.

You have to be the kind of man who cheerfully does the dirty work and never demands any credit.

You are seldom interviewed on TV and feature writers never tell your life story. You get your rewards from seeing your team win.

Memory recalls Cody Risien, the prototype offensive lineman, leaping in glee when the Browns defeated Houston on a late long pass from Bernie Kosar to Reggie Langhorne this season.

Risien did not throw the pass or catch it, but he was as happy as those who did. Football is a brutal, vicious game, but this is the kind of selfless attitude that exemplifies the sport at its best.

Risien is the Browns' dean of offensive linemen. In his eighth season, the tackle has emerged as one of the club's leaders, a six-foot, seven-inch tower of good sense and affability.

"He's very important to the stability of our group," says offensive line coach Howard Mudd, a three-time all-pro at guard. "He teaches the young guys how to play and think. They have an inherent faith in him.

"But at the same time, he doesn't think he knows everything. When another guy makes a good play, he's liable to ask him, 'How did you get that job done?' He is very tough competitor, but his style is not to hit a guy in the back or go around looking for piles to throw himself into."

There have been occasions when even the gentlemanly Risien lost his temper in the violent world of football. "One guy, Ben Williams of Buffalo, used a head slap on me until he retired," Risien said. "It was very aggravating."

Risien admitted there have been occasions when he has punched an offending rival or grabbed a facemask in the fury of the scrimmage battles. "I don't think I did it deliberately," he said. "I'm human, too."

Intelligence is another common attribute of offensive linemen, who perform different duties on the various plays. Risien's pedigree shows he has brains.

His father was a senior vice president of a bank in suburban Houston. Unfortunately, he never saw his son play pro football. He died at 46 when Risien was a rookie in training camp.

"The last communication I had with him was in the hospital before I went to camp," Risien recalled. "He told me with a great degree of certainty I'd make the team. He knows I have."

The Browns' offensive linemen are like a little club. They kid each other about their lack of renown and fine each other for minor transgressions.

The fines can range from pennies to four or five dollars for such things as being offside in practice or falling down awkwardly. The money is used for the annual linemen's party at a downtown restaurant the last week of the season.

"Tom DeLeone, Doug Dieken and Robert Jackson will make guest speeches this year," Said Risien.

They are three former Browns offensive linemen of note.

Risien has come all the way back from the knee injury that cost him the entire 1984 season. Last year, he played adequately, but not supremely.

"He wasn't really sure his body would work after the injury," Mudd said. "Now, he's confident he is sound and is having a year comparable to 1983."

That was the season when United Press International picked him for the first team in the American Football Conference and USA Today named him to the first team of its All-National Football League roster.

A superior pass blocker, the 280-pound Risien admits the years of punishment take their toll on the body.

"I remember Clay Matthews (the linebacker who had had the locker next to Risien's for years) saying that when he was young, you never saw him in here on Tuesdays," said Risien, referring to the team's day off. "Now, I'm in here every Tuesday, too, getting the soreness out in the whirlpool."

Risien has no trouble listing his biggest thrills. "The best one was when I got my first chance to play," he said. "It was against Pittsburgh. They threw me into the lions' den to replace George Buehler and I did well against Steve Furness and Gary Dunn. The other big thrill was the whole 1980 season. That was a fairy tale."

It ended with Brian Sipe throwing the infamous interception

against the Oakland Raiders. "I couldn't believe it," Risien said. "I thought, 'This fantasy season can't be over.' To this day, I feel that way."

Risien, 29, has always wanted to play 10 years in the NFL, which would mean two more seasons. "But the way this team is playing, I might stay longer," he said. "I think we're at the beginning of something."

As the Browns head into their showdown with the Cincinnati Bengals tomorrow, let's hope Risien is right.

Postscript: The Browns routed Cincinnati, 34-3, then stormed through the playoffs before losing to Denver in the conference title game, when John Elway engineered the famous drive.

Indians 1950s–'60s

"He'd throw at anybody"

EARLY WYNN *Apr. 15, 1999*

Early Wynn one of the best pitchers the Indians ever had, died in Venice, Fla., last night at the age of 79.

The Hall of Famer had health problems for several years, said his daughter, Sherry Van Tilburg of Venice. He had suffered a heart attack and a stroke in recent years.

Insisting on being independent, he refused offers to move in with his daughter's family. Instead, he lived in an assisted living center. He used a walker until becoming ill in January.

Burly Early won 300 games and lost 244 from 1939 to 1963.

He achieved his greatest success with the Indians, winning 20 or more games four times in the 1950s. He was a member of the quartet of Tribe pitchers known as the Big Four, along with Bob Feller, Bob Lemon and Mike Garcia.

Wynn won 23 and lost 11 in 1954, when the Indians won the American League pennant with 111 victories, the league record for a 154-game season.

After being traded to Chicago, Wynn won the Cy Young Award for the pennant-winning White Sox in 1959, posting a 22-10 record at age 39.

Wynn was known for his intensity on the mound. "He was serious about every pitch, every game," former Indians pitching coach Mel Harder said. "He liked to have fun, but he was tough to get along with on the days he was pitching. Hitters knew it.

"He'd throw at anybody, whether it was Joe DiMaggio or Ted Williams."

Wynn once recalled that when he joined the Washington Senators as a rookie in 1939, manager Bucky Harris had a standing rule. "If you had two strikes on a batter and were ahead in the count, you had to knock him down with a pitch or you were fined $25," Wynn said.

Wynn jocularly denied that he would throw at his grandmother if necessary. "Only if she was digging in," he said.

The right-hander would down hitters who hit the ball through the middle or players who bunted on him.

In 1949, when a Detroit pitcher twice floored teammate Larry Doby, the first black player in the American League, Wynn knocked down the pitcher on four straight pitches when he came to bat.

"Doby is on my team," said Wynn, a Hartford, Ala., native. "If they hurt him, they hurt me. I've got to teach them manners."

His former manager agreed. "He was one of the best competitors I ever saw," said Hall of Famer Al Lopez, who managed Wynn through most of his career with the Indians and Chicago.

"He would go deep into the count on hitters almost every time. He just wouldn't give them a good pitch to hit."

Wynn led the league three times in innings pitched, twice in strikeouts and once in earned run average. He threw 290 complete games.

He was also a good hitter, belting 17 career homers and hitting as high as .319 in a season. He was often used as a pinch-hitter.

Wynn became a polished pitcher after coming to the Indians at age 29 in one of Cleveland's best trades. After the 1948 season, team owner Bill Veeck sent Eddie Robinson, Eddie Kleiman and Joe Haynes to Washington for Wynn and Mickey Vernon, a first baseman.

He had a 72-87 record for weak teams in Washington.

When he joined the Tribe, Harder told him he would have to learn to throw a curve and a change-up and to pitch to spots.

"He developed a real good change-up," Harder said. "He had such confidence he could throw it on counts of 3-1 and 3-2, where most pitchers would throw fastballs. He learned to throw a curve with a lot of spin on it, with a small, sharp break."

From 1949 to 1957, he won 163 and lost 100 for the Indians.

Wynn liked to have fun off the field, engaging in stunts such as putting Limburger cheese in rival catcher Clint Courtney's glove.

He wrote a weekly sports column for the old Cleveland News. He was not afraid to criticize General Manager Hank Greenberg, American League President Joe Cronin or sportswriters.

Greenberg, with whom Wynn often had contract problems, complained that the News was "using" the pitcher to build circulation. Wynn's top pay with the Indians was about $45,000.

After his record slipped to 14-17 in 1957, the Indians traded him and Al Smith to Chicago for star left fielder Minnie Minoso.

Wynn returned to the Indians as a free agent in 1963, needing one victory to reach his goal of 300. At age 43, he failed in several tries at No. 300, including a complete-game 1-0 loss.

He reached the milestone July 13, 1963, pitching the first five innings of a 5-4 victory in Kansas City.

Wynn served as the Indians' pitching coach in 1964, and did the same for the Minnesota Twins for three years.

He was inducted into the Baseball Hall of Fame in 1972, making an emotional speech in which he said he had achieved his three goals: being an All Star, pitching in a World Series, and making the Hall of Fame. "Thank you very, very much," he said, with tears in his eyes.

His first wife, Mabel, was killed in an auto accident in 1942.

The family said funeral arrangements were pending.

Revered Slugger Overcame Broken Ankles, Bad Knees; Life Cut Short by Robbery

LUKE EASTER *Sep. 29, 1987*

Even though he was murdered, it would be wrong to say Luke Easter was a tragic figure. The former Indians first baseman packed a lot of thrills and fun into his life.

Everybody loved Easter, even the Indians fans who occasionally booed him.

He was the classic example of that most popular type of ballplayer—the big guy who could slug the long ball.

On June 23, 1950, Easter hit a home run that has come to be accepted as the longest in the history of the Stadium. It came off a 3-0 pitch from Washington's Joe Haynes and landed in the upper deck in right field.

Sports writer Hal Lebovitz of the Cleveland News measured the blast at 477 feet, running a string from home plate to the seat into which the ball crashed.

In his three full years with the Indians, from 1950-52, Easter averaged 29 home runs and 102 runs batted in, hitting between .263 and .280.

Easter's fielding was another thing, something that irritated the fans. But he never became angry over the criticism. "I love the fans," he said, flashing his golden-toothed smile. "They're my friends."

He did not speak the words in a clownish way. Easter was a street-wise man with excellent people skills.

Sadly, nobody will ever know how good Easter could have been in baseball. Because of the nation's racial attitudes, his best years were spent on the outside of organized baseball, first in softball and then for the Homestead Grays and Cincinnati Crescents of the Negro Leagues.

He was 35 by the time he played his first full year in Cleveland, although he gave his age as 28.

Easter arrived after a sensational half-season with San Diego of the Pacific Coast League, an Indians farm team, in 1949. The 6-4½, 240-pound left-handed clubber had hit .363 with 25 home runs and 94 RBI, by late June.

Indians fans could hardly wait to see him play.

But then one of his knees gave out. Easter came to Cleveland on crutches, needing an operation. "This won't stop me from playing baseball," Easter said on June 26, 1949, in an interview in the Majestic Hotel. "I overcame two broken feet, so why should I worry?"

In 1941, both of Easter's legs were broken at the ankles in a car accident. From then on his legs were never right. He wound up having two knee operations while he was with the Indians, and constantly played with his legs wrapped in bandages.

Dr. Don Kelly, the Indians' team physician, called Easter one of the most courageous men he had ever met. "I love the guy," said Kelly in 1952.

Easter, like many ballplayers in those days, behaved as though he played for the pure enjoyment of the game, not the money. After he broke in with 45 at-bats in 1949, Tribe General Manager Hank Greenberg called him in for a contract talk.

Easter told Greenberg to sign the contract for him. "Don't you want to know how much it calls for?" Greenberg asked.

"No, whatever you say is all right with me," Easter said.

He was paid $7,500 for hitting 28 homers with 107 RBI and a .280 average in 1950, surely the biggest bargain in baseball.

His low point came when manager Al Lopez, annoyed by his fielding and .208 batting average, optioned him to the Indians, Indianapolis farm club in June 1952. Lopez hinted that Easter's big-league career might be over.

Easter took the demotion calmly. "He said he'd be back," recalled his widow, Virgil, who still lives in Cleveland. "All he said was that Lopez was the boss."

Easter hit well in Indianapolis and returned to the Indians in July. From then to the end of the season, he relentlessly attacked the baseball, winding up with his career-high 31 homers and 97 RBI.

Frank Gibbons of the Cleveland Press called his performance baseball's most dramatic story of 1952 and said Easter was one of the most remarkable people the game had seen since Babe Ruth.

Easter was always in good spirits, a fine team man who was always eager to congratulate a teammate for good work. Once, when Al Rosen hit a home run, he leaped up in glee and knocked himself out by hitting his head on the dugout roof.

His most famous escapade occurred during a train trip, when a couple of strangers got into a card game with some of the Indians and fleeced them. Tribe pitcher Early Wynn caught one of the men dealing from the bottom of the deck and began to attack him, while the other ran away.

Easter calmed down Wynn, the future Hall of Famer. "If you hit him, you could get into trouble," Easter said. "Let me take care of it."

Easter ordered the culprit to play against him in a game of gin rummy. Soon Easter cleaned out the man and then gave his teammates all the money they had lost.

"How come you were so sure you were going to win against a guy who could deal from the bottom of the deck?" one of his teammates asked.

"I can deal from the middle of the deck," Easter replied.

In 1953, Easter reached his top pay of $20,000 and was also involved in a Cleveland sausage-making business. His face was put on the sausage wrappers with the message, "If you want to hit like Luke, you have to eat like Luke."

Everything was looking good, but finally, at 38, his legs gave out after his foot was broken when hit by a pitch from Lou Kretlow of the Chicago White Sox.

Wynn, who loved Easter like a brother, drove him to the hospital. "He wanted to carry me up the steps himself," said Easter. "He sure is some guy."

He was finished with the Indians after playing 68 games in 1953 and six in 1954.

But Easter was far from through with baseball. He became a big star in Buffalo and Rochester of the International League, hitting

36 homers in 1956 and 40 in 1958. His 1956 salary was $12,500, excellent money at a time when 95 percent of Americans made less than $10,000 a year.

Easter played until he was 50, although nobody knew his real age. "He just enjoyed playing," his wife said.

Virgil, a retired court reporter, said Easter always shrugged off racial insults, including the times when he and other black players could not stay in the same hotel as their teammates. "He didn't like it, but he adjusted," she said.

After retiring from baseball Easter got a job at TRW, Inc. in Euclid, working as a polisher. A supervisor said he was popular with other workers and recognized his leadership potential. Easter soon became a union steward, a job he held until his death.

On March 29, 1979, Eater was shot and killed by two men outside a bank in Euclid. He had just cashed more than $40,000 of fellow workers' paychecks, something he did every week, and was on his way back to work. Two men rushed out of a parked car, shot him, grabbed the money and fled. One of the men was a fired TRW employee, who knew of Easter's routine.

The hoodlums were chased by police and captured after a shootout. One was sentenced to life in prison. The other got 15 years to life.

An estimated 4,000 mourners filed past Easter's coffin in the House of Wills funeral home. Another 1,000 people, including Mayor Dennis Kucinich, Indians General Manager Gabe Paul and Hall of Famer Bob Feller, packed the Mount Sinai Baptist Church for the funeral service.

Cleveland honored the ballplayer by renaming Woodland Hills Park as Luke Easter Park. A bust of the ballplayer who was never too old overlooks the sandlot playing fields he loved.

Remembering the Big Bear

MIKE GARCIA *Jan. 29, 1984*

It was 8:13 a.m. yesterday. Mike Garcia, 60, was lying on a bed in St. John Hospital, getting a dialysis treatment for his kidneys. In the next bed, a 22-year-old man, getting the same help, quietly strummed a mandolin.

It was a long way from that room to the days when Garcia was one of the best baseball pitchers in the American League.

They just put two needles into me," said Garcia. "They're as big as nails. I'll have to stay here for three hours while they drain the excess fluid."

"He'll lose six pounds while he's here," said Lynn Guminiak, his young nurse.

"That's a heck of a way to go on a diet," Garcia said valiantly. He weighed 235 pounds in his golden time of the early 1950s when he won 79 and lost only 41 in four consecutive years for the Indians. Now, he is 180.

"That's my kidney over there," said Garcia, pointing to a six-sided, foot-high box that was connected to his arm by tubes. The box purifies Garcia's blood, a task his ailing kidneys can no longer handle.

"It's like changing an oil filter," said Garcia. "I'm getting to know so much about this, I'm talking like a doctor."

Garcia always was a kidder, one of the most popular players on the Indians. He would needle media pals, hide typewriters and plant phony rumors.

"I come in here three days a week," said Garcia. "You feel drained when it's over. Sometimes I feel okay. Sometimes I'm bad. The more they pull out of you, the worse you feel. I need a lot of rest and I have to watch what I eat. My wife and daughter watch me like a hawk."

On the wall of the hospital room is an autographed picture of Garcia in his pitching days. "We replaced Tom Selleck with Mike," said Guminiak. "My father told me all about his pitching."

He was called the Big Bear then. Indians second baseman Joe Gordon christened him when he was a rookie. He hollered at Garcia, "Grande oso," Spanish for big bear. Garcia asked him why he called him that and Gordon replied, "Because you walk like a big bear."

The name stuck. Garcia used it for his Parma dry cleaning business which he ran for about 20 years until forced out by illness.

"I'm diabetic to start with," said Garcia. "Diabetes wrecks your organs. When I went to California to visit my sister last August, my ankles blew up like balloons. I felt rotten, so I came back to Cleveland. I was so sick, I didn't even want to talk. In the hospital, I told them to do something, even if it was wrong." That was when the dialysis began.

In his heyday, Garcia's fastball was one of the best in baseball.

His first two years, he threw nothing else. As a rookie in 1949 he won 14 and lost five, earning a munificent $5,000. His salary was doubled the next season. The most he ever got was $35,000. Today, he'd get a million easily.

"Sooner or later, I have to get a kidney transplant," said Garcia. "I've got nothing to lose. What I'm doing here is buying time while they learn more technology. It's rough, but what are you gonna do?"

"About 70% of transplants are successful," said Guminiak.

It was more fun going back to the snug blanket of baseball memory. "The hitter who gave me the most trouble was Yogi Berra," said Garcia, speaking of the old New York Yankees catcher. "He was so strong, you could fool him on a pitch and he'd still hit it out. From the waist up, he was really stacked."

Next August, the Indians are planning a 30th anniversary reunion of the 1954 team that won 111 games. Garcia was 19-8 that season. The plan is to bring in the Yankees' old-timers too. "That's gonna be something," said Garcia. "I'm really looking forward to it."

The Señor Looks Back

AL LOPEZ *Dec. 3, 1985*

Al Lopez, the last successful manager the Indians have had, was back in town last night for the Mike Garcia bash.

The Señor, 77, looks good, just about the same as when he gave up deep thinking in the dugout 16 years ago. He was troubled with a nervous stomach through much of his managerial career.

"I quit managing because I couldn't sleep or eat," he said sipping a beer.

Lopez led the Indians to five second-place finishes and a pennant from 1951–56. He later won another flag with the Chicago White Sox. His winning percentage of .581 is the 10th best in baseball history.

Lopez had a simple managing philosophy. "I just tried to treat my players the way I wanted to be treated when I was playing," he said.

But there was more to it than that. Dick Donovan, the old pitcher, once explained why Lopez' teams always did so well.

"He kept us all under here," said Donovan admiringly, pressing his thumb on the table.

"I think what he meant was that they all respected me," said Lopez. "We had rules, but I don't think anybody was ever afraid of me."

As well as Lopez did here, the Indians were not fully appreciated. That was why he left. "In 1955, we came home two games in front with two weeks to go," he said. "We were playing Detroit and had a crown of about 5,500. I was disappointed. It looked like people were getting a little tired of it and maybe they needed a change. That crowd stayed in the back of my mind."

The next year, the Tribe finished second again and Lopez decided to leave.

It is hard to believe, but Cleveland fans complained about the Tribe then almost as much as they do now. They were disdainfully tagged the second-place guys who couldn't beat the New York Yankees.

Even when they were winning 93 games, the fans charged them with playing dull baseball, depending on strong pitching and the long ball instead of speed.

Can you imagine how they would storm the gates now if the Indians had a second-place team that had great pitching and power hitters such as Al Rosen, Larry Doby and Luke Easter?

"You'd draw two million with a winner now," Lopez said.

Most old-timers say players were better in their day. Lopez disagrees. "They're just as good today, even with expansion," he said.

The feeling here is that Lopez' 1954 Indians, who set the league record with 111 victories, would have annihilated this year's world champs, the Kansas City Royals.

But Lopez wouldn't concede that. "You hate to say you're better," the Señor said. "But I do think we had the best pitching staff in baseball history."

There is not much doubt there. Bob Feller, Bob Lemon and Early Wynn are all in the Hall of Fame. Garcia, the fourth member of the Big Four, was, at times, the best. Over a period of four years, the Big Bear averaged 20 victories. He won 59.4% of his games lifetime.

"He would take the ball any time you wanted him to," said Lopez, referring to Garcia's willingness to relieve in a pinch. "He could throw as hard as anybody."

After Lopez left Cleveland, the Indians went into an immediate decline and have occupied the baseball slums since. "The Big Four got old and Herb Score got hurt," is how Lopez analyzes the situation. "And then the Indians stopped coming up with good pitchers in the farm system." Score won 36 games his first two years before his career was ended by an eye injury.

Lopez also helped make a pivotal decision that hurt the Indians, trading Minnie Minoso to Chicago in 1951. The White Sox wanted either Minoso or Harry Simpson. Lopez felt Simpson would become a superstar. He spent two seasons grounding out to second base for the Indians while Minoso became a great player in Chicago. Had Minoso stayed here, the Tribe almost certainly would have won a few more pennants in the 1950s.

"Minoso didn't have a position," said Lopez yesterday, looking back across the ruins of one of his few bad guesses. "I think Simpson was too tight. He tried too hard. He was just like Larry Doby, who should have been great."

Doby, the Indians' first black player and a splendid center fielder, was still good enough to lead the league in homers twice and in runs batted in once.

The only other move for which Lopez was criticized was his refusal to use Feller in the fourth game of the 1954 World Series. The Señor, down three games to zero, went back to his first-game starter, Lemon, who lost.

The fans wanted Feller, the sentimental favorite, to have a chance to win the only World Series game of this life.

"I'd still do it today," said Lopez, who obviously doesn't give up his beliefs easily. "That Minoso trade didn't hurt us that much either. We had plenty of power."

It is generally believed that it is more difficult to manage today because of the players' high salaries, long-term contracts and agents.

But Lopez said he would still want to manage if he were young again. "I might be conceited, but I think I could handle it."

He probably could. The Señor was always a winner.

Boos Couldn't Deter Kirkland in 1961

WILLIE KIRKLAND *Jul. 3, 2001*

Indians fans loved to boo Willie Kirkland. It wasn't his fault, but his timing was bad when he arrived in Cleveland in 1961. Kirkland was caught in the backlash of the Rocky Colavito trade. The fans were still furious that their idol had been sent away for Detroit's Harvey Kuenn the previous year. They had a natural skepticism toward anyone who tried to fill Colavito's big, spiked shoes in right field. Kuenn had been booed the year before and had been dispatched to San Francisco for Kirkland and pitcher Johnny Antonelli.

Now it was Kirkland's turn to hear the inverted cheers. It was too bad. Kirkland was a nice fellow. He wore conservative, well-tailored suits and carried an umbrella. He never caused anybody trouble. Although his casual demeanor on the field camouflaged it, he tried hard all the time. He was a tall, strong guy with power and a terrific arm.

He never complained about the treatment, although he looked kind of lonely. He had been yanked away from San Francisco, where two of his closest friends were future Hall of Famers Willie Mays and Willie McCovey.

In spring training, the three Willies would huddle deep in right field for secret conversations that invariably ended in laughs and slaps of the hand.

Kirkland had two memorable outbursts in Cleveland. In July 1961, he made the record book by hitting four home runs in four straight at-bats. Even that did not work out right. The feat took place during two games four days apart and was separated by two walks and a sacrifice.

As a result, it did not get the attention it deserved. Nevertheless, there is Kirkland's name in the record book, probably forever, along with superstars such as Jimmie Foxx, Hank Greenberg, Mickey Mantle, Stan Musial and Manny Ramirez, for most consecutive homers in two games.

It is doubtful, even in these days of orgiastic slugging, that anybody will hit five homers in five straight at-bats.

Kirkland hit his first three off Chicago's Cal McLish on July 9, driving each of the balls deep into the right-field stands at the Stadium. They were his 12th, 13th and 14th of the season. Indians manager Jimmy Dykes and a wild pitcher cost him his chance to hit four in a game, something that only three American Leaguers have done.

After his third homer, he was walked. Then Dykes, impervious to history, had him bunt for a sacrifice with two on and nobody out and the Indians losing by a run in the ninth inning. The Indians lost anyway when Vic Power hit into a double play.

Afterward, Kirkland was asked how he felt about not having a chance to hit the fourth. "I would have liked another crack at it," he said. "But I'm not complaining. Maybe I would have hit into a double play."

Asked if he thought about ignoring the bunt call and swinging away, Kirkland said: "It never crossed my mind. I hope to be around this ballclub for a while." He was not going to risk the manager's wrath by disobeying orders.

That was the last game before the All-Star break. When the Indians came back July 13, Kirkland walked in his first at-bat against Pedro Ramos of Minnesota. But in the third, he crashed a home run deep into the Stadium's right-field upper deck, near the foul pole. That made it four homers in four trips, because walks and sacrifices are not counted as official at-bats.

In his next game, he homered off Clevelander Ken McBride of the Los Angeles Angels for five homers in three games. That first season in Cleveland was Kirkland's best in the majors. He hit 27 homers and drove in 95 runs, career highs in both departments.

He signed for $18,000 in 1962. "I got a nice raise," Kirkland said. "I hope I get another one next year."

"Willie was a mama's boy," one of his old friends said. "He lived at home with his mama. Every year he'd buy a new car and give his old one to his mama."

Kirkland acknowledged his nerves got to him early in the season because he was trying to live up to Colavito. "I pressed," he said. "Then I decided to give it that I-don't-care attitude and I got better. Doggone, if I'd only had a fair first half I'd have gone way over 100 RBI."

Kirkland had reached his peak at age 27. His numbers went down the next two years. But he still emerged with perhaps his most memorable game of all on June 13, 1963, when he hit a home run in the 19th inning to defeat the Washington Senators, 3-2, in the nightcap of a doubleheader.

At the time, it tied a team record for the longest game, three innings short of the current club mark. It is still the longest game in Indians history to be decided by a homer. Kirkland connected off Jim Coates at 1:13 a.m., four hours and 33 minutes after the game began. About 1,000 of the original crowd of 12,377 in Cleveland Municipal Stadium was still in the seats. The left-handed-batting Kirkland, who was hitting .200 going in, drove in all three Cleveland runs. In the 11th inning, he homered off tough lefty Claude Osteen to tie the game. He had singled in a run off Osteen in the first inning.

Kirkland talked about the booing fans after the game: "They're funny. After I hit into a double play, a fan yelled, 'Why don't you go back to Jacksonville?' Then I hit the homer in the 11th and the same guy was yelling for me like I was Babe Ruth.

"You can't let them get to you. They want to see you throw the bat or something. But you mustn't do that, because if you do, they'll boo some more."

He finished the season hitting .230 with 15 homers and 47 RBI, and was traded to Baltimore for Al Smith. He wound up with Washington in 1966, then went to Japan.

Unlike many Americans, he thrived in Japanese baseball. He learned the language, played there for several years and married a Japanese woman.

Now 67, he could not be located for this story. He is said to be living in Detroit.

A Sickening Thud

Herb Score *May 6, 1997*

The Julio Franco liner that broke the jaw of Detroit's Willie Blair on Sunday brought back memories of one of the most devastating games in Indians history.

It occurred in the Stadium 40 years ago tomorrow, when Herb Score was hit in the right eye by a line drive off the bat of Gil McDougald of the New York Yankees.

It is often said that the Rocky Colavito trade began the Indians' long descent into baseball futility, which lasted until the early 1990s. But the injury to Score might have been an even more seminal event.

Score was 23 and the most overpowering left-handed pitcher in baseball. In 1955, when he was the rookie of the year, he won 16 games. The next season he won 20. In both years, he led the American League in strikeouts.

He looked like a pitcher who would win 20 a year for the next 10 summers.

The 1959 Indians, who finished five games behind pennant-winning Chicago, probably would have won that flag with Score at full efficiency.

"He was as good as you can get," said former Indians pitcher

Bob Lemon, 76, a Hall of Famer. "If he hadn't been hurt there's no telling what he would have done."

McDougald, 68, said: "He was faster than Sandy Koufax, no question about it. And his curve just dropped out of the clouds. Right from the start, everybody looked at him and said: 'Hall of Fame.'" Two weeks before the injury, Hall of Famer Tris Speaker said: "If nothing happens to him, this kid has got to be the greatest."

Although he had some glistening moments after the accident, Score never recaptured his old form. Now, he is better known as the Indians' radio play-by-play man for the last 30 seasons. Most young players and fans have no idea of his old talent. "Every once in a while some player on another team will come over and ask me for an autograph," said Score, who doesn't take himself seriously. "Probably his father told him to do it." Score, 63, said he will not be thinking back to the anniversary of the event.

"I'm getting so old I forgot I played," he said. "I'll be married 40 years in July. That's the only anniversary I think about."

McDougald, on the other hand, was driven out of baseball by the incident. "It was cemented in my mind," he said. "It made me realize the game was not that important. Herb was one of the good guys. I told my wife that as soon as I could establish myself in business I'd walk away, and I did." He retired in 1960 at age 32.

Score missed the rest of that 1957 season, but looked as though he was going to be all right early in 1958. "I struck out 13 or 14 in my second start," he said. "But then we got rained out and I didn't work for 10 days."

Score pitched again on a cold, rainy day and felt a pain in his arm in the sixth inning. He kept pitching and finished the game, but soon after that he went on the disabled list for most of the year. Score has insisted that it was the arm injury, not the blow to the eye, that finished him. "I lost something on the ball," he said.

He had his moments, however. In 1959 he won nine games by the All-Star break. "I was pretty good but fortunate," recalled Score, who did not pitch with his former dominance. He did not win another game the rest of the year, finishing 9-11. In 1961, after he was traded to the Chicago White Sox, Score beat the Indians with a two-hitter, striking out 13. "I can't explain that one," he said. It was his last major-league victory.

McDougald, speaking from his home in Spring Lake, N.J., remembered the first time he saw Score pitch after the accident. "He was recoiling, short-arming the ball," said the old infielder. "It looked like he was getting ready to get the glove up and get into fielding position. When you come back too quick you're like shell-shocked. It's natural. After what he went through, you're like a boxer, defending yourself. No question he wasn't following through the way he had been."

Lemon recalled: "Herb got off to a good start the next year, but then a ball was hit back through the box and it brought back memories. He became mechanical, like doing it by numbers. He wasn't the same Herb. He wasn't bringing it like he used to, not holding anything back. He didn't just throw the ball and let the hitter beware. Now, it was like he was thinking: 'Let the pitcher beware first and then throw the ball.'"

Score dismisses such speculation. He pointed out that he had been hit by liners several times before the critical injury, on the chest, arm and leg. In high school he was hit on the head. "I did not have a Spalding Guide delivery," he said of his all-out style. "I often thought I might get hit on the back by a liner because I followed through so hard I was looking at the center-field scoreboard when I finished."

Score was going for his third straight shutout of the world champion Yankees, dating to the previous season, when he faced them in the fateful 1957 game. He retired leadoff man Hank Bauer. McDougald, the second batter, hit him with the liner on a 2-2 pitch. "He threw it low and away," said McDougald. "And I just flicked it. The next thing I remember is watching Herb go down. All I recall is seeing blood. I don't recall running to first. I was very upset." The ball caromed to third baseman Al Smith, who threw out McDougald. "I never saw the ball," said Score.

Indians manager Kerby Farrell and Yankees manager Casey Stengel rushed to the mound, along with several players. Score lay prostrate on the mound, with blood pouring out. Indians first baseman Vic Wertz ran toward Score, took one look and stopped 10 feet away, then turned back.

"As soon as I hit the ground I prayed to St. Jude," Score was quoted as saying. "I was afraid I wouldn't be able to see." The Plain Dealer bannered the story across the top of Page One: "SCORE HIT IN EYE BY LINE DRIVE."

Score was taken off the Stadium mound on a stretcher and driven to Lakeside Hospital, his head wrapped as though he had a war wound. "I've been in pain before but this is the worst," the Cleveland News' Hal Lebovitz quoted him as saying. "I feel like screaming." Score was given sedation.

Score suffered a broken nose, cut right eyelid and considerable swelling and hemorrhaging of the right cheekbone and eyebrow. When his mother, Anne, heard about the accident at her home in Lake Worth, Fla., she exclaimed: "Oh, those beautiful blue eyes."

"I had my eyes covered for two weeks, wondering if I'd ever see again," recalled Score. "When something like that happens, you find out your priorities."

Lemon was called in to pitch and was given all the time he needed to warm up. "I went to the mound after they cleaned up the blood," he said. He held the Yankees to six hits the rest of the way, winning, 2-1.

McDougald was in tears after the game. "The main thing I wanted to know was if he was going to lose his eye," said McDougald. The next day he and teammates Bauer and Yogi Berra tried to visit Score at the hospital, but no visitors were allowed. Dr. Charles Thomas, the eye specialist who was treating Score, called McDougald every day to update him on Score's injury. The young pitcher received thousands of cards and letters from all over the nation.

The previous week, McDougald had hit Detroit pitcher Frank Lary on the hip with a liner. After the Score incident, he almost hit Baltimore hurler Skinny Brown, who went down with his legs and arms flying in all directions.

McDougald would never have hit Score with his original batting stance. When he first came up in 1951, McDougald batted with a wide-open stance. He hit .306 as a rookie, but by 1954 his average had gone down to .259. In 1955, Stengel told him: "If you want to stick around you better change your stance." So, McDougald closed up the stance and practiced hitting the ball up the middle. "I never would have reached that low, outside pitch with my old stance," McDougald said.

In a strange coincidence, McDougald also was hurt when teammate Bob Cerv hit him with a ball during batting practice. That led to a progressive hearing loss after his retirement. "I was deaf for 15 years," said McDougald. He had to sell his thriving building maintenance business because he could not talk to anyone on the phone.

In 1994, McDougald's hearing was restored when an electronic device was implanted in his head. Now, he makes speeches urging the hearing-impaired to undergo the same operation. "It's a simple operation," he said. "It's much better than a hearing aid." Score, meanwhile, has lived the pleasant existence of a baseball sportscaster for all these years. He is respected in the community and he and his wife, Nancy, have three grown children and eight grandchildren.

"Maybe it's better the way things worked out for Herb," said McDougald. "Sometimes when adversity strikes it's for the best." When asked to list his top baseball thrills, Score recalls the doubleheader he pitched against Boston with teammate Bob Feller on May1, 1955, his rookie year. Feller threw a one-hitter to win the opener, 2-0. When Score came out of the Stadium dugout for the second game, a fan yelled at him: "That's a tough act to follow." So Score struck out 16, yielding four hits, in a 3-1 victory. Another highlight is his 20th victory in Kansas City in 1956. Lemon and Early Wynn had each won No .20 the previous two days.

Too bad we will never know what might have been.

He Stole the Show—and Home, Twice in One Game

Vic Power *Aug. 14, 1999*

It was not an important game. Hardly anybody was at the Stadium to see it.

But 41 years ago today, Vic Power of the Indians did something that nobody else has done in the major leagues in 72 seasons.

He stole home plate twice in a game.

He was not aided by being on the front end of a double steal. He did it alone, challenging the pitchers and pulling off baseball's most exciting play. Twice, in the space of about 45 minutes.

"Nobody is ever going to break that record," Power, 67, said from his home in Guaynabo, Puerto Rico. "To break it, you'd have to steal home three times in a game.

"But I didn't do it to set a record. Whatever I did in baseball, I was playing to win."

Plain Dealer baseball writer Harry Jones wrote that day that it was one of the most thrilling games ever on a big-league diamond. In the eighth inning on Aug. 14, 1958, Power drove in a run with a single to give the Indians an 8-7 lead over Detroit. Then he stole home with Bill Fischer pitching and taking a full windup. "It was easy," Power said. "I got a good jump."

The Tigers tied it in the ninth, so Power came back with his third hit and swiped home for the winning run in the 10th with Frank Lary on the mound.

Moreover, he did it with the bases loaded, two outs and Rocky Colavito at bat. Colavito, the Indians' leading slugger, had hit his 25th and 26th homers in the game.

Amazingly, Power stole only one other base all season. Power was motivated by his dislike of the Tigers and one of their coaches, hot-headed and fast-talking Leo Durocher. "The Tigers and Boston were always throwing beanballs at me," Power said. "I don't know the reason, but I didn't like it." When Power faked his second steal of home on the first pitch to Colavito, dancing up the baseline, he quotes the late Durocher as yelling to Lary: "Don't worry about that monkey. He's just trying to make you wild."

The angry Power retorted, "Now I see why Laraine Day divorced you." Durocher had been married to Day, a popular movie star of the 1940s and '50s.

Power faked again, racing dangerously close to the plate, before again turning back. With the count 2-and-1 and Lary taking a windup, Power started again, then kept going into immortality, sliding and easily beating the tag of catcher Charley Lau to the delight of the crowd of 4,474.

"The pitch was low and away," Power said. "They never had a chance to get me."

He thought the odds were against Colavito getting another hit since he had had such a big day already.

In the eighth, Power swiped home with the Indians' No. 2 slugger, Minnie Minoso, at the plate. Both times, Power went on his own. Ten other major-leaguers stole home twice in the early years of the century. Power is the only man to do it since Doc Gautreau of the Boston Braves on Sept. 3, 1927.

The steals helped the Indians break a five-game losing streak and improve to 56-59, good for fifth place. The Tigers were in fourth. "I think it was easier for me to steal home than second," said Power, explaining why he had a mere three steals all year. "I wasn't fast enough."

He never stole more than nine bases in a season and totaled 45 for his 12-year big-league career.

The straight steal of home is hardly ever seen these days. Asked why, Power said: "You have to be tough to steal home. Today, they don't want to be hurt. They're making too much money." Power's top salary was $48,000, while playing for six teams, including the Indians from 1958 to 1961.

Power, whose real name is Pellot, is a retired scout for the Anaheim Angels and runs baseball clinics in Puerto Rico. He is in pretty

1. Satchel Paige pitched with flair. He got batters out with pitches like the Trouble Ball, the Bat Dodger, and the B-Ball ("When I throw it, you be out."). *Page 15* (CSU)

2. Bob Lemon in his prime, after setting down the side once again. He pitched for the Indians in two World Series: 1948 and 1954. *Page 18* (CSU)

3. The indomitable Bill Veeck, flamboyant owner of the Indians, shows off his wooden leg to a group of young admirers. His credo was, "Let's have fun at the ballpark." Fans did. *Page 21* (CSU)

4. Russ Christopher pitched his heart out—almost literally. *Page 27* (CSU)

5. Lou Boudreau, with the stance every Cleveland boy copied. More than a great shortstop, he was a natural leader. *Page 25* (CSU)

6. Jim Hegan gives son Mike some catching pointers. Hegan frequently caught both ends of doubleheaders and caught 142 of 154 games in 1948. "You couldn't throw a ball past him," Bob Feller said. *Page 33* (CSU)

7. Pat Seerey and wife, Jeanne, two happy people. "Fat Pat" had a picture-perfect swing but lacked the hand-eye coordination to make contact regularly. *Page 36* (CSU)

8. Gene Bearden, the surprise of 1948. *Page 43* (CSU)

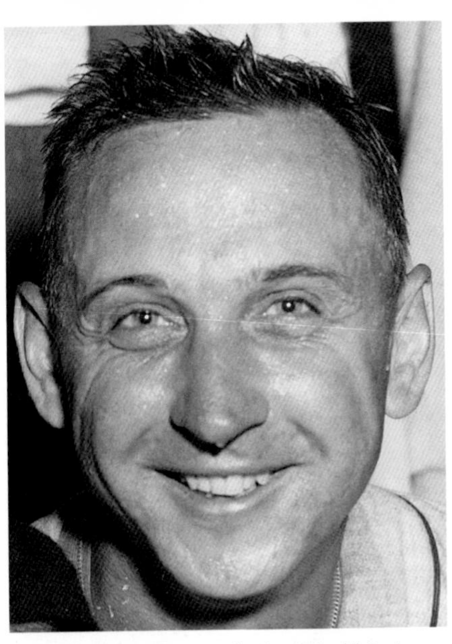

13. Steve Gromek won the key World Series Game in 1948. "I had a good rising fastball . . . but Boudreau told me he'd fine me $250 if I ever threw a curve." *Page 53* (CSU)

14. Ken Keltner throws a ball off the Terminal Tower in a publicity stunt. On the field, the third baseman always looked at the ball before throwing to first, a habit that drove his pitchers crazy. *Page 56* (CSU)

15. Dale Mitchell was as quick as a jackrabbit and one of the most difficult men to strike out. *Page 59* (CSU)

16. "Big Bill" Willis was actually pretty small for a lineman, but he played big enough to reach the Pro Football Hall of Fame. *Page 63* (CSU)

17. Paul Brown, a small-town boy from Norwalk, ran his team like a dictator and created a football dynasty. "If anybody here is playing just for the money, you can get up and leave right now," he told his team. *Page 78* (CSU)

25. Don Cockroft, two-gun kicker, has a secure place in the Browns' record book. *Page 89* (CSU)

26. Brian Sipe led the Kardiac Kids to glory and heartache. "It was better we went out with a bang instead of a whimper," he said. "The way we lost people will always remember us." *Page 96* (CSU)

27. Doug Dieken, the man they couldn't oust. Every summer brought a new challenger for his job, but Dieken ultimately stayed in the lineup for 203 straight games. *Page 99* (CSU)

28. Cody Risien, a true team player. *Page 108* (CSU)

29. Sam Rutigliano, the most likable coach in Browns history, always knew how to laugh. When the Browns lost a tough game, Rutigliano consoled his team with the immortal line, "Eight hundred million Chinese don't even know you played." *Page 92* (CSU)

30. Earnest Byner (left) and Kevin Mack both ran for 1,000 yards in the same season. *Page 101*
(Tony Tomsic)

31. Burly Early Wynn, always in charge. Jokers claimed Wynn would throw at his own grandmother if necessary. "Only if she was digging in," he replied. *Page 111* (CSU)

32. Luke Easter could hit 'em a mile. His baseball career was cut short by knee trouble—at age 50. *Page 113* (CSU)

33. Mike Garcia, "The Big Bear," was a charter member of the Big Four. *Page 116* (CSU)

34. Señor Al Lopez led the great 1954 team to 111 victories despite a nervous stomach. He quit managing because he couldn't eat or sleep. *Page 118* (CSU)

35. Willie Kirkland wouldn't let the boos get to him when fans criticized him for not being Rocky Colavito. Then he went out and hit four consecutive homers himself. *Page 120* (CSU)

36. Herb Score, when he really had it. "He was as good as you can get," said Bob Lemon. "If he hadn't been hurt there's no telling what he would have done." *Page 123* (CSU)

37. Vic Power, called a showboat for catching fly balls one-handed, said "If God wanted players to catch with two hands, he would have put gloves on both hands." *Page 127* (CSU)

38. Rocky Colavito, darling of the Cleveland fans. The highlight of his career was hitting four consecutive homers. "I remember everything about that game," he said. *Page 130* (CSU)

39. Jim Piersall battled with pitchers, umpires, scorers, fans, and sportswriters . . . but he was a great interview. "Probably the best thing that happened to me was going nuts," he wrote in his autobiography. *Page 134* (CSU)

40. Gene Green, who almost quit the Indians while on a West Coast road trip. *Page 138* (CSU)

41. "Sudden Sam" McDowell, raring back to fire. He was a ball of fire off the field, too. *Page 141* (CSU)

42. Luis Tiant, the Cuban Comet, had the most entertaining delivery of any pitcher. *Page 143* (CSU)

43. "There's something wrong with Tony." Tony Horton was obsessed with hitting but couldn't handle the outs. *Page 146* (CSU)

44. Larry Nance, the leaping Cavalier. *Page 151* (Paul Tepley)

45. Mark Price, the Cavaliers' small star, dribbles past John Stockton. *Page 155* (Paul Tepley)

46. Lenny Wilkens was a winner on and off the court. *Page 158* (CSU)

47. John Battle, intense and emotional, fought his way to the NBA. *Page 163* (Paul Tepley)

48. Johnny Bower, Cleveland's favorite goalie, finally made it to the NHL at age 34. *Page 165* (CSU)

good health, but takes pills to control high blood pressure. He is divorced and has a son and a grandson. He gets a $3,000 baseball pension each month.

Power was one of the most interesting players of his time and was a great defensive first baseman. A four-time All-Star, he earned seven Gold Gloves. He was a friendly person but was constantly involved in feuds and hassles.

He was called a showboat because he caught everything with one hand. In 1961, Indians manager Jimmy Dykes told him to keep doing it. "Never argue with success," Dykes said.

"Now they catch everything with one hand," Power said. "If God wanted players to catch with two hands, he would have put gloves on both hands."

Power was so handy in the field that he played every position but pitcher and catcher in the majors. "I'm proud of that," he said. "They didn't do it for show. They put me in those positions because they were trying to win." He played third base, with Mickey Vernon on first, the day he stole home twice.

Latins and blacks were not numerous in the big leagues in his playing time, and Power went through the usual insults. In Kansas City, Mo., he sat down in a restaurant and was told he would have to leave. "We don't have Negroes," the waitress said. "I don't want a Negro, I want a steak," Power replied.

In Power's native Puerto Rico, there was no segregation. It was a culture shock when he came to America. "When they segregated me, I got mad," Power said. "It made me want to beat them in baseball." He had numerous fights and imbroglios. In a game in Boston early in his career, he made a leaping catch on a line drive off the bat of the eccentric Jim Piersall, then heard somebody yell a racial epithet from the Boston dugout.

"I called time and went to the Boston dugout," Power said. "I asked who called me that. Piersall told me to get back to first." Later in the game, Piersall reached first base. Power, still angry, told his friend, pitcher Bobby Shantz, to try a pickoff play. When Power got the ball, he slapped it hard on Piersall's neck. "I wanted to fight Piersall, but the umpire stopped me," said Power. "I'll never forget what Piersall said: 'You don't want to kill me. I've got a big family to support.'"

The retort made Power start laughing. Piersall was the father of nine children. Later, the two played together on the Indians and got along well.

Power was in several beanball fights. "I didn't get mad at the pitchers as much as the managers," he said. "The pitchers were just following orders. So I went to managers Al Lopez [White Sox], Casey Stengel [Yankees], Bill Rigney [Angels] and Pinky Higgins [Boston]. I told them the next time I was hit I was going after them in the dugout. I finally got some respect. I know Stengel told his pitchers, 'Don't wake him up.'"

Power was a good hitter, averaging .284 with 126 homers while using a 36-inch, 36-ounce bat. His high was .319 with the Kansas City Athletics in 1955.

He remembers his first visit to Cleveland, going 0-for-16 against Indians pitchers Bob Feller, Bob Lemon, Early Wynn and Mike Garcia.

Another memorable confrontation occurred at the Stadium when Power was with the Indians in the late 1950s. An elderly fan behind the first-base dugout yelled insults at Power throughout the game. "He kept calling me a showboat," Power said. Power finally went to the stands and shouted back at the fan. It was not until he read the newspaper the next day that he found the man was Ohio State football coach Woody Hayes.

Power came to the Indians with shortstop Woodie Held from Kansas City in a 1958 trade for promising outfielder Roger Maris, who later broke Babe Ruth's home run record with 61 in 1961. "I'm proud of that," said Power. "If it wasn't for me, Maris wouldn't have beaten Babe Ruth. He would have played in Cleveland, where it was hard to hit homers. When Kansas City traded him to New York, he had that short right field in Yankee Stadium."

Power, who watches three or four major-league games a day on cable TV, has one regret, that he never played in the World Series. "But I enjoyed my days in baseball," he said. "Even when they beanballed me."

Four Home Runs in Succession

Rocky Colavito *Jun. 10, 1999*

Rocco Domenico "Rocky" Colavito was in a slump going into the Indians' game in Baltimore on June 10, 1959. He had only three hits in his last 28 at-bats on that balmy Wednesday evening 40 years ago tonight. There were rumors he might be traded to Boston for slugger Jackie Jensen.

Colavito, never one to be easily discouraged, bounded up the dugout steps to take batting practice, saying hello to a group of Cleveland baseball writers. They asked him about his slump. "What slump?" he said. "I'm not in a slump."

"When are you going to start hitting?" Harry Jones of The Plain Dealer asked.

"You never know, Harry, maybe tonight," Colavito replied.

Colavito then went out and had the greatest slugging game in Cleveland baseball history, hitting four home runs in four successive at-bats, one off Jerry Walker, two off Arnold Portocarrero and the last off Ernie Johnson. The right-handed hitter pulled all four balls into the left-field stands, hitting them in the vicinity of 375 to 425 feet. It was the sixth time since 1900 that a major-leaguer had hit four homers in a game. Despite all the home runs flying out of ballparks today, only four more men equaled Colavito's feat in the succeeding four decades.

Colavito remains the last American Leaguer to slam four homers in a game. He, Lou Gehrig and Mike Schmidt are the players to hit four in succession.

Clevelanders watching the game on TV in living rooms and taverns cheered and slapped each other on the back as the Indians won, 11-8, in the midst of a hot pennant race. Colavito was one of the most popular players in Cleveland sports history. Up to then, no player had hit more than two home runs in a game in Baltimore's spacious park.

"I remember everything about that game," said Colavito, 65, from his home in Bernville, Pa.

He has in his den the ball he hit for the fourth homer. He has been offered a lot of money for it but will not sell. It would be like selling a part of his life, he said.

Spud Goldstein, Indians traveling secretary during the 1940s and 1950s, retrieved the ball after the game from the fan who caught it. "He gave the guy three autographed balls and $25 for it," Colavito said.

That was before the memorabilia craze drove up the price of such a prize.

Colavito said he never made a penny off his heroics. Frantic Frank Lane, Indians general manager and Colavito's nemesis, did not give him a bonus and barely acknowledged the performance.

"The only offer I got came from Ed Sullivan," continued Colavito, referring to Sullivan's highly rated Sunday night TV show. "He was going to give me $500 to come on the show the next Sunday. But we had a 14-inning game in Washington—Mudcat Grant pitched all the way for us—and I never made it to New York in time." At the end of the program, the disappointed Sullivan waved goodbye to the audience and said, "Good night, Rocky Colavito, wherever you are." He never received the $500.

Colavito made $28,000 that year, good pay for a 25-year-old player in 1959, but a trifle compared with today's baseball salaries. The top wage of his 13-year career was $70,000, which made him one of the highest-paid players of his time.

Colavito recalled that he walked his first time up against Walker in the historic game. "Nobody remembers that," he said. He cracked his first homer off Walker with a man on in the third inning. "The ball hugged the left-field foul line," Colavito said. "I knew it was long enough. It was just a question of whether it was high enough." It was.

The bases were empty when he homered off Portocarrero in the fifth. This was the best of the lot, sailing deep into the stands far from the foul line. In the sixth, he again connected off Portocarrero, with a man on.

"Both were on good pitches, sliders that hit the outside part of the plate," Colavito recalled. "I was able to reach over and get them."

Colavito was ecstatic, but the best was yet to come. His roommate, pitcher Herb Score, was sitting on the dugout steps as Colavito got off the bench to hit in the ninth. "Go up there and hit the fourth one," Score shouted.

"I said I'd be happy to get a single," Colavito recalled. "But Herb said, 'Bull. Go up there and do it.'"

Johnson was the Orioles' ace reliever. Colavito later heard that Johnson vowed in the dugout that Rocky would not hit another homer. Johnson's first pitch was high and inside. "I just raised my chin and the ball went under it," Colavito said. "I was seeing the ball real good. He probably thought I'd be looking away for the next pitch so he came back up and in with another fastball. I was looking for it and connected.

"I was thrilled. I was aware Gehrig had the record because he was my brother Vito's favorite ballplayer, and mine too, until Joe DiMaggio came along."

The Bronx-born Colavito, son of an Italian immigrant, trotted around the bases as the Baltimore crowd of 15,883 gave him a standing ovation.

Colavito jumped on home plate with both feet, tipped his cap to the crowd and raced into the dugout, where he was swarmed by his teammates.

Pitcher Gary Bell, who had started the game, came out of the shower with a towel on and shook Colavito's hand in the dugout. Colavito shook hands with every person he could find, including the bat boy and clubhouse attendants.

Grant played the Rocky Colavito Cha Cha Cha on his guitar in the clubhouse.

The Plain Dealer carried the story in a six-column headline across Page 1, "Colavito Slams Four Homers, Tribe Wins." The victory kept the Indians in third place, 1 game behind first-place Chicago and a half-game behind the Orioles.

The outburst, which included six runs batted in, gave Colavito 18 homers for the year. He would finish with a league-leading 42 homers and 111 RBI as the Indians wound up in second place behind Chicago.

Ten months after the game, Lane traded him to Detroit for batting champion Harvey Kuenn, shocking Cleveland fans and beginning a downward slide during which the Indians stayed mostly in the second division until their recent revival.

Indians fans loved Colavito for his slugging and powerful arm. He looked the way a ballplayer should look, tall and strong. And he would sign autographs for hours after games. Small boys imitated the stretch he employed when he came to the plate, grabbing both ends of the bat and pulling it back over his shoulders and down to his hips. They mimicked the way he punched his glove twice before catching routine fly balls. Bobby-soxers idolized him. "Don't knock the Rock," was a civic byword.

Colavito played 13 years in the majors, hitting 374 home runs, more than his idol DiMaggio, who had 361. Colavito had more than 100 RBI in six seasons, two more than Hall of Famer Mickey Mantle.

Life is good for Colavito these days. He and his wife, Carmen, will celebrate their 45th wedding anniversary in August. They have three grown children, Rocco, 43; Marisa, 42; and Steve, 32, and five granddaughters. Colavito is in good health and makes occasional appearances at card shows. He sounds exactly the way he always did, voluble and friendly. He enjoys hunting.

Colavito maintains a casual interest in baseball, even though it is not the game he once knew. He cannot understand why teams sacrifice bunt in the first inning or steal bases when they are leading, 10-0. He is convinced the ball is much livelier. "We had strong guys when I played, like Mickey Mantle, Harmon Killebrew and Frank Howard, but when they hit the ball off the end of the bat, it was an easy fly," he said. "Now, you see little guys getting homers on balls off the end of the bat. But it's been good for baseball. The game needed a boost after the [1994] strike."

Colavito has one regret. He does not have a tape or film of his four-homer game. He asked the TV station for one soon after, but it had been destroyed. "In those days, they didn't save the tapes," he said. They simply ran another game tape over the previous one. The tape might be gone, but nobody can take away Colavito's game for the ages.

Outfielder's Antics Overshadowed Real Baseball Talent

JIM PIERSALL *Jun. 26, 2001*

Jimmy Piersall was the noisiest ballplayer the Indians ever had. He was always talking, often at the top of his voice, on the team bus, in the clubhouse and on the field.

In three tumultuous years in Cleveland, from 1959 to 1961, he was a riotous package of fun, trouble and skill. The center fielder battled with pitchers, umpires, sportswriters, scorers and fans. He also was a great guy to interview.

Most fans loved him. "They knew I wasn't two-faced," he said. He recorded two songs, "Please, Jimmy Piersall," and "Rookie of the Year," and talked/sang them in shows at the Hippodrome, Olympia, Elysium and Berea theaters.

It is good to see Piersall has lost none of his spirit at age 71. "I feel great," the old rascal said from his home in Illinois. "I had a triple bypass in 1976 and a quadruple bypass in 1984. I asked my doctor how many more years I have left and he said, 'You're too ornery to die.'"

He had nine children by the time he was 31 and playing for the Indians and now has 25 grandchildren.

Piersall, who used to broadcast Chicago baseball games and still does three radio shows a week, said he is set financially. He and his second wife, Jan, to whom he has been married for 20 years, own two houses, one in Arizona.

"I'm the gooney bird that walked to the bank," he said. "I'm doing better than most of those guys who said I was crazy."

He had detailed his emotional and mental breakdown as a Boston Red Sox rookie in his best-selling book "Fear Strikes Out." After his retirement as a player, Piersall wrote another book, "The Truth Hurts," in which he said in the first line: "Probably the best thing that happened to me was going nuts. Nobody knew who I was until that happened." He had been institutionalized. After his recovery, most baseball people thought Piersall was deliberately putting on a show with his antics. Others thought he was still suffering from the effects of his illness. Maybe a little of both was true.

Bob Hale, 67, a former pinch hitter with the Indians and now a retired school principal, said: "When there were 40,000 in the stands or the game was on TV, you could expect Jimmy to make something happen. I think it was calculated. But he was a fine player and a lot of fun."

Former outfielder Tito Francona, 67, agreed. "Jimmy was smart as a fox," he said. "Every time he got kicked out of a game, he made more money. People sent him money to pay his fines. I remember a game in Yankee Stadium where he ran to second base and did jumping jacks. Then he ran behind the monuments and sat down."

Rocky Colavito, 67, recalled the time he was playing next to Piersall in the Indians outfield in Detroit. "He was in center and I was in right," said Colavito. "All of a sudden, I saw him running to the 395-foot sign in center where two guys were sitting by themselves. He came back laughing. I asked him what happened and he said, 'Those two guys have been yelling at me through the whole game. I just spit in their face.'"

In Cleveland's Municipal Stadium, Piersall would sit on top of the fence. Bleachers fans would yell, "Hey, Jimmy, the men in the white coats are coming." The quick-witted Piersall would answer back. "I didn't mind if they yelled at me," Piersall said. "But when they came on the field, it was a different story."

That happened twice within three weeks in 1961, both in Sunday doubleheaders against the Yankees. A crowd of 56,307 at the Stadium saw a burly fan run at Piersall in center. He wanted to shake his hand. "You touch me and I'll kick you in the rear," Piersall said, reasoning the man could have a knife. The fan squared off at Piersall, then ran. Piersall punted him. Then, in front of 57,824 at Yankee Stadium, two fans, 17 and 18, charged him, calling him a nut and throwing punches. He had shouted at the populace in defense of teammate Vic Power, who was being booed. Piersall defended himself well, landing punches and another field goal as teammate Johnny Temple and police helped out. The skirmish took the play away from Roger Maris and Mickey Mantle, who were waging their epic duel for the home run title. Piersall refused to press charges after the melee.

"I've had 117 fights and that's the first time I've ever won," he said. Aside from the escapades, Piersall had talent. When he came up with Boston in 1952, Yankees manager Casey Stengel said he was the best right fielder he had ever seen. He had a great arm then, but injured it after a throwing contest with Willie Mays. Piersall became a brilliant center fielder, a quick man who always got a good jump on the ball. He was smart and canny, knowing exactly where to play hitters.

When Francona replaced Piersall in center for Cleveland in 1959, Jimmy would stand in the bullpen and position him. Once, with Elston Howard of the Yankees up, Piersall told Francona to move toward right center. Francona, figuring the right-handed Howard would pull the ball against the pitcher, who did not have much speed, shifted toward left center instead.

But Howard hit the ball to right center. "That's the last time I didn't listen to Piersall," Francona said.

Piersall was a good hitter, too, averaging .272 in 17 seasons. He led the league in doubles once and hit as many as 18 homers. His best season came with Cleveland in 1961, when he hit .322. He had trouble with manager Joe Gordon as the Indians almost won the 1959 pennant. "Joe didn't like me," Piersall said. "We should have won the pennant that year. It was the best club I was ever on." The late Gordon was quoted as saying: "So help me, before I'm through I'm going to belt Piersall."

"You couldn't dislike Jimmy," Colavito said. "He was fun. He had a commercial deal with Neptune Sardines and would always bring some to the clubhouse."

"He said the sardines were the reason I hit .363 in 1959," Francona said.

Piersall would answer almost any question an interviewer asked. He was friendly with noncritical writers, but he always seemed to be feuding with somebody in the press. In Minnesota, he ordered two Twins writers out of the clubhouse. On at least one occasion, he threw a baseball at a sportswriter from center field during warmups, missing by 10 feet. He circled writers who were smoking cigarettes like a caged lion. "If you want to talk to me, you'll have to put out that cigarette," he said.

He frequently argued with official scorers and umpires. He regrets the power umpires have assumed today. "You can't even look at an umpire anymore," he said. "Baseball can be a very dull game. People don't come to see the umpires."

He prided himself on getting opposing players angry, hoping to distract them. "Now the players pat each other on the ass," he said.

Piersall burst on the scene as a rookie with the Red Sox in 1952. He suffered a breakdown from the pressure of trying to make the team and began doing things never before seen on baseball fields.

He ran up the screen behind home plate; spread his arms in imitation of an airplane when running to first base; dropped his bat and imitated the pitcher's motion; left the plate and ran to first to give a stage whisper to a runner. When an umpire called him out on strikes in the minors, he pulled a water pistol and sprayed the plate, saying, "Maybe now you can see it." All this was told in "Fear Strikes Out." It was later made into a movie, starring Anthony Perkins. Piersall hated Perkins' portrayal because the actor was so unathletic. His father, played by tall, domineering Karl Malden in the movie, was actually a small, friendly man, judging from a visit he once made to the Cleveland dugout. "The book was the truth," Piersall said. "The movie was not my story."

When the Indians traded Piersall to Washington for Dick Donovan and Gene Green, he expressed happiness to a Cleveland baseball writer. "I don't have to read your stuff anymore," he said. "You and those two columnists. You guys are killing baseball in that town. But I like you anyway. We're pals, right, even though I think you're a [expletive]."

Piersall went on to play with the New York Mets, where he ran himself into everlasting legend by trotting around the bases backward after hitting his 100th home run. "Yeah, but don't forget I was a good ballplayer, too," he said. That he was.

The Short Jump of Gene Green

GENE GREEN *Jul. 11, 1971*

The Downstairs Room, in its heyday Cleveland's gaudiest night spot, is gone. Midnight adventurers cast nostalgic glances at the parking lot that stands where it used to be until it was torn down some months ago.

Eight, ten years ago the room was the sporting set's favorite hideaway. You'd see all the baseball players there and many of the football players, along with the pickpockets, daring young ladies and celebrities from respectable pursuits.

If you wrote all the things that happened there you'd make Jim Bouton's book Ball Four sound like the Boy Scout Manual. In fact, they were having so much fun that one year the American League barred all its ball players from going there, which caused considerable grumbling.

Often when I think of the place, I remember Gene Green, the old Cleveland ball player who maybe had more fun there than anybody.

Green was not only a valiant man with a scotch and soda, he was also an invaluable news source. He'd feed me a lot of good inside stuff, but his major contribution to sports literature came when he decided to jump the team in 1963.

Green wasn't playing enough to be happy and when the Indians left Los Angeles for a flight to Washington one morning I noticed he wasn't on the plane.

"Where's Green?" I asked Birdie Tebbetts, the manager.

"I don't know and I don't care," replied the Bird, who was not enchanted with the Green personality.

Sitting down on the plane next to the scholarly second baseman, Jerry Kindall, I mentioned that if Green didn't contact the team when it arrived in Washington I was going to write a story speculating that he had quit the club.

Kindall glanced up from the book he was reading and looked at me from above his glasses and down his nose. "That's preposterous," he said.

"I'll remind you you said that if it turns out to be true," I said.

We reached the capital and still no word from the prodigal. I was convinced Green had stayed in L.A. where he had many friends to help him forget his troubles.

I knew his haunts and began making phone calls. I found him feeling no pain in a bistro called Ernie's and he had no inhibitions about saying what was on his mind.

He wasn't going to come back, he wanted to be traded, he wasn't making enough money and he didn't like Tebbetts.

I had the story all to myself and I phoned it in to the paper and walked triumphantly into the hotel lobby. The Green mystery was now the only topic of conversation. Nobody else knew where he was and ball players and writers congregated in little groups talking about it.

Tebbetts and his general manager, Gabe Paul, strolled into the lobby, having just finished a merry dinner, and I announced I had located Green. It wasn't as good as Stanley finding Livingston but it was a hell of a story at that time.

The other writers begged to know the details and Tebbetts and Paul were just as curious.

When I told them what Green had said Tebbetts hit the ceiling and called Green every name in the book while I happily wrote down all his quotes. The gist of Birdie's diatribe was that Green was a poor excuse for a major league ball player and that if he didn't like sitting on the bench he could quit and become a truck driver.

The next day Green arrived, penitent. He was happy to be back and I was happy because I had my story. I reminded Kindall that he had said the idea was preposterous.

Likable Swashbuckler in Trouble

PETE RAMOS *Aug. 12, 1979*

Too bad about Pedro Ramos, who was arrested and charged with a felony in a $2 million cocaine bust in Miami, Fla., recently. The old baseball pitcher, who won 116 games in 16 years in the majors, was one of the most likable athletes I ever met.

I don't know if Ramos is guilty or not, but I do know that former jocks often get into trouble because they can't adjust to being one of the peons after years in the spotlight. Ramos was a swashbuckler who lived it up better than almost anybody in his heyday.

I first met him in spring training of 1962 when the Indians acquired him in a trade for Vic Power and Dick Stigman. He was badly overweight when he reported, a rash under his ribs serving as testimony to a winter of a reckless diet.

But he worked off the suet willingly, running in the outfield sun. He moved like a young stallion, with perfect form. You could have put a teacup on his head while he was galloping at full speed and it wouldn't have fallen off. He was often used as a pinch runner. He kept challenging Mickey Mantle, the fastest man in the league, to a match race for $1000, but Mantle always laughed it off.

Ramos quickly established himself as a genial guy around the Cleveland clubhouse. He possessed a curious mixture of childishness, naiveté and bravado and loved to be interviewed and photographed.

Even though he couldn't read English, he would sit for hours on airplanes looking at pictures in the sports pages. One day he said to me, "A friend of mine say you make fun of me in an article." He didn't mind. He relished the attention. Needed it.

He would only get angry when he spoke of his mother, who was living in Castro's Cuba. "If the U.S. invades I will be the first one on the beach," he said grimly. "My mother is sick and needs medicine. If I could help her I'd quit baseball today."

He was easily the most generous ballplayer I ever knew. Most of them have the first penny they ever earned, but Ramos would actually buy drinks for sportswriters. One day in Washington he took the unprecedented step of taking all the Cleveland writers and broadcasters to lunch at a fancy restaurant.

An extremely dashing man, he loved the fans. I can still see him signing autographs at ballparks around the league, hair brilliantined, big cigar in mouth, talking expansively to his public.

He was married to Miss Cuba of 1960, a stunning brunette. "You should see my first wife," Ramos said. "She look just like Elizabeth Taylor."

Ramos' personality was always geared toward the entertainment world. He often said he would like to be an actor in cowboy movies after his baseball career ended. They didn't call him Pistol Pete for nothing.

One night in 1963, Ramos attended a backyard party that sportscaster Jimmy Dudley threw for the whole team at his Bay Village home. Ramos was dressed in a cowboy outfit – tight black pants, black shirt, and black hat. Two revolvers hung from holsters at his sides. He looked just like the Cisco Kid.

A row of party lights were strung across Dudley's yard. At the height of the revelry, someone suggested to Ramos that he shoot out the lights. He pulled out his guns, aimed and was about to fire when someone suggested it might not be too good an idea.

That was typical of Ramos. He was willing to go along with anything people wanted. "I like to make people hoppy." He said.

Ramos himself must not be very "hoppy" now.

Postscript: Ramos was put on probation. In 1981 he violated his probation and was sentenced to three years in prison. He became recreation supervisor at a farm prison, pitching in softball games, and was released after a year. He has not been in trouble since. He now has a cigar company, Pedro Ramos Cigars.

"Sudden Sam" was Consistent for Weak Tribe Teams

SAM McDOWELL *Jul. 24, 2001*

Most pitchers do not throw a one-hitter in their entire careers. Sudden Sam McDowell was so talented that he threw one-hitters in two consecutive games in 1966.

Both very easily could have been no-hitters. "Getting a no-hitter is 100 percent luck," said McDowell, 58, who lives in suburban Orlando, Fla.

On April 25, 1966, the fast-balling McDowell gave up a bloop, two-strike single in the sixth inning to Jose Tartabull of Kansas City in a 2-0 Cleveland victory in front a cozy gathering of 5,227 at the Stadium.

"I jammed the heck out of Tartabull," recalled McDowell. "I was going for a strikeout, but he hung in there." Shortstop Larry Brown batted in both runs with a single in the sixth inning off Roland Sheldon.

After the game, McDowell credited his veteran catcher, Del Crandall, who had been acquired after a long career in the National League. "We're working together in sort of an easy rhythm, like a dance team," he said.

The Indians were undefeated with eight victories in what would become a 10-0 start under manager Birdie Tebbetts. Six days later, on May 1, McDowell overpowered the Chicago White Sox, 1-0, beating Tommy John.

Don Buford got the cheapest kind of hit, a bloop over first base, just inside the right-field line, in the third inning. Brown again got the winning hit, singling in Pedro Gonzalez in the second. A mere 9,655 saw the game at the Stadium as the Indians moved to 11-1.

"Sam's been great in all his games," Crandall told Chuck Heaton of The Plain Dealer. "I've never seen his slider better."

"Two straight one-hitters is hard to believe," said Buford. "That's great pitching. I didn't get much wood on the ball."

The rawboned 6-6 McDowell, who was lean and mean then, had become the second American League pitcher since 1900 to throw two consecutive one-hitters. The other was Whitey Ford of the New York Yankees in 1955. Since then, Dave Stieb of Toronto (1988) has done it. Three National Leaguers—Rube Marquard (1911), Lon Warneke (1934) and Mort Cooper (1943)—achieved the feat.

Still only 23, McDowell became a favorite subject with the media. He was on the cover of Sports Illustrated. He was being compared with Sandy Koufax as the next great left-hander.

Then his arm got sore. "I had a slight tear of the rotator cuff," McDowell remembered. "They didn't know how to fix rotator cuffs in those days. I got a shot of Novocain and kept pitching." He finished 9-8 that season, leading the league in strikeouts with 225 and posting a 2.87 earned run average.

McDowell, who was chosen one of the 100 top Indians in history, rebounded to have consistently outstanding seasons for mostly weak teams in Cleveland. He was 18-14 for a last-place club in 1969 and 20-12 for the fifth-place Indians in 1970. "My best year was 1968, when I had a 1.81 ERA. I was able to throw the ball where I wanted to and how I wanted to," he said. He was 15-14 that year.

He won five league strikeout titles, going as high as 325 in 1965, when he was 17-11. He had six seasons in Cleveland when his ERA was under 3.00.

McDowell disputes his long-held image that he preferred tricking batters to simply firing the ball past them. For his career, he struck out 8.86 batters per game, fourth-best in baseball history behind Randy Johnson, Nolan Ryan and Koufax.

He has no qualms admitting he had an alcohol problem, however. He was in several off-the-field scrapes before leaving the Indians in a trade for San Francisco's Gaylord Perry after the 1971 season. He remained addicted to alcohol and also used amphetamines through the rest of his career in baseball, winding up with a 141-134 record in 1975.

He was still hooked when he retired and became a successful salesman for an insurance company in Pittsburgh, his hometown. He had to hit rock bottom before he finally went into rehabilitation. "I had lost my wife, my home, my job, and was sitting on a curb in Monroeville [Pa.] one night with 35 cents in my pocket," he said. "My gas tank was empty and I was trying to figure out if I should buy a hamburger or 35 cents worth of gas." He went to the restaurant.

When he woke up the next day, he was in a rehabilitation center. "Everything has been fine since," he said. "My parents and brothers pulled me through. They refused to let me lie to myself."

He has not had a drink in 22 years.

"I should have been a lot better pitcher," McDowell said. "I was a real jerk, but I don't regret anything else I did. If I hadn't been a drunk, I wouldn't be where I am. I might never have helped the people I helped."

McDowell became a therapist and alcohol and drug counselor for the Texas Rangers and Toronto Blue Jays. In suburban Orlando, he is involved in building a retirement village for athletes. He lives alone but is close to his former wife.

He relishes a compliment once paid to him by former Indians manager Alvin Dark, who called him an outstanding clutch pitcher. "I liked challenges," said McDowell. "When Denny McLain said he couldn't wait to pitch against Cleveland because it was like getting a rest, I asked Alvin to move me up a day so I could pitch against him. I beat him. The same thing happened with Vida Blue." McLain, of Detroit, and Oakland's Blue were two of the league's best pitchers. So was Sudden Sam, when he really had it.

Tiant Was Unforgettable in Spring 1968

Luis Tiant *Aug. 7, 2001*

Luis Tiant wasn't just another good pitcher. He was one of the most entertaining hurlers in baseball history. His choreographed windup had a wide range of motions. He would bob his head, turn his back on the batter, look skyward or into the field boxes, then deliver the ball from a bewildering array of angles, overhand, sidearm or even underhand. "I didn't do it for show," Taint, 59, said. "I did it to get batters out. Players would tell me, 'We can't tell where the ball is coming from.'"

Tiant was at his best in the spring of 1968, when he threw four straight shutouts. It is an Indians club record and one short of the American League mark of five in a row, set by Doc White of Chicago 97 years ago.

It was an unforgettable season for the Cuban right-hander. A few weeks after the four straight zeroes, he struck out 19 while winning a 10-inning game, 1-0. "That was the best game I ever pitched," he said. "I had everything."

He won 21 and lost nine in that sensational 1968 season, while leading the league with an earned run average of 1.60 and in shutouts with nine.

His fastball burned up hitters' bats. "I'd say 75 percent of my pitches were fastballs," he said.

"The fastball is the best pitch in baseball. It's like having five pitches, if you move it around."

"Tiant had a backup curveball," said Joe Azcue, 61, who was his favorite catcher. "It never broke. His change-up was so-so. But he had pinpoint control and could bring it, about 95 miles an hour. And he had a hell of a move to first base. He liked to talk to the hitters. He'd say, 'Hit it baby.'"

The stocky Tiant, who was listed at 6-0 but was really only about 5-9, was one of the club's most likable players of the era. A clubhouse joker, he loved cigars and smoked them anywhere, including the shower. He was nicknamed "Looie" or "El Tiante." "It was fun playing behind him," said former third baseman Max Alvis, 63. "He'd get on the rubber and throw in a hurry. Everybody was on their toes because he was always around the plate. He had bulldog competitiveness."

Tiant began his spectacular shutout streak on April 28, 1968, throwing a two-hitter over the Senators in Washington for a 2-0 victory. Senators slugger Frank Howard struck out on Tiant's hesitation pitch. "I give him shoulder, back, foot and the ball last," Tiant told the Cleveland Press.

"He threw everything at me but the ball," Howard said.

Tiant was considered the Indians' fourth starter on a strong staff that included Sam McDowell, Sonny Siebert and Steve Hargan.

On May 3, Tiant fired a three-hitter over Minnesota at the Stadium, throwing 122 pitches in a 4-0 triumph. The Plain Dealer said, "a surprisingly good crowd of 5,106" saw the action. That shows the condition Cleveland baseball was in then. Tiant needed only two hours, 12 minutes to win. "Pitching is 85 percent luck," he said. He also complimented Azcue. "He speak my language," said Tiant in broken English. "Duke Sims is good too, but he no speak Spanish." Four days later, Tiant hurled his third straight zero, beating the Yankees, 8-0, in New York on a five-hitter in which he delivered 129 pitches. He fanned 10 and hit a two-run single. On May 12, Tiant stepped into the Cleveland record book with a four-hit, 2-0 shutout of Baltimore at the Stadium in which he struck out nine. His ERA fell to a dazzling 1.03. "I'm hitting the spots," said Tiant. "I've got control like I never had before."

Tiant was upset because the Orioles, who had Hall of Famers Frank and Brooks Robinson1, complained about his hesitation pitch. But umpire John Flaherty ruled it was a legal pitch if nobody was on base.

During the four shutouts, Tiant yielded 14 hits and struck out 35. On May 17, Tiant went after White's record of five straight blanks. "I am feeling the pressure but I am not scared," he said. The Orioles finally stopped Tiant at 41⅓ straight shutout innings when Boog Powell hit a three-run homer in the sixth inning in a 6-2 defeat of the Indians at the Stadium. A crowd of only 14,125 watched the heavily promoted game. The Indians were 17-14, three games out of first place.

Tiant hit his zenith on July 3, with his 19-strikeout game, most in Indians history. The game was scoreless in the 10th when the Twins put men on first and third with nobody out. With a crowd of 21,125 on its feet and screaming, Tiant struck out John Roseboro, Rich Rollins and pitcher Jim Merritt to surpass Bob Feller's mark of 18 K's, which was done in a nine-inning match. The Indians won in the bottom of the inning when the immortal Azcue singled in Sweet Lou Johnson.

Tiant threw 135 pitches. "I've never seen a fastball thrown so hard for so many innings," said Roseboro, who had caught Sandy Koufax and Don Drysdale with the Los Angeles Dodgers.

Giddy over his 21-9 record, 254 strikeouts and 19 complete games, the Indians brass hoped to make Tiant even better. They told him to forsake his usual practice of pitching in winter ball and rest. It was a classic case of trying to fix something that had nothing wrong with it.

"When you're used to pitching, you have to keep your arm going all the time," Azcue said. "He lost two feet on his fastball."

"I got a sore arm," said Tiant, who dropped to a 9-20 record in 1969. "It took me two years to get over it." The Indians quickly gave up on Tiant, 29, trading him and Stan Williams to Minnesota for Dean Chance, Graig Nettles, Ted Uhlaender and Bob Miller on Dec. 10, 1969.

Tiant eventually resurfaced with the Boston Red Sox, where he won 20 or more games three times in eight years. He won a World Series game in 1975, beating Cincinnati. "I threw 163 pitches and we won, 5-4," he said. "Today they take them out after 90 pitches." Tiant ended his 19-year career in the majors with a 229-172 record, including 49 shutouts. Some people think he belongs in the Baseball Hall of Fame. Nobody who saw those four shutouts and 19 strikeouts will argue.

The Pressure was Just Too Much

TONY HORTON *Jul. 31, 2001*

Tony Horton left the glamour, glory and tumult of Major League Baseball and disappeared into oblivion with startling rapidity. In one of the major tragedies in Indians history, Horton, 25, suffered an emotional breakdown in the midst of a doubleheader at the Stadium.

The slugging first baseman never played baseball again and has seldom been heard from since. He is 56.

Horton's exit from baseball took place on Aug. 28, 1970, during a twi-night doubleheader against the California Angels. He went 1-for-4 in the first game, which the Indians lost. Veteran shortstop Larry Brown, who was on the bench, was worried by Horton's demeanor at first base in the nightcap. "He was kind of staring," recalled Brown, 61. "I told [manager] Alvin Dark, 'He's not here. You've got to get him out of there.'" Horton went hitless in two at-bats in the second game. After his second out, he snapped. "Tony threw a fit," said Brown.

Michael Coyne, then an assistant to Indians clubhouse director Cy Buynak, was in the dugout and saw the incident. "Tony grabbed Dark and shook him real hard for several seconds," said Coyne, now owner of McMahon-Coyne Funeral Home. "Dark then said, 'Tony, you're finished for the day. Go to the clubhouse.'" The manager told Brown to go with him and keep an eye on him.

When Horton arrived in the clubhouse, he expressed dismay about his poor hitting and said, "I failed my mother." "No, you didn't," said the sympathetic Buynak, who was a good friend of Horton's. "You've got 17 home runs." In those days, a 20-homer season was good work.

Brown stayed with Horton in the clubhouse. He was baffled by the scene. "Tony went to every player's empty locker and talked about each guy," Brown recalled. "He talked about who was a man and who was not a man. I was trying to figure out what was going on." The team doctor came in and wanted to take Horton to a hospital. Buynak said Horton was unwilling to go. "All I need is sleep, Cy," he said. He was not hospitalized that night.

The next day, Horton appeared in the clubhouse wearing sandals and an Indians shirt. "That was the strangest day of my life," recalled Sam McDowell, 58, who was to pitch and win his 19th game that day. "When I came in, Dark said, 'There's something wrong with Tony.'"

Horton wanted to talk to McDowell, who was not a particularly close friend. "Tony talked to me like we were long-lost brothers while I got dressed," McDowell said. "Mostly he talked about having a bad year. He couldn't understand why he wasn't hitting. Petty things were bothering him. He was nervous. I was compassionate. He needed a sounding board. When I went to the bench, he sat down next to me until I went out to warm up. That was the last time I saw him on the ballclub."

Horton went into a hospital soon after that. The Indians covered up the story. Dark told the media that Horton would miss some games with a strained groin and physical exhaustion. About 10 days went by before they said he would be out the rest of the season.

In January, they announced that he had been in a hospital since September and that he would miss the 1971 season. McDowell saw Horton about a year after the crackup. Horton contacted him when the Indians were playing in California. "He had been under therapy and wanted to see some of the guys," McDowell said. "A few of us, Duke Sims was one, went to see him. He was fine. But apparently it caused a major problem."

Horton suffered a relapse after the visit.

In a brief Plain Dealer interview in 1973, Horton said: "I never think about playing baseball again." He said he had a small investment business at the time. Since then, he has not been interviewed.

Those close to Horton offer a variety of opinions for his breakdown. Everybody talks about his intensity.

"If he hit a homer, he wanted to hit the next one farther," said Max Alvis, 63, former Indians third baseman. "He used to squeeze the bat harder and harder."

"You'd see him grinding the bat," said former pitcher and roommate Sonny Siebert, 64. "He was very intense, and it finally caught up to him. He had a high desire to do well and couldn't relax under pressure."

Mentor restaurateur Tony Alesci was one of Horton's best friends. "I'll never forget the time he hit two homers," Alesci said. "He was pounding his fist and saying, 'If I'd only hit one more we would have won.'"

Buynak recalled that Horton, who came to Cleveland from Boston in a trade for Gary Bell in 1967, was obsessed with hitting 50 homers in a season. He would give himself impossible goals, figuring how many he had to hit in the remaining games to reach the mark.

His best hitting season was 1969, when he hit .278, with 27 homers and 93 runs batted in. But he had not been able to get the kind of raise he wanted from Dark in 1970 and was upset about that. Brown remembered Horton's weaknesses. "He swung at bad pitches all over the place," he said. "If he had a 3-0 count, he would swing even if the ball was over his head. And he was the worst baserunner I ever saw."

Siebert recalled a moment of levity. "Steve Hamilton threw him a blooper and Tony either popped up or struck out," said Siebert. "Tony crawled back to the dugout on his knees for a joke."

"We didn't think he had that kind of sense of humor," said Hank Kozloski, then an Indians beat writer and now one of the Indians' official scorers. "Maybe it wasn't humor."

Even before his demise, bachelor Horton had a reputation as a champion ladies man. "If Tony was in a restaurant eating breakfast and he saw a pretty girl, he'd take off and try to meet her," Brown recalled. "But he was religious. I think he was torn in two directions."

"Tony was a good-looking young guy," said Alesci. "He was not a drinker, but he loved to eat and he loved girls. But he was very selective. He was in love with Kathy Bauman."

Bauman, from Independence, was a Miss Ohio and a finalist in the Miss America pageant. "She was one of the most beautiful girls I ever saw," said Syd Friedman, director of beauty pageants.

"She told me that she and Tony were going to get engaged," said

Buynak, who is now head of the visitors' clubhouse at Jacobs Field. Bauman is said to be married and living in California.

Alesci said Horton, who received a big bonus to sign with Boston out of high school, never wanted to be a baseball player. "He wanted to go to USC," Alesci said. "He was doing something he did not want to do."

Variety

Cavaliers, Barons, Negro League Baseball,
Olympics, High School & College

Touch of Class

LARRY NANCE *Mar. 13, 1988*

The old piano still sits in his mother's house, a symbol of Larry Nance's boyhood.

Minnie Nance insisted that her son take piano lessons. "I pushed him," she said from her home in Anderson, S.C.

Larry dutifully endured piano lessons for five or six years. He got pretty good, too, playing at Sunday School and when company dropped in.

"But he didn't like it," his mother recalled. "He liked basketball. When he started playing basketball, he quit the piano. We laughed at him."

Obviously, Nance made the right career choice when he passed up the chance to complete with Vladimir Horowitz and Van Cliburn.

The 6-10 forward with the astonishing leaping ability is one of the quality players in the National Basketball Association. His career shooting percentage of 56.4% going into this season is the fifth-best in the history of the league.

Since he was acquired by the Cavaliers in a trade with the Phoenix Suns on Feb. 25 he has become the franchise's ornament of hope in the drive for the playoffs.

Area fans have already fallen in love with him. After watching him swoop around the basket like an agitated condor in his first game at the Coliseum as a member of the Cavs Wednesday, they gave him a couple of standing ovations.

It became quickly apparent to the fans in this rust belt town that Nance, despite his physical gifts, is no prima donna. He did a lot of menial work in his debut, grabbing the tough rebound and making the outlet pass. When the guards were pressed, he came back from the basket to help bring the ball down court.

On defense, he was constantly shouting to his teammates to let them know where the picks were being set. Even though he may be the most electrifying slam-dunker on the club, he reveled in seeing his mates make the jam, slapping their hands in congratulation.

He looked like a man who was going to fit in very quickly.

"I was in shock when I was traded," Nance said. "I had a lot of good friends in Phoenix. I planned to spend the rest of my life there. Other than that, I don't regret leaving the team. This organization is a lot classier. Lenny Wilkens (coach) expects you to act like a pro without him having to yell at you."

Even his mother now likes the trade.

"I was very, very upset when they moved Larry," she said. "I didn't know how he was going to like it. I was worried for him. But he called me the other day and said he was happy about going to Cleveland. That made me feel so good. Now he's a little closer to me. Phoenix was so far away and I don't like to fly. As soon as I can, I'm planning to come to Cleveland to see some games."

Carl Stegall, who coached Nance at McDuffie High in Anderson and still stays in touch with him, offered another insight.

"The trade will help Larry because I think he got kind of disgusted in Phoenix," Stegall said. "He wasn't getting much publicity. He should have been on the All-Star team every year."

Consensus throughout the league is that the Cavs got the better of the deal. Typical of the opinion are those words from two of Nance's former teammates, veterans Maurice Lucas and James Edwards.

"It was a total surprise to everybody in the NBA that Phoenix even thought of trading Nance," said Lucas. "He's a great player and I'm a big fan of Mike Sanders, too. He's a real sturdy player."

Sanders also came to the Cavs in the trade for Mark West, Tyrone Corbin and Kevin Johnson.

Edwards said: "The Cavs got the best of the deal because they got a forward who can do everything Nance should have made the All-Star team this year. He's a sparkplug."

With Cavs fans expecting so much from Nance, there is a lot of pressure on him. He says he can handle it.

"I can play under pressure," Nance said. "I want to be the great player they want me to be."

It is said that Nance harbors deep resentment over the fact he has been selected for the All-Star Game only once in his seven-year career.

"He doesn't talk about it much, but you can see it in his face," said Suns coach John Wetzel.

"It's something I strive for every year," said Nance. "It hurts my feelings when I'm not picked."

The continued slights are the reason Nance has never participated in the Slam Dunk contest since winning the first one at the All-Star Game four years ago. Nance won that contest with an unequalled move in which he slammed two balls during one high-flying maneuver.

"I don't want to travel all the way just to slam dunk," he said. I'd rather take the three days off at the All-Star break and spend them with my girlfriend.

Nance's sensational shooting percentage is built around his jumping ability and his refusal to take bad shots. He will convert a lot of lobs into stuffs. "He doesn't want to hurt his team by taking low-percentage shots," said Wetzel.

Despite his brilliance, Nance had been held in low esteem in several basketball stops. Herman Boseman, his junior varsity coach at Hanna High in Anderson, told him not to bother coming out for the team because he wouldn't make it.

Boseman, now a plant manager in Anderson, explained his shockingly wrong decision.

"He had a basketball in his hand all the time, but he hadn't developed," Boseman said. "He was very slender and not as mature as the other kids. He was about 5-9. The kids I kept grew to 5-11 and he grew to 6-10. No way I could tell that. We kid about it all the time. I see Larry a lot."

Because of Boseman's rejection, Nance quit Hanna and went to McDuffle High in Anderson. The coach there was, and is, Carl Stegall, who immediately saw his potential.

"My wife asked me one night, 'What do you have on the team this year?'" Stegall said. "I told her I've got a kid who's going to play pro ball. Larry wasn't the best player I ever had in high school. But he was the one with the most potential. But none of the colleges wanted him. They couldn't recognize talent."

Nance was about to enroll in a junior college when he got his one and only scholarship offer from Clemson coach Bill Foster.

"A lot of people didn't think he was Division I material," said

Foster, now the coach at the University of Miami (Fla.) "But he ran easy and had some graceful moves that caught the eye. By Christmas of his freshman year he grew three inches and put on 30 pounds."

"I was growing so fast I kept outgrowing my shoes," Nance said. "My mother had to keep buying me new ones."

Foster, like everyone else Nance has played for, said he was a pleasure to coach.

"He came from a two-parent, very religious family that had great values," Foster recalled. "His daddy drove a truck all over the U.S. Later he bought his own bus."

Nance's father died two years ago from heart trouble. He hardly ever missed seeing Larry play in college and high school.

The strong hand of Minnie Nance was always present, too.

"He was a sweet child," she said. "I'm proud of him, just as I am of my other three boys. None ever got into trouble. But I spanked them all. I put the whammy on all of them."

Even though Nance had a great career at Clemson, he was only the 20th pick in the first round of the 1981 NBA draft.

"Everybody goes by body type in the NBA," said Foster, guessing why Nance was ignored for so long. "Larry was a hard guy to figure. He played center in college, but he had the build of a small forward."

There is one huge void in Nance's career. He has never played on a team that won a championship.

"In my senior year at Clemson, we lost the game that would have put us in the Final Four," Nance said. "UCLA upset us, and they didn't belong on the same floor with us. I regret never being on a champion. Maybe it will happen with this team."

Postscript: The Cavs never did it. They were always stopped by Michael Jordan and the Chicago Bulls. Nance retired in 1994 with a 16.8 scoring average with the Cavs. He is the team's second-leading career shot-blocker, behind John "Hot Rod" Williams.

Choir Boy Gets Chorus of Praise from Foes

MARK PRICE *Apr. 12, 1988*

Mark Price remembers the first time he saw his future wife. He was the basketball star at Georgia Tech University and was cruising around the campus in a car driven by his roommate, Craig Neal. Price spotted a nice-looking blonde coed and said, "There's a girl I'd like to go out with sometime."

Then he forgot about it. Young people make hundreds of remarks like that and forget them the next minute.

A few weeks later, roommate Neal was in the Georgia Tech library with another girl and again saw the future Mrs. Price, whose name was Laura Marbut. He asked his girlfriend to tell her that Price would like to meet her. "Who's Mark Price?" asked Marbut. She knew nothing about basketball. But the girl coaxed her into giving her phone number.

Price called Marbut. Their first date was at a basketball game. "I played one of my worst games," Price recalls. "But I knew I was OK when she said,'You sure played good.'"

That was almost three years ago. They were wed last year. "Now she tells me everything I'm doing wrong," Price said with a laugh.

Not many people are criticizing Price these days. He is the Cavaliers' major surprise of the season as they fight for a National Basketball Association playoff spot.

The six-foot-tall workaholic is averaging 15 points a game as one of the highest-scoring point guards in the league. He dashes around like a fugitive frantically escaping the police. He happily dives for any available loose ball.

He is a choir boy off the court, but on it he sings a different tune. As the point man in the Cavs' attack, he brings the ball up in a confident, almost insolent, manner. He avoids eye contact with the player guarding him. "I don't want anybody to read me," he says. Sometimes you look a guy in the eye and he can see if you're tired or worried."

He does not try to put on a show. He relies on fundamentals. His first step is as quick as that of any guard in the NBA, enabling him to blow past more heralded performers.

Even though he looks like a nice boy who should be shooting in a quiet suburban driveway, it is wrong to underestimate his physical ability. His college coach, Bobby Cremins, said Price dominated in the Atlantic Coast Conference, which is loaded with top players and is often called the best college league in the land. He was the greatest player I ever coached," says Cremins.

His quickness is a shock," said Chuck Daly, coach of the division-leading Detroit Pistons. "He's a major-league point guard. He has to be among the three most improved players in the league."

Said Doc Rivers, Atlanta All-Star guard: "The sky's the limit for Mark. He's the best outside shooter of any point guard in the league. He's tough and quick. Nothing rattles him. I tried to post him up because I'm bigger than he is. He wouldn't allow it."

Kevin Johnson, the Cavs' No. 1 draft pick last spring, had no qualms about Price beating him out of a job. "Price is awesome," Johnson said from Phoenix, where he was traded Feb. 25. "He's playing point guard as well as anyone in the NBA. There is no doubt he deserved the job over me. The amazing thing about him is that he plays just as well in practice every day. His energy is unbelievable."

Price is secure in comparing himself to the other point guards in the league. "The best ones are the guys everybody knows about, like Magic Johnson, Isaiah Thomas and Maurice Cheeks," he said. "Then there are all the other guys who are just as good. At this level, they're all great." In other words, he takes a back seat to nobody in his own mind.

The funny thing about Price's glittering season is that he was almost the odd man out. The Cavs indicated they had no confidence in him by drafting Johnson and by making the aborted trade for Jim Paxson, another guard. John Bagley was another point man who was still available.

"Everybody was talking about Johnson and Bagley playing the point," Price said. "I was worried but I didn't let it bother me."

He was angry about the way he had played in his rookie season last year. He shot only 41% from the field. He blamed it on his newness in the NBA, combined with his midseason marriage and appendectomy. "I hadn't shown them the way I could really play," Price said. On a visit to his hometown of Enid, Okla., he sat down with his father, Denny, 50, and discussed his precarious situation. His father, a former NBA assistant coach, told him to return to basics, get back into a gym by himself and start working.

Mark took 500 shots a day all summer, usually working out at the Coliseum with teammate Craig Ehlo. When Ehlo wasn't available, Price's wife fielded balls as he shot. By the time the Cavs opened training camp, Price was in top shape, lean and mean.

Fortunately, he also had a coach in Lenny Wilkens who gave him an honest chance to win a job, instead of simply handing the post to Johnson. "It would have been very easy for him to start the No. 1 pick," Price said. "A lot of times it's very political. But I was given a legitimate opportunity."

Price is playing so intensely that it is natural to wonder if he will burn out. "I don't think so," Rivers said. "You never burn out if you love the game. At least not for 10 years."

Cremins said, however, that Price gets tired and needs extra rest. Cremins played him the full 40 minutes of every game, but gave him time off in practice.

Price admits he gets tired when he plays two nights in a row. But he cannot cut back. "I always go 100 percent," he said. "It's the way I was taught by my mother and father." An amateur psychologist would suspect that Price plays with such frenzy because he is trying unconsciously to please his father, who was an outstanding player.

"My dad was the only hero I ever had. He was a great shooter," Mark says. "Even when I was in high school he could beat me in a game of HORSE."

The Price family was a close one, steeped in the Southern Baptist religion. His mother, Ann, would play the piano at home while dad and the three sons sang gospel songs. The elder Price never spared the rod when the boys did something mischievous. "I always used the belt on the boys," he said. "In today's society, they'd probably call it child abuse."

Said Price: "He would tell us to pick out the belt we wanted to be spanked with. They were all thick." Price, the All-American boy, was whupped for doing such things as playing with matches and setting a field on fire and for throwing water-filled balloons at passing cars. "In Enid you had to find things to do," he explained.

Those were exceptions. Price's boyhood was built around religion and roughhouse sports with his brothers. He was a good quarterback in eighth-grade football and played excellent shortstop in baseball. Like many young boys, however, he was afraid to stand in and hit a fastball.

This is interesting, for Price looks fearless as he bounces off NBA floors for loose balls. This takes every bit as much courage as facing a speeding baseball. "I dive for the ball because sometimes it gets fans and teammates into a game," Price said. "Other guys dunk. I have to do other things."

When Price got to Georgia Tech, he still considered himself primarily a scorer. Cremins wanted him to penetrate and pass. He wanted to penetrate and shoot. "Sometimes he would give me dirty looks," said Cremins. When the coach found what a deadeye Price was, he gave him the green light to shoot from anywhere.

This scoring mentality is one reason that Price does not rank high in NBA assists. "I wasn't a true point guard in college," he said. "It's something I'm still learning."

Through it all, Price retains his deep religious feelings. He hasn't had a drink of alcohol since he was eight years old, when he had a beer at a friend's house. No doubt Denny got the belt out for that one. Price attends chapel meetings before every Cavs home game.

"When he came here I wondered if this guy was for real," said Cremins, referring to Price's religious inclinations. "Then I saw him sing in church. I'll never forget him. He won't back off from anybody. He was unique."

NBA rivals are beginning to find that out. "He's a great point guard," said New York Knicks rookie-of-the-year candidate Mark Jackson, who was burned for 24 points by Price the other night. "He's as tough as they come."

Wilkens Fights Right to the Top

LENNY WILKENS *Feb. 29, 1988*

Life is funny. You take a kid who has every advantage. His father is the board chairman. He gets $100 a week in spending money from the time he is 10 and a Corvette for his 16th birthday. Then he winds up broke, drinking wine under a bridge or snorting cocaine in a bath tub.

Then there is a fellow like Lenny Wilkens, who started out with very little. He never owned a basketball or a baseball glove as a boy. Yet, on the graph of success, his life has been one continuous line upward. Very few problems. Very few controversies.

The facts are there. Wilkens was a great basketball player. Basketball Digest says he was the fifth-best point guard in National Basketball Association history. For 15 years he has been a top coach, winning the NBA championship in 1979 with Seattle. Now he has the baby Cavaliers heading toward a playoff spot, developing faster than anyone expected.

To really understand Wilkens you have to go back more than 49 years to his boyhood in one of the toughest neighborhoods of Brooklyn, N.Y. His father, a chauffeur, died of a bleeding ulcer when Lenny was five. His mother struggled to support her five children. An old friend, New Yorker Shelley Kaplan, says Lenny was practically raised by Father Thomas Mannion, a Roman Catholic priest. Wilkens was his altar boy at Holy Rosary Church.

"He was like a big brother to me," Wilkens says. "He was always challenging me to do more, giving me responsibility. One year he made me coach of the girls basketball team."

Mannion, still at Holy Rosary after all these years, disclaims credit for Wilkens' success. "Lenny was extremely well prepared for life before I ever met him," said the priest. "He had the psychological structure to accomplish anything in life by the time he was 8. He was a good student, but not because he was trying to please the teachers. He didn't need to be noticed. He could have become a professor at Providence College if he hadn't gone into basketball. As an altar boy, he was as good as he is at anything else he does."

Wilkens carries a lifelong love of the church, attending mass every Sunday. In this area, he goes to St. Basil's Church in Brecksville and St. Mary's in Hudson.

"Lenny's only problem as a boy was to pretend to be a member of two warring gangs so that he could cross town and survive," Mannion laughed. The streetwise Wilkens convinced both gangs, the Madison Street Boys and the Kingsboro Street Boys, that he was on both of their sides, even though they were battling each other.

But Lenny still ran into the kind of crime that plagues many inner city youths. Once, when he was playing basketball in a schoolyard, two thugs appeared and robbed everybody at knifepoint. "When they shook me down all they found in my pocket were rosary beads," he recalls.

In his first year of high school two boys stole his swim trunks and began throwing them around the classroom. The teacher was too terrified to do anything. "I knew I had to fight," Wilkens recalls. "If I didn't, everybody in school would be picking on me." Wilkens went after the rascals in the classroom. He pushed one boy's hat down over his eyes and punched the other.

The same sort of toughness is visible in Wilkens today. If you doubt it, sit near him during a game and listen to him exhort his players and officials. He is not bashful about his yelling. But he is too cagy to get thrown out of a game. He has been ejected only three times in 15 years of coaching. Twice he did it on purpose to wake up his team. "It worked both times," Wilkens says. "We won both games."

Wilkens always worked after school, delivering groceries, stocking shelves in supermarkets, even cleaning houses. He gave the money to his mother. Joe Mullaney, his basketball coach at Providence College, got him a summer job in the New York garment district, working for Shelley Kaplan. "He was one of our best employees, even though he only made minimum wage," said Kaplan. He was a shipping clerk packing girls' sweaters. He never missed a day."

Wilkens never encountered any sustained hostility until he began playing for the St. Louis Hawks in 1960 at a time when about 70% of the players in the NBA were white. "There was a lot of bigotry on that team," said Kaplan, who is still his close friend.

"The white players never said anything racial to me," said Wilkens. "But you could tell how they felt in comments they made about other black players."

He recalls going into a restaurant with black teammate Sihugo Green and seeing some other Hawks there. "They acted like they didn't know us," said Wilkens.

Wilkens credits St. Louis coach Paul Seymour for making his life with the Hawks more comfortable. "He was a very good person," says Wilkens. "Then once I became a regular, the other players began treating me better."

Seymour would not play Wilkens regularly right away. If he made a mistake in a game, he would yank him immediately. Once, after a practice in which Wilkens did well, Seymour said, "Rook, why don't you play like that all the time?"

Wilkens responded in a rare burst of rebellion. "How would you know? You take me out every time I make a mistake."

Seymour put him into the next game and let him stay in. He had a good game and became a NBA fixture for 15 years. It seems he belongs in the Hall of Fame. His playing numbers are far superior to other honorees. For one example, he was in nine NBA All-Star games. Hall of Famer Bill Bradley was in only one. Frank Ramsey, another Hall of Famer, was never an All-Star.

"I don't think about being in the Hall," Wilkens says. "I'm only interested in the job I'm doing now."

Bob Pettit, the Hall of Famer who was Wilkens' teammate on the Hawks, recalls his ability.

"He had tremendously quick hands, he stole a lot of balls," said Pettit, now a New Orleans banker. "I remember a game in his rookie year when he sank two foul shots after time ran out to put us in overtime."

Joe Mullaney, his college coach, said, "He played a relaxed game, then connected like a snake and stole the ball. I used to watch him steal balls and say, 'I can't believe this guy. He never sweats.'"

Kaplan was surprised at his NBA performances.

"I told him not to go into pro basketball," he said. "He couldn't shoot, he could jump only as high as the curb, and he could only go to his left. And he was small."

Yet Wilkens averaged 16.5 points a game. In NBA history, only Oscar Robertson has more assists.

Zelmo Beaty, a former Hawks teammate, gave Wilkens a wonderful tribute on ESPN-TV recently saying he always knew how many shots each player on his team had taken, making sure to pass the ball to the big men in equal parcels.

"I knew I could go to the basket anytime I wanted," Wilkens said. "But I wanted to keep the other players happy so they would stay in the game. You have to reward your big men for running the floor, fighting for position." He coaches the same way today.

"He's a player's coach," said Cavalier guard Mark Price. "Being a former player he can empathize with our ups and downs better than a coach who never played at this level. He knows how tired you can get."

Occasionally you can see Wilkens become angry on the bench over a misplay. Having been so gifted himself, he probably finds it hard to understand a gaffe. But he controls himself.

"He doesn't degrade you in front of the players," said Price. "If you do something he doesn't like, he'll talk to you as a person, rather than talk down to you."

Mel Monheimer, a Seattle agent when Wilkens had some problems there, said, "Lenny's biggest fault is that he stops talking to a player when he gets mad at him and he has no idea why. Then, the player walks around saying, 'What did I do?'" Wilkens denied it. He has no doghouse in Cleveland.

The most difficult period in Wilkens' career came during the 1981–85 season, when his Seattle team finished with a 31-51 record. Several unnamed players criticized his coaching. Jack Sikma, the star center, was reportedly one of them.

"I never realized I had so many problems with Sikma," Wilkens says. "My door was always open. But he said things that disappointed me."

Sikma, who has been traded to Milwaukee now, says, "We were all unhappy in Seattle because we had always been winners and we suddenly had a bad year. But I think Lenny was good for my career and hopefully he'd say the same about me. We're on good terms now."

Wilkens also had trouble with Dennis Johnson, the star of his 1979 NBA championship team. Lenny wound up trading him to Phoenix for Paul Westphal.

"I was a young coach and he was a young player," Wilkens says. "A lot of things bothered him. We're very friendly now."

Phoenix found the talented Johnson a hard man to satisfy, too, trading him to Boston for Rick Robey.

After the 1985 season, Wilkens was kicked upstairs to the post of Seattle general manager. But he still felt he had some coaching left in him. He approached Wayne Embry, who had just been named Cavs' general manager. Embry hired him to coach the Cavs last year.

"The one-year break recharged me," Wilkens said. "But I don't think I'm coaching any different than I ever did."

"He's a happy man anytime his team holds the opposition to less than 100 points in a game, win or lose," said Kaplan explaining Wilkens' coaching philosophy as well as anyone.

Embry points out that Wilkens gives his assistants, Dick Helm and Brian Winters, the freedom to coach.

"Brian was such an excellent shooter, he wants him to work with the players," Embry said. "Last year Brian was reticent because he was a rookie coach, but Lenny told him, 'If you see something, don't be afraid to say so.'"

Helm, a long-time Wilkens aide, organizes practices and drills, along with influencing Lenny's personnel decisions. In a recent victory over Washington, Wilkens was ready to send in Ron Harper for Craig Ehlo in the stretch run. But Helm suggested he leave Ehlo in there. Wilkens reconsidered. Ehlo wound up making the game-saving block of a shot for a Cavs victory.

Wilkens appears to be having more fun than at any time since his Seattle teams appeared in consecutive NBA finals in 1978 and 1979. He did not get angry last month, for instance, when Harper publicly stated that he felt the Cavs' offense was too conservative, not pushing the ball up the court quickly enough.

"Ron's a young player," he smiled, nullifying a potential hassle with his enfant terrible. Maybe at times he was right. Ron and I communicate all the time."

Wilkens came here with a reputation of being wary of the press, the result of what he feels was unfair treatment by a Seattle writer.

"If I was a vindictive person, I could have sued for libel and won," Wilkens says. His only ground rule with reporters is that if they print a critical story about him, they also call him to get his version of the story on the same day, rather than wait until the next day and write another story. He has not exhibited hostility to writers here. In fact, he goes out of his way to be accommodating.

"I'm a private person," Wilkens, 50, said. "I don't like too much exposure. My belief in God comes first, my family is second, and third is my work."

Always a Battler; Helped Feed Family at 12

JOHN BATTLE *Jan. 1, 1992*

Cavaliers guard John Battle learned a long time ago that life is a struggle.

He was born and raised in the ghettos of Washington, D.C., where he had to grow up fast.

"It was really rough," Battle said. "I was pretty much on my own from the time I was 12 years old. My mom was with us, but we had 10 kids in the family. I worked in department stores and delivered newspapers to put food on the table. My mom never had to buy me anything after I was 12."

That early life is reflected in Battle's style of play. He brings an intense, emotional presence to the Cavs, who have an image of being a businesslike team that relies on cool finesse. Actually, the Cavs play as hard as anyone. Most of them—Mark Price is an exception—just don't exhibit their emotions as much as Battle does.

He is wired for action as soon as he steps on the floor, hustling, almost pugnacious, anxious to beat the other guy. He gets mad when things go badly and leads the cheers when they go well. "That's the way the game should be played," Battle said. "If you don't have that attitude, the game is not exciting. You can't play as though it's just a job."

Coach Lenny Wilkens, whose Cavs have won six in a row, appreciates Battle's style. "He'll fight you for position," Wilkens said. "He's smart and aggressive. If you take a cheap shot at him, he'll find the right time to get you back."

Battle, a 6-2 shooting guard, says he is always ready to help a teammate in the event of any rough stuff. "If somebody approaches one of my teammates, I'm the first one to help," he said. "Either do it (fight) or get on with the game. If somebody takes a cheap shot at a teammate, I'll give him one back. These are my teammates. I can't do anything without them. We have to stick together. I hope they feel the same way about me."

Wilkens scorns the idea that Battle is the "policeman" some observers have felt the Cavs need, but the coach says, "We're not going to be pushed around."

Actually, Battle has a background in police work. He graduated from Rutgers University with a degree in criminal justice and spent a year as an intern at Rahway State Prison in New Jersey, learning various police assignments.

"When I finished I was supposed to know everything a prison warden would do," Battle said. He dealt closely with prisoners. Once he and the entire prison staff were quarantined in the prison overnight after a murder by one of the inmates.

Battle said he never had any problems with the prisoners. "I was playing basketball at Rutgers so most of them knew who I was," he said. "They'd talk basketball with me."

Battle was at Rahway when the famed "Scared Straight" movie was made, in which inmates screamed at troubled teen offenders, trying to shock them into understanding the horrors of prison life.

Battle, 28, has another distinction. He is the best-dressed player on the Cavs. "I just like to feel good," he said of his penchant for fashionable threads. "When you feel good about yourself, it carries over to the floor. When I come to work, I like to dress well. I like to wear suits because they make a statement."

Battle's playing is also making a statement. He combines with Craig Ehlo to give the Cavs plenty of hustle and scoring at the two guard. Battle is shooting 94.3% from the foul line, having made his last 25 free throws. In the last nine games, he is averaging 12 points and shooting 56%.

The high-jumping Battle constantly comes around screens to get good shots around the foul line. "That's how I survive in the NBA," said Battle, who knows all about survival.

Glory Unmasked

Johnny Bower *Feb. 6, 2002*

Johnny Bower, the Hockey Hall of Fame goaltender, has 240 stitches on his face.

That is because goalies did not wear masks for much of his career, which extended from the mid-1940s through 1970 and included nine seasons with the Cleveland Barons. Hard-rubber pucks, flying at upwards of 100 miles an hour, often crashed into the netminders' faces.

The stitches have faded, but Bower wears their remnants proudly, as a symbol of his courage and endurance.

In fact, some of the stitches were not necessary. "We had an insurance deal where we would get five dollars for a stitch," Bower, 77, recalled in a phone interview. "If the doctor needed only two stitches, I'd tell him to give me a couple more so I could get another 10 bucks."

They don't make 'em like that anymore.

Bower tried masks a few times late in his career but never liked them. "I couldn't see the puck around my feet and if there was a guy on the other side of the net I couldn't see him at all," he said. So he sacrificed skin for performance.

Bower, whose uniform No. 1 will be retired by the Barons on Feb. 15, along with the late Freddie Glover's No. 9, was one of the most amazing athletes ever.

He is considered the finest goalie in the history of the American Hockey League, with 45 career shutouts. But he did not move up to the National Hockey League to stay until he was an elderly 34 years old.

"I figured I had two, maybe three years left when I went to the NHL," Bower said from his Toronto home.

But he fooled himself and everybody else in hockey. His greatest years were yet to come. Bower was the Toronto Maple Leafs' goalie for another 11 seasons, performing on four Stanley Cup champions. He did not retire until he was 45.

There is a streak of longevity in his family. His father lived to 92. Bower underwent a heart bypass operation a year ago but says he feels strong. "I'm looking forward to coming to Cleveland for the ceremony," he said. "What a thrill and honor to be remembered by people when you left so long ago."

Bower first joined the Barons in the 1945-46 season, when he was 21. His last name then was Kiszkan. He changed it to Bower the next season. He played nine years on those Barons teams that won the Calder Cup three times in his tenure and made a habit of packing the old Cleveland Arena under owner Al Sutphin, General Manager Jim Hendy and coaches Bun Cook and Jackie Gordon. His agility earned him the nicknames "Panther Man" and "The Great Wall of China," the latter bestowed by Geoffrey Fisher of the old Cleveland News.

Among his Cleveland highlights: In the 1957-58 season, he set an AHL record by not allowing a goal for 249 consecutive minutes and 51 seconds. He had three shutouts in the streak. He made 78 saves in a four-overtime Calder Cup battle against Pittsburgh in 1953, finally losing, 1-0, to rival Gil Mayer. The game lasted five and a half hours and did not end until 1:55 a.m. He still led Cleveland to the 1953 title in seven games.

"Pittsburgh was supposed to walk all over us, but Bower made the difference," said Gordon, 73, from his home in Vancouver, British Columbia. On several occasions, Bower had to leave the ice in great pain to be stitched or have teeth yanked after being struck by pucks, then returned to play in the same game.

"Johnny was quick and agile," said Gordon, who doubled as a high-scoring forward. "He had a knack of bouncing up after he hit the ice. He was a hard worker. Even in practice, he'd get mad as hell if you scored on him. He was as good at keeping the puck out of the net as anybody I've ever seen."

Bower fondly recalls those Barons teammates of Cleveland's golden hockey age.

"Freddie 'The Fox' Thurier was the best playmaker we had," he said. "Tommy Burlington had unbelievable talent, but he couldn't play in the NHL because they had a rule against hiring a guy with one eye. Les Cunningham had the best wrist shot I ever saw. He looked like he was telegraphing it, but it always went where you didn't expect. Johnny Holota was strong on rebounds in front of the net. Tommy Williams wore glasses but he was a good defenseman. Glover (second-leading career scorer in AHL history) hated to lose and always gave 150 percent. He should have been in the NHL too." Those players flourished when only six teams were in the NHL, rather than the 30 of today. The Barons were often called the seventh-best team in hockey.

Bower got his first shot in the NHL in 1953, when the New York Rangers acquired him from the Barons for goalie Emile "The Cat" Francis, defenseman Steve Kraftcheck and Jack Stoddard. He had a 2.60 goals-against average in 70 games for the Rangers, but was dumped after one season. "New York is rough if you don't win," Bower said. "We finished in last place and Gump Worsley got my job." The Rangers shipped Bower to their Providence farm team in the AHL, where he took the Reds to the Calder title, beating Cleveland in the finals.

By February 1958, Bower was back with the Barons and having a superlative season. The Maple Leafs made a big offer for him in midseason. Hendy allowed Bower to decide whether he wanted to go to Toronto, according to Barons historian Gene Kiczek in his book, "Forgotten Glory." Bower decided to stay with the Barons. "I didn't want to let my teammates and the fans down," he recalled. "I had been here for so long I considered Cleveland my home. I loved Cleveland." He and his wife of 53 years, Nancy, were married in Trinity Cathedral here.

"We were making a good living in the AHL," said Bower. 'Some guys were getting $3,000 to $4,000 for six months work a year. I had a hamburger joint in Prince Albert, Saskatchewan, and did very well there in the off-season."

Bower had worked himself up from his rookie pay of $1,600 with the Barons. "That's tip money for some guys today," Bower chuckled. "We played for the love of the game. Money is good, but you got to want to play."

The low Arena prices for tickets, only $2.60 for rinkside in 1950, for example, contributed to the meager salaries.

Toronto drafted Bower in the summer of 1958, but he was still reluctant to leave Cleveland. He finally agreed to go to the Maple Leafs when Hendy told him he would be suspended by hockey authorities if he refused.

The rest is hockey history. Bower had 37 NHL career shutouts, won two Vezina trophies as the best goalie in the league and was voted the eighth-best goaltender of all time in a 1995 poll. He is the oldest goalie (44) ever to play in a Stanley Cup playoff game. His career goals-against average per game in the NHL was 2.52. Bower was elected to the Hall of Fame in 1976.

The Glory Years of the Barons

RED WILLIAMS *Feb. 10, 1985*

The girl walked into the sporting goods store to pick up her ice skates.

The friendly old proprietor greeted her warmly and gave her the sharpened skates. "You sure brought in some snow, didn't you?" he joked. "Maybe you'd like to buy some skis next time."

The girl replied pleasantly and left with her skates. She could not be expected to know that the nice old man was a popular player in the days when the late Cleveland Barons ruled the American Hockey League.

The man was Tommy (Red) Williams. He was kind of a cult figure because he played fine defense and almost never took a shot. The fans liked him because he was smart and totally unselfish.

In the season of 1955–56, for instance, Williams did not score a goal in 60 games. He had 15 assists. He never scored more than four goals in a season in his 17 years in pro hockey.

"My shot couldn't break a pane of glass," Williams recalled. "The year I got four goals, I got two of them by flipping the puck high in the air. Then it came down on its edge and took a crazy bounce into the net."

Williams is almost forgotten now, except during those lunchtime conversations between old Cleveland hockey aficionados. One of the best parts of this job is looking up legendary athletes who have slipped into oblivion. It is a kick to strum the chords of memory.

"My health is good," said Williams, 61. "I feel it a little in my legs, though. I have to wear support hose." He and his partner, Ed Kozdron, own Burgoyne Sporting Goods in Rocky River.

Williams wears a gold watch that has the letters AHL CHAMPIONS in place of the numbers. He has boxes full of pictures of his old teammates in his store. An old fan could lose a whole afternoon reliving the days of Les Cunningham, Fred Thurier, Earl Bartholome and Bobby Carse.

Williams has a couple of scars on his chin, and another on his forehead, souvenirs of long-ago hockey wars. You sense he is self-conscious about them. But they gave him the romantic look of an old warrior.

He opens his mouth and pulls a bridge containing four false

teeth from the top of his mouth. "They were knocked out in Cincinnati," he says. "I was high-sticked after the play was over. I was looking another way and the guy hit me in the mouth with his stick. King Clancy, the Cincinnati coach, was so mad he released the guy right after the game."

It is hard to believe now, but in those days hockey players did not wear helmets as they do today. Even goalies played without masks. Many a goalie had 200 stitches in his face.

It was good for the spectators. You could see what the players looked like in their pompadours and crewcuts. The players thought nothing of it. Hockey had always been played bareheaded.

"Cal Stearns got a head injury once and they gave him something like a football helmet," Williams said. "But somebody squawked and they wouldn't let him wear it after a couple of games."

Williams recalled his first game with the Barons. "I was called up on Christmas night in 1948," he said. "I was lucky enough to get my hip into a guy and send him for a pretty good spill. The crowd gave me a big hand."

The Cleveland fans who would jam the Arena 10,000 strong every Saturday night loved the big hitters.

"They always ragged Johnny Holota," said Williams, speaking of the late center who scored 52 goals one season. "They called him a pot hanger. He didn't crash into players. I didn't do it very often either. I was a stick checker. But every once in a while I would get carried away."

One of Williams' best friends was Johnny Bower, the goalie who went on to become a big star in the National Hockey League. Bower even moved in with the Williams family in Saskatchewan. One summer when they were in their early 20s, Williams and Bower bought a used car and toured all of Canada, from the Calgary Stampede to Banff National Park. Bower was Williams' best man when he married his wife of 32 years, Eunice.

"We were like brothers," said Williams wistfully. "But I haven't talked to him in years. It's just one of those things, you wonder how it happens."

Williams still loves hockey, watches it on cable TV. He says the game is still about the same, except for the curved sticks. He feels today's players cannot be as accurate with their shots and passes as the old-timers were with their straight sticks.

Wayne Gretzky, currently the god of hockey, is considered by many to be the best player ever, but Williams criticized him a bit.

"I make my wife mad when I talk about Gretzky," he said. "I probably shouldn't say anything about him since he scores so much and his endurance is so remarkable, but he is loose with some of his passes.

"My biggest thrill was watching Bobby Orr and I got a bigger kick out of Gordie Howe than Gretzky, too."

"When Orr had his great years they were really picking on him, too," said Williams, referring to the violence of hockey. "One time the whistle blew and Orr was standing there relaxed and an opponent knocked him out with a check.

"That's what is so remarkable about Gretzky. He never gets hurt. Usually, they do anything, play dirty, to get the No. 1 guy out there."

It sounded as though Williams calmly accepts the barbarity of hockey. But he does not. He regrets the viciousness and feels the referees are doing a poor job in curbing it.

He still hates to think of the demise of the Arena, where he spent eight years. "I loved that place," he said.

So did a lot of other people.

Owens Thrilled the World in 1936, but Riches Didn't Come with the Fame

JESSE OWENS *Sep. 25, 2000*

There was never a runner who looked quite as good as Jesse Owens. As you can see in that one film clip that is shown again and again on national television, the late Clevelander had a style that was as smooth as a baby's powdered bottom.

"He ran effortlessly, like he was sitting in a chair," recalled Harrison Dillard.

Owens was a worldwide sensation in the 1936 Olympics, when he won four gold medals.

With track-and-field drama unfolding at the current Olympics, this is a good time to remember his brilliant and sometimes troubled career.

"His problem was that he was born about 50 years too soon," said Dillard, of Shaker Heights, who won four gold medals in the hurdles and sprints in the 1948 and 1952 Olympics. "If he were running today, he would undoubtedly be a wealthy man."

As an indication of the esteem in which he was held, in 1950 the nation's sports editors voted Owens the leading track athlete of the first half of the 20th century. Jim Thorpe, who had won the decathlon and pentathlon in the 1912 Olympiad, was second in the vote, with Paavo Nurmi, who had won three distance events in the 1924 Games, third.

Owens was born in Oakville, Ala., in 1913 and moved to Cleveland with his family at age 11.

Clevelanders had known about him since he was at Fairmount Junior High, when he astounded coach Charley Riley by running 100 yards in 10 seconds flat on a sidewalk course set up on E. 107th St. near Carnegie.

"No eighth-grader can run that fast on a sidewalk," Riley exclaimed, looking at his stopwatch. He was convinced the next day when Owens did it again.

Later, at East Tech, Owens tied the world 100-yard record at 9.4 seconds and won three events in the U.S. scholastic track championships.

He was already married by then. He had eloped with Ruth Johnson when he was 16 and she was 15. By the time he graduated from Tech, he already had a daughter. Eventually, he and Ruth had three daughters.

Owens burst into the nation's consciousness in 1935, while running for Ohio State in the Big Ten championships at Michigan. In the span of about an hour, Owens set world records in the 220-yard dash, the 220 low hurdles and the broad jump, and tied the world mark in the 100.

By the time he arrived at the Olympics, he was acclaimed as the greatest sprinter in the world. The three Cleveland newspapers gave him maximum coverage, using wire service reports to detail his exploits on the front pages.

On Aug. 3, 1936, Owens won the glamorous 100-meter race in 10.3 seconds, tying the Olympic record. He started out third in a soft rain, took the lead at the 30-meter mark and won by a full stride over Ralph Metcalfe.

The crowd of 100,000 at the Reichsport showered Owens with thunderous cheers, but some newspapermen started a controversial myth that persists to this day. They wrote that German Chancellor Adolf Hitler, who preached Aryan supremacy, snubbed Owens.

They say he left the stadium just before he ran, so he wouldn't have to shake his hand.

Owens discounted the story at the time and for the rest of his life. In 1972, he said, "I didn't know I had been ignored until the Olympics were over. I got a phone call from somebody asking me about it. I didn't know what they were talking about."

Owens followed up his 100 victory with triumphs in the 200 meters and broad jump, setting Olympic records in each. He also led off the victorious 4 x 100 relay for a fourth gold.

In a reflection of the times, the Associated Press called him "the Ebony Antelope." At this point, Owens was as popular as any athlete in the world. Berliners mobbed him for autographs. He modestly signed, "Yours sincerely, Jesse Owens."

The city of Cleveland staged a welcome-home parade for him that ran for 12 miles. Owens and his wife sat atop the backseat of an open convertible as the crowds yelled, "Jesse, Jesse." One of the children who saw him that day was Dillard. "Owens smiled and winked at me and my pals," Dillard remembered. "He said, 'Hi, kids.' That was great stuff."

At Public Hall, Owens gave an emotional six-minute speech, saying, "I have been in many places in the last two months, but this is the greatest reception I have ever seen. It makes me proud to be a Clevelander."

After that, his financial problems began. "He had trouble finding a job," said Dillard. "Conditions stunk."

At first, his future looked good. Comedian Eddie Cantor reportedly offered him $40,000 to appear with him for 10 weeks. The story created a front-page splash at a time when the average workingman was making $30 a week. The next day, Cantor refuted the offer, saying it was made by his publicity man.

That began a long and checkered odyssey through the financial maze. Owens, who had won $250 in an amateur singing contest at Public Auditorium in 1930, toured with an orchestra, singing, tap-dancing and handling the baton. He also danced with the famed Bill "Bojangles" Robinson. He made a movie in which he played a detective. He toured with a basketball team called the "Jesse Owens Olympians." He ran a 100-yard race against a horse in Havana, and another against a horse at Bay Meadows in California. He ran in professional track events.

"It was honest labor," Dillard said. "He had a family and did what he could to get paid."

The Amateur Athletic Union, which hated to see athletes make money, suspended Owens for the sin of being a professional. Unlike contemporary track greats Michael Johnson and Carl Lewis, he was banned from making a living at what he was best at—big-time track.

In 1938, Owens opened a dry cleaning establishment on Cedar Ave. That year, he was appointed to a $1,080-a-year Cleveland playground job, but was removed before he began, probably for political reasons.

On Oct. 11, 1938, the Internal Revenue Service said he owed $746.20 in delinquent taxes.

In 1939, he declared bankruptcy.

A 1942 article stated that he had made $50,000 from his Olympic fame, but that he was too good-hearted, and that he was victimized by phony friends.

In 1946, running in full baseball uniform and spikes, he beat Indians outfielder George Case, the base-stealing king of that era, in a 100-yard race at the Stadium, charitably winning by two steps between games of a doubleheader against the St. Louis Browns. His winning time was 9.9.

Later, at age 40, he could still run 100 yards in 9.7 seconds.

Possessed of excellent people skills, Owens drifted into the personnel and public relations field, working out of Chicago, Detroit and Philadelphia. The Ford Motor Co. and baseball's American League were among his employers. He was in demand as a public speaker and made appearances on behalf of clients all over the country. In 1966, he had a setback when he was fined $3,000 for income tax evasion. Later, he opened a successful public relations firm in Phoenix.

In 1972, he returned to Germany to write a series of articles for The Plain Dealer on the Olympics in Munich. The Germans were thrilled to see him back. ABC aired a TV special, "Jesse Owens' Return to Germany."

On March 31, 1980, Owens died of throat cancer at age 66. He had been a cigarette smoker for years.

There was a move to have Cleveland Municipal Stadium renamed in his honor, but it fell through.

The Germans named a thoroughfare in his honor in West Berlin in 1984, with his widow and three daughters attending the ceremony. TV stations all over the world carried the news, decorating it with that marvelous clip of Owens running.

A Champion 50 Years Ago

HARRISON DILLARD *Jul. 31, 1998*

Cleveland became known as the City of Champions in 1948, and it was not merely because the Indians, Browns and Barons won titles. Clevelander Harrison Dillard, a student at Baldwin-Wallace College, scored a sensational upset victory in the 100-meter dash in the Olympic Games 50 years ago today.

Dillard's victory is one of the most storied in Olympics history because he was not competing in his specialty, the high hurdles, in which he was the best in the world.

In a fluke, Dillard had failed to qualify in the hurdles in the U.S. trials, finishing last. Considered an outsider in the 100, he somehow beat the fastest men in the world in the Olympics in London. The victory was greeted with huge headlines and cheers from Cleveland sports fans, who had followed Dillard's spectacular career.

He was inspired to become a track man when his idol, Jesse Owens, was honored in a parade after winning four gold medals in the 1936 Olympics. Dillard was standing at E. 63 and Central Ave. with friends when Owens rode by.

Owens, who preceded Dillard at East Tech, looked straight at the 13-year-old boy and his pals, winked, and said: "Hi, kids, how are you?"

"We thought it was the greatest thing in the world that our idol had actually spoken to us," Dillard recalled. "That was when I first thought about getting into the Olympics."

The gifted Dillard starred at Kennard Junior High, East Tech and B-W, becoming a fixture on the sports pages. He held the world hurdles record of 13.6 seconds and won 82 consecutive races before losing the week before the '48 Olympic Trials, when he ran four heats within 30 minutes, competing in both the sprint and the hurdles.

If there was a lead-pipe cinch going into the Olympic Trials in Evanston, Ill., it was that Dillard would make the team as a hurdler. All he needed was a top-three finish. Things began well as Dillard qualified in the 100 in the trials, finishing third. Then came the hurdles fiasco. Incredibly, Dillard began crashing into hurdles, banging into the second, fourth and sixth barriers. His rhythm gone, he pulled up at the seventh hurdle and finished last as Northwestern's Bill Porter won in 13.9 seconds.

"I was greatly disappointed," Dillard said. "But I had already qualified in the 100, so I wasn't devastated. I still felt I was the best hurdler in the world but that it was not meant to be in 1948."

On the ship sailing to the Olympics, people kept offering sympathies to Dillard because of his failure in the hurdles. But Dillard and his coach, B-W's Eddie Finnegan, were not listening. They set out to win the 100. Knowing his only chance to win was to start quickly, Dillard practiced his starts continually. "I lost four pounds from all the work and weighed 148," said the 5-10 Dillard.

He ran well in the preliminaries in Wembley Stadium, winning all three heats, but he still was not given much chance in the 100. "Mel Patton, Barney Ewell and Lloyd LaBeach were the favorites," Dillard said. "I was just there."

Patton, from the University of Southern California, was the world record holder. Ewell had been a top competitor worldwide for years. LaBeach, from Panama, was considered the favorite. Dillard felt confident. "I tried to visualize myself winning," he said. He told Ewell, his friend and roommate: "I'm going to beat you."

Ewell, from Lancaster, Pa., said: "You're crazy." A crowd of 83,000 packed Wembley Stadium for the 100 final, with six runners competing. "The king and queen of England and the princesses were there," said Dillard, who had the outside lane. "It was a gorgeous day, in the low 70s. The track was not the fastest in the world, but it looked beautiful, with red dirt made from bomb rubble from the war."

The practice on the starts paid off, as Dillard sprang to a lead at the gun. "Bing, I hit it perfectly," he said, a glint in his eye as he relived the moment in his Shaker Heights home. "At 50 meters, I was three to five feet ahead, which is a pretty good margin in a sprint.

"I was just hoping the tape would hurry up and get here. It seemed like a mile away. Patton, Ewell and LaBeach were all tremendous, long-legged sprinters. I knew they'd be coming." Dillard tried to relax and keep driving. He wanted his head to stay down, not flop around.

At the end, he threw himself at the tape and felt it hit him across the chest. From the corner of his eye, he saw somebody else lunging for the tape. It was Ewell in Lane 2.

"I felt I won," said Dillard, who waited calmly for the decision. "Barney felt like he won and went into a dance of celebration, jumping up and down. His chest had hit the tape, too. But LaBeach, who came in third and had a look at both of us, told Barney: 'Mon, you don't win. Bones win." Bones was Dillard's nickname.

It took two minutes, but the photo finish upheld Dillard's opinion. He had won in 10.3 seconds, tying the Olympic record. He went over and consoled Ewell. "He was heartsick," Dillard said. "He was 31, and he knew he would not be around for another Olympics."

Finnegan and Jack Clowser, Cleveland Press sports writer who was the only Cleveland reporter on the scene, ran onto the track and hugged and congratulated Dillard. "We did it," shouted Finnegan.

When Dillard returned to the Olympic village that night, a group of about 50 athletes applauded as he walked into the room for dinner. It was a tribute he has never forgotten. A couple of days later, he was one of three or four U.S. athletes chosen to attend a reception in Buckingham Palace. "There were about 25 Rolls Royces in the courtyard," he said. "I was really impressed."

Dillard won another gold medal when he ran on the winning 4x100 relay team with Lorenzo Wright, Ewell and Patton. He ran the third leg, with Patton as anchor.

In 1949, Dillard received a direct financial benefit from his victory when Indians owner Bill Veeck hired him as a team publicist at $125 a week. "That was as much as some of the players were making at the time," Dillard said.

In later years, Dillard worked for the board of education. An accomplished speaker, he gave many talks in schools. He became head of business operations for the board and retired five years ago.

Dillard, 75, and Joy, his wife of 42 years, have three grandchildren. He likes to walk for exercise. He had prostate cancer surgery four years ago and has been fine since.

After his 1948 triumph, Dillard continued to run. In the 1952 Olympics at Helsinki, he won the hurdles in 13.7 seconds, a record at the time for the Games. He won another gold in the 4x100 relay. He considers his 1948 victory the thrill of his career. "Winning the first one is always the dearest," he said. "In 1952, it was just vindication. That was the one I should have won in '48."

The Only White Player in the Negro Leagues

EDDIE KLEP *Dec. 12, 1997*

Nobody paid attention when Eddie Klep's troubled life ended 16 years ago.

There were no obituaries about the former baseball player. He was cremated and buried in a relative's grave in his hometown of Erie, Pa.

Only his widow Ethel and a few relatives grieved. "I think about him every day," said Ethel, 75, from her home in Erie.

Now Klep is hot.

A member of the Society of American Baseball Research is writing a book about his life. A song, "The Ballad of Eddie Klep," has been recorded and is sung in concerts. Feature writers are doing newspaper articles on him.

Klep's legend has been revived because he is the white Jackie Robinson.

The stocky left-handed pitcher was the only white man to play in the Negro Leagues.

He performed briefly for the Cleveland Buckeyes in 1946, the same year the Brooklyn Dodgers broke the color barrier by signing Robinson for their Montreal farm team.

Klep had come off the sandlots of Erie, starring in the fast Glenwood League. He had a 26-6 record in 1945. Before that, he won six letters in football and baseball at Erie East High. The Buckeyes, the Negro League champions in 1945, signed him after he handcuffed them for three innings in an exhibition game, said the Cleveland Call and Post, the black newspaper.

"I saw him pitch," Ethel said. "It was fun watching him. He had a strut and that Me-God attitude. He was a damn good-looking boy. If he was half-way sober, he'd go nine innings."

The Call and Post was enthusiastic when Klep joined the Buckeyes, headlining the story across the top of the sports page. A full-length photo of Klep in his pitching motion was put alongside the team's established stars on the eve of the season opener. "White Hurler Augments Cleveland's Drive to Retain Negro Baseball Title," the headline said. Sportswriter Jimmie N. Jones called him one of the most promising pitchers on the staff.

Willie Grace, 78, a former Buckeyes outfield star who lives in Erie, roomed with Klep. "I wanted to make him feel at home," Grace said. "He was a nice kid, a happy-go-lucky guy. He liked to laugh and talk and have fun with the other guys. Everybody took to him. But he liked the bottle. Sometimes he'd take two or three days off."

Klep's most publicized incident occurred in Birmingham, Ala., during warmups for a spring training exhibition game. The white police evicted him before the Buckeyes played the Birmingham Black Barons. They told him to leave the park or the game would be stopped. They did not want white men playing on the same field as blacks. "We were mad as hell about it," Grace said. "We raised our voices, but there was nothing we could do. The cops, there were about five of them, didn't care."

Klep went to his hotel and changed clothes. He was not allowed to stay with his teammates in their hotel. He returned to the ballpark and sat in a box seat, but again the police appeared. They told him he would have to move to the white section of the seats. Klep complied.

Buckeyes owner Ernest Wright, who signed Klep, traveled to Birmingham to protest the treatment of his pitcher. Wright said that, in keeping with the American way, Klep should be free to play with the team of his choice.

The Call and Post headlined Wright's trip, saying the Buckeyes would defy the Alabama police and keep the white ballplayer. About a week later, Klep set another precedent when he pitched for the Buckeyes in Atlanta against the Crackers, another black team. A crowd of 12,000 packed the park to see Klep pitch. The Call and Post said Klep did a good job, giving up two hits and a walk in three innings. However, he was charged with three runs because of loose fielding by his "jittery" infield.

Klep's regular-season debut came against the Indianapolis Clowns. Coming on in relief with the bases full, he gave up two two-run singles, one of them by Reece "Goose" Tatum, who also played basketball with the Harlem Globetrotters. Not long afterward, Klep was let go.

"I felt sorry to see him go," said Grace. "He was a good pitcher with a nice fastball, but we knew he couldn't make it in our league. He had to pitch against some of the best players in the world. But Wright, who was a shrewd judge of talent, thought he had a legitimate chance."

"He was a good pitcher when he wasn't out the night before," said Ethel.

Ethel said Klep never talked much about his time with the Buckeyes. "He was only upset that he couldn't stay with the team at all of the hotels," she said.

His release by the Buckeyes was another in a long line of setbacks for Klep, beginning with his father's death in a 1937 railroad accident when Klep was 18. "From there on it was bad," Ethel said. Family members said his father's death changed Klep. Klep began breaking the law and was arrested several times for crimes such as larceny, disorderly conduct and assault and battery. When arrested, he gave a variety of occupations—truck driver, waiter, painter, clerk, laborer.

Through it all, Ethel tried to stay with him. They met when she was 18 and he was 22, in 1941. She had fallen in love immediately. "He could charm the birds out of the trees," she said. "His mother told me not to marry him, but my mother insisted I do." Their wedding date was set for March 17, 1941, but it had to be postponed when Klep took an overdose of Mercurochrome. Klep and Ethel finally married on the second try in August and lived together, off and on, for 12 years.

"Eddie was a ball," said Ethel. "We'd go walking outside when it was snowing and we'd go to wrestling matches."

But Klep continued his wayward life. Police records show that on Sept. 9, 1946, he was convicted of burglary, larceny and receiving stolen goods and was sentenced to three to six years in prison. He was released on parole Sept. 29, 1948, but returned to prison on April 4, 1950, for parole violation. He was discharged Sept. 9, 1952.

Shortly after, Klep moved to Buffalo and then to Los Angeles. Ethel did not see him again until 1975, when she went to Los Angeles to visit their son and to see her granddaughter. "Eddie was in a home of some sort," Ethel said. "He had his arm in a sling, but except for that he was still good-looking. He didn't know who I was."

Ethel and Klep have two grandchildren and three great-grandchildren. "He doesn't know what he missed," she said. Klep died in Los Angeles from the effects of alcoholism in 1981. He was 62.

"He was cremated out there and they sent the ashes here," she said. "They put Eddie's ashes in the same casket as his brother, Julius."

They are buried in a family plot with the husband of Klep's

niece. But the names of Eddie and Julius are not on the tombstone. Ethel said she would like to have Klep's ashes. But she lacks the money to have them exhumed. "When I die I'd like to be cremated and be buried with him so we can be together," she said.

Days Are Long for Former Outfielder

SAM JETHROE *Jan. 10, 1995*

The cheers have long since subsided for Sam Jethroe, 72. The 1950 National League rookie of the year, Jethroe sits in the bar he owns in Erie, Pa., holding a small, sharp-faced dog in his lap. "Wherever I played, the fans always liked me," said Jethroe, who was with the Boston Braves of the NL and also the Cleveland Buckeyes of the Negro League. "Whenever I'd get on base they'd holler, 'Go, go, go.'"

The dog growls when a stranger comes nearby, but it looks completely comfortable in the arms of the old ballplayer. "She was on the steps outside one day and I gave her some water and food," Jethroe said. "She came back the next day and she's been here ever since. I never knew her name, so I call her Gal."

A customer enters and Jethroe rises to serve him, with Gal trotting faithfully behind him. The customer obviously is a regular, for he doesn't say a word. Jethroe doesn't, either, but pours him a glass of wine and scoops up the money the man puts on the bar. Jethroe has owned this 100-seat establishment for five years. It has seen better days.

The glass in the sign in front is broken. The front door is locked and needs repairs. Customers enter by a rear door. Asked how business is, Jethroe replies, "Slow."

He wears a smile, but he moves slowly, slightly bent. "I've got high blood pressure and I take some pills for that," he said. "My sugar is up a little but I don't take insulin shots. My feet hurt. If my feet didn't hurt, everything would be all right."

Jethroe suffered a disaster on Nov. 19. The house he and his wife, Elsie, had owned for 45 years burned down. "It started on the rear porch and went inside," Jethroe said. "Everything in the kitchen was burned out. We didn't even have a plate. The only thing that was left was a television set."

"We lost everything," said Elsie, who has been married to Sam for 52 years. They never had any children, but raised a foster daughter, who has given them grandchildren.

"I didn't have any house insurance," Jethroe said. "They scratched me because the crime rate was too high." The Erie Fire Department says the blaze is under investigation. Elsie is staying with their daughter; Sam is living in quarters behind the bar.

He spends all his time at the bar, opening up about 9:30 a.m. and closing around midnight.

"I'm trying to get $10,000 together to buy another house," Jethroe said.

Jethroe is used to tending bar. He had a better place in Erie for 30 years, but it was lost to urban redevelopment. Another shocker occurred Dec. 10, when a gunman killed a man in the washroom of Jethroe's bar, putting six shots in his back. The murderer escaped and remains at large. Jethroe was in the bar when it happened.

"It was a fight that started somewhere else and they wound up here," Jethroe said. "They were from out of town.

"Running a bar is a tough business. The hardest part is keeping the peace between customers. When people get to drinking you never know what might happen."

Jethroe, who was 6-1 and 178 pounds at his peak, always relied on diplomacy to calm down antagonistic revelers. "But lots of times I had to go outside and fight them too," he said. He does not employ a bouncer. "They give me more respect than they would a bouncer," Jethroe said.

He is used to being interviewed about his baseball days. "One guy came from Washington," he said. "They had all the cameras in here. Another guy came from Toledo. I get calls all the time. They say they're writing a book."

He was brought to Jacobs Field to participate in the official ceremonies when the Indians retired Larry Doby's number. He was flown to California to play in the Roy Campanella Classic Golf tournament. He makes appearances at card shows and gets letters from fans who want his autograph.

"People want me to sell them my awards, but I won't do that," he said.

His rookie of the year plaque is in the bar. He received it after hitting .273, with 18 homers, and leading the majors with 35 stolen bases in 1950 for the Braves.

"That's the highlight of my career," the old switch-hitting leadoff man and center fielder said.

His second season was almost a duplicate of the first. He hit .280 and 18 homers, stole 35 more bases to lead the majors again, and scored 101 runs.

Those numbers would make him a multimillionaire today. "They pay .135 hitters a million now," he chuckled. His average fell to .232 in his third season with the Braves, but he stole 28 bases. That was the end for him. He was through in the majors at age 30.

What happened?

"Don't ask me, ask Charlie Grimm," Jethroe said. The late Grimm was the Braves' third-base coach and took over as manager during the 1952 season. He was one of the most popular men in the game.

"I didn't like him calling me Sambo and I told him that," Jethroe said. "He said it wasn't nothing."

At the end of the season, Jethroe was traded to Pittsburgh, where he batted once in 1953, then was sent to the minors for the rest of his career.

"I wasn't upset," Jethroe said. "I played in Toronto for four or five years and liked it. The Braves had some good young black players coming up at the time, like Hank Aaron and Billy Bruton. Maybe they figured there'd be too many black players. I don't have a grudge."

Jethroe, as the only black player on the Braves, roomed alone and often had to stay in different hotels than his teammates. Before coming to the majors, Jethroe played six years for the Buckeyes, from 1942–47. The native of East St. Louis, Ill., hit .353 in 1944 and .393 in 1945. The Buckeyes won the Negro League championship by beating the Homestead Grays in 1945. "We played in League Park and the Stadium," Jethroe recalled. "We would draw 7,000 or 8,000 fans. I never liked the Stadium. It was too cold, even in July. But it was a great thrill beating the Grays."

As the star of the Buckeyes, Jethroe's name occasionally was in Cleveland headlines in those days. The newspapers would give only perfunctory coverage to black baseball.

When he first came to the majors, Jethroe was paid the minimum of $5,000. "I was making more in black baseball," he said. His top pay in the majors was $12,000.

Jethroe does not get a pension because he did not play the required five years in the majors, which was the rule at that time. Today, a player becomes vested for a pension in his first season. "I don't have a grudge about it," Jethroe said. "A rule's a rule. That's about it. But it sure would be nice to have a pension."

Ahead of His Time

MIKE MEDICH *Feb. 11, 2003*

Mike Medich was a giant. At a time when many basketball centers stood 6 feet, Medich was 6-5. Everybody in his family was tall. His father and two brothers were the same height he was. His mother was 5-10.

"Mike resembled Mom," his sister, Mildred, said. "He had her curly hair. Mike was her youngest son and her favorite. When he died, she was never the same. She died of a broken heart."

Medich, who died under harsh circumstances at the age of 29, was the LeBron James of an earlier era. His power and skill made him a Cleveland basketball legend at Benedictine High School.

Medich's most spectacular game came on Dec. 19, 1945, when he set a state scoring record of 59 points in a 75-29 victory over West High. The sensational outburst put Medich's name on top of every newspaper sports page in Cleveland.

To put the astounding 59-point effort into perspective, Cathedral Latin defeated St. Ignatius, 26-24, on the same night in that low-scoring period.

Medich's scoring record stood in Cleveland for about 20 years, until it was exceeded by Phil Argento in the 1960s.

Medich scored almost all of his points in his big game near the hoop, putting in rebounds and taking passes for short shots. Playing with four fouls, he scored 22 points in the last quarter. "When we saw something big was going to happen, [coach] Norb Rascher told us to keep giving Medich the ball," recalled former teammate Ed Cercek, 74, of Brecksville.

In the previous game, Medich had scored 41 points against Barberton, prompting Rascher to say: "He's the most natural center I've ever seen. He has everything and does everything right."

His former teammates remembered the 240-pound Medich. "He looked like a lumberjack," said Paul Vavrek, 74, of Euclid. "He was all muscle and no fat. Most big guys in that time had bad hands, but Mike could catch everything."

Joe Stipkala, a retired FBI agent who lives in Upper Marlborough, Md., was on the Benedictine junior varsity team behind Medich. He often scrimmaged against him and saw every game he played. "He was a dominator, a huge force," Stipkala, 73, said.

"He was unusually well-built, with a tapered waist and large shoulders, and very mobile."

Medich led Benedictine to a 15-0 record and the city championship that season. The Bengals held three teams to fewer than 20 points, defeating Collinwood (44-17), Central (68-12) and Holy Name (67-10) in consecutive games.

"Medich was the main reason for those low scores," Stipkala said. "He swatted away a lot of shots."

The Bengals defeated West Tech, 49-44, for the Senate title before a standing-room-only crowd at Public Hall. By that time, teams were swarming around Medich like Lilliputians around Gulliver and he was held to only 17 points, almost eight below his season average of 24.8.

At that time Cleveland teams were not playing in the state tournament. Madison Square Garden invited Benedictine to play New York's best schoolboy team after the season, but the Ohio High School Athletic Association refused to give the Bengals permission to participate. OHSSA rules said all high school basketball should be completed by March 22. The game was scheduled for March 30.

Clevelanders were upset over the ban. Mayor Thomas Burke said he would see what could be done to allow Benedictine to play in New York. Gov. Frank Lausche was asked to intervene. But OHSAA Commissioner Harold Emswiler turned down all pleas.

"We were disappointed," Vavrek said. "But studies were the main thing in school then. It's not like today, where school teams can go all over the country."

That ended Medich's career at Benedictine. He played only one full season of basketball at the school after transferring from Duquesne (Pa.) High School.

Medich was a mildly controversial figure from the start. It was commonly whispered in those days that Benedictine had imported Medich and his close friend, Rudy Schaffer, in order to become a power in Cleveland sports.

Medich and Schaffer turned Benedictine into a Cleveland prep powerhouse. Both starred in football and basketball, and the school soon began winning championships.

"Medich and Schaffer put the school on the map in sports," Stipkala said.

As a sophomore center at Duquesne High, Medich had led his team to the Pennsylvania state championship.

His sisters recall his happy home life in Duquesne. They watched all of his games and remember him as a likable youth who never caused anybody trouble. "He was younger than me," said Mildred Luptak, of Duquesne. "But he acted like he was older. When we'd go to dances, he'd come and get us after the dance. He'd walk us home."

His nickname was "Socko," because of the way he could sock the ball through the basket.

Nobody has a clear answer about what made Medich leave his large, close, Serbian-speaking family in Duquesne and transfer to Benedictine, where he was among 25 or so other boarders in the school monastery.

"He had some kind of trouble," said Father Placid Pientek, a Benedictine monk and priest. "The parish priest in Duquesne felt a change of environment would do him good."

"He felt a lot of animosity, being a sophomore with a lot of seniors on a state championship team," said Mildred. "He said he couldn't take it. He said he wanted to go somewhere else."

Bob Tedesky, who later became one of John Carroll University's basketball greats, played on the Duquesne title team with Medich. He said that coach Bill Lemmer was a taskmaster who often yelled at his players. A member of the Medich family said the coach was a tough disciplinarian who did not know how to handle youngsters, which might have been a major reason why Medich left.

At that time, several Benedictine priests hailed from the Duquesne area, about 12 miles from Pittsburgh. Father Louis Hudak, who later became principal of Benedictine, was visiting friends there and met Medich and Schaffer. He invited them and a few other students to visit the school. They liked it and decided to transfer. Tuition and board totaled $200 for the school year.

"Everybody was really mad when Mike went to Benedictine," said his cousin, Gabriel Medich, of West Mifflin, Pa. "We felt we'd win three state championships in a row with Mike."

"Mom felt badly about him going to Cleveland," said Helen Lia, one of Medich's sisters. "But when she met the caliber of people there she knew he was in good hands. Mike felt very much at home at Benedictine. He became friends with Chuck Noll [a student who later became the Pittsburgh Steelers coach] and he had three or four of his Duquesne friends there."

Photos in the school newspaper showed him happily shoveling snow on the sidewalks and waiting on tables at the school cafeteria.

Medich was soon involved in another controversy. He and Schaffer played a full season of football for the Bengals as juniors.

However, after Medich scored 34 points in the first two basketball games, he and Schaffer were suspended for the season. Out-of-town transfers were supposed to sit out a whole year of athletics.

He was a marked man when it was finally his time to play basketball as a senior. One newspaper writer, referring to his suspension, called him a notorious "bad man, basketball's Public Enemy No. 1" and a "dangerous dead shot."

In reality, Medich was just the opposite. "He was a gentle giant," said Cercek. "In the warm-ups before games, Rascher would tell me to push him around a little to fire him up. The only time I saw him get upset was when the Cathedral Latin band played 'The Pennsylvania Polka' and the Latin students called him a 'farmer.' He wanted to go into the stands. We had to hold him back."

Medich had his worst game against Latin. He was held to eight points before fouling out in the third quarter, but Benedictine won, 36-35, on Ed Jankura's foul shot.

After graduation, Tedesky wanted Medich to come to John Carroll. The Blue Streaks were playing teams like Georgetown and Notre Dame in those days. "Mike could run, rebound and play defense like crazy and was a good outside shot," recalled Tedesky, 76, from his home in Plano, Texas.

According to Tedesky, Medich went to Carroll briefly before dropping out. He was not the most enthusiastic of students. Later, he attended the University of West Virginia for a short time. Unlike LeBron, he had no NBA job waiting for him. It was unheard of at the time for high school players to go directly into pro basketball.

Medich returned home and followed his brothers into the Merchant Marines, traveling all over the hemisphere. He was a soldier in the Korean War, then became a military policeman. After his discharge, he went back to the ships as a seaman and got married.

He suffered a terrible death in 1958. Mildred said her brother had abdominal pains while working on an oil tanker and was put ashore by himself in Barcelona, Venezuela, to find a doctor. "A truck driver took him to a clinic," Mildred said. "They thought he had a ruptured appendix, but when they operated they found it was a perforated duodenal ulcer. He died on the operating table."

Medich was buried in Venezuela. Mildred, after enlisting the aid of a U.S. senator, was able to get his body exhumed and shipped back to the U.S. after five years.

"He was given a beautiful service on the shore in Baltimore," she said. "The seamen stood at attention, flags were flying, and he was put in a hearse and brought back to Duquesne."

Now Medich lies next to his mother in a grave in Versailles Cemetery in McKeesport, a few feet from his father's grave. "That was my mother's last wish," said Lia. "She wanted Mike to be buried next to her."

The Best Basketball Player St. Ignatius High Ever Had

DAVE DEMKO *Feb. 19, 1978*

Dave Demko was the best basketball player St. Ignatius High ever had, making all-scholastic three times in the early 1950s.

Only 5-11, he was wily, silent. He performed with a touch of insolence and seemed to be in total peace on the floor. It belonged to him.

But he was one of those people whose greatest triumphs come early in life. After the glory years at Ignatius, it was mostly downhill. He died of a heart attack on Oct. 24, 1976 at the age of 43.

It is appropriate to discuss him now, when the scholastic basketball tournaments that he so often dominated are again being contested.

So the other day I went to his home on the near West Side, where he had lived with his widowed mother until his death.

The white frame house had a "Beware of Dog" sign on the front porch. The snow had not been shoveled away. I knocked on the door, but there was no answer.

I want to a neighbor's house to inquire about Mrs. Demko's whereabouts. "Oh, Betty died last year, almost a year to the day after Dave died," she said. "All she ever thought about was him. She had five albums filled with his clippings. After his funeral she went to May Company and had four oil paintings made of him. They cost $500. She kept one for herself and gave the rest to relatives. She and her husband saw every game Dave played in.

"Dave's father, you know, died only a couple of months before Dave did. In a year and a half the whole family died, all from heart attacks. They were good people, worked hard, saved their money. It's a shame they all went so fast."

The house is empty now while the Demko estate is being settled. The thieves have discovered it. Just before Christmas somebody broke in and stole nearly everything of value inside. The garage has been broken into also.

"Dave was a quiet guy," the neighbor continued. "He'd go to work, come home. He'd be around the house all the time. Sometimes he'd come on the porch and smoke a cigarette. When you'd go into his house, he'd be watching TV, and when you came in he'd go to his room and stay there. On weekends he played golf or went fishing. Every summer he and his mother and her friend would go up to Canada and fish.

"Dave's only problem was that his mother never let him get married. She was against every girl he ever took out. She always said the women of today weren't worthy of him.

"Then, after he died, she said she was sorry that she hadn't let him get married. 'At least I'd have some grandchildren,' she said. Dave listened to his mother. When she told him to do something, he'd jump."

Demko worked as a delivery man for the Board of Education. Also a good baseball shortstop, he had received three letters from major league teams offering him tryouts.

"He wanted to go, but his mother was afraid he wouldn't take care of himself," said the neighbor. "So he stayed home." Other neighbors and friends verified Mrs. Demko's complete hold on her only child.

The trail then led to the other side of town, to Fred George's Scoreboard Inn, at 886 E. 200th St. It is a spacious, two-room bar filled with sports artifacts and memorabilia.

The bartender was John Wirtz, who coached so many Ignatius teams to championships before his retirement a few years ago. Wirtz, 63, was his usual burly, affable self. "I come in to open up for Fred a few mornings a week," he said.

We were soon joined by the white-haired Fred George, the proprietor, who lives upstairs with his wife and two sons. George, 60, coached Demko in his junior year at Ignatius. Wirtz had him as a senior.

"John and I were pallbearers at Dave's funeral," said George. "He looked good, like he could have gotten up and played."

"Dave was the most complete player I ever coached," said Wirtz. "He led us in scoring, assists and even rebounds, short as he was. He had great timing, fast hands."

"He had a great sense of where the ball was going to be," agreed George. "He had a real soft hook shot with either hand and could dribble well with either hand."

Wirtz recalled the night Demko threw in 57 points against Glenville to miss Mike Medich's Senate record of 59 for Benedictine.

"He had 27 at the half," said Wirtz, "and the other kids said, 'Mr. Wirtz, let him play all the way and we'll feed him.' I sat him out for the first three minutes of the second half because he had three fouls and then I put him in the pivot and he just started, wheeling and dealing from there. He could play inside or outside."

Both men said Demko was a quiet, but popular youth at Ignatius, one who never shirked duties or got into mischief.

"The Jesuit priests treated him like a son," said George. "Father John Rossing and Father William Sullivan were his guardian angels."

Demko was not a brilliant student, but let us not forget that the Ignatius curriculum features few fresh air courses.

"Father Rossing would tutor him for an hour and a half in freshman Latin," said George. "I had him in freshman algebra. He was the kind of kid who could learn if you'd take him to the blackboard and explain things."

"I had him in business law when he was a senior," said Wirtz. "He was a willing kid."

After graduating from Ignatius, Demko went to Dayton University, where he captained the freshman cage team. "He was one of the best prospects they ever had," said George, "but he and the books just didn't hit it off."

"I always felt he'd have finished college if he'd come to John Carroll (where George was coaching). He'd have had more help with the books there, like he had at Iggy. I worked to get him to come to Carroll."

Demko's stay at Dayton was marked by a wager he made with Bill Ewell, the Flyers' 6-10 center. He bet him a milk shake he could hit Ewell with a pass he wouldn't see during a scrimmage.

"Sure enough, Dave hit him in the chest with a pass that day," laughed Wirtz, "You had to be alert with him. If you weren't you were liable to get hit in the face with a pass."

Demko dropped out of Dayton after a year, then went into the army. His college days never resumed.

"I saw him often after that," said Wirtz. "I ran into him a lot at the West Side Market and he came to all the Ignatius games until he died. He only lived a couple of blocks away."

"We sat together through a lot of those games," said George. "It was a great shock to him when his dad died. He had been a great local athlete too."

I looked up at the wall above the bar. There was an article up there, written by Vince Lombardi, the late Green Bay football coach. "What It Takes To Be No. 1," it was entitled. Next to it was a picture of Wirtz and George when they came to Ignatius as young coaches in 1948.

Wirtz looked at George, and the strings of memory were humming. "Dave could really play, inside and outside," he said.

George nodded. "He had a real nice funeral," he said. "A lot of the guys who played with him were there." There was nothing left to say.

Football Star, War Hero

JIM MARTIN *Feb. 14, 2000*

Former Clevelander Jim "Jughead" Martin, a member of the College Football Hall of Fame, had a wildly successful gridiron career from the standpoint of team championships.

He was a lineman, playing both ways, on the Notre Dame teams that won three national titles and went unbeaten from 1946 to 1949, winning 38 games and tying two.

Then he played 14 years in the NFL, performing on championship teams with the Browns in 1950 and the Detroit Lions in 1952, 1953 and 1957.

Today Martin, 76, lives in Wildomar, Calif., with his daughter, Beverly, and 12-year-old grandson, Peter. "I feel great," he said in a telephone interview. "I'm old and I'm diabetic, but I'm happy."

Martin grew up in the Cleveland neighborhood of E. 79th St. and St. Clair. He was nicknamed by a friend at the Yale movie theater after he got a short haircut.

"I always liked that nickname," Martin said. "When they called me 'Jughead' it meant they liked me."

He attended East Tech High School, playing football for legendary coach Humphrey Harmony. "He was tough," Martin recalled.

A superb physical specimen at 6-2 and 215 pounds at his peak, Martin loved to swim at Gordon Park. That skill came in handy when he joined the Marines in the middle of World War II in 1943. He was in a reconnaissance unit, swimming 1,000 yards in the dark to Japanese-held islands, then going ashore to determine where the enemy strength was concentrated. Sometimes he came so close to the enemy he could hear them talking.

"We were dumped off destroyers at Tinian and Saipan and then we swam back," he said. "It was tough. I lost a good buddy right next to me."

Martin was decorated with a Bronze Star.

After the war, Martin went to Notre Dame, playing under coach Frank Leahy on the great teams that featured Johnny Lujack, Emil Sitko, George Connor and Leon Hart. Martin was co-captain with Hart in 1949.

He also found time to win the heavyweight boxing championship of Notre Dame.

In 1950, the Browns drafted him in the second round. Cleveland, playing in the NFL for the first time, won the league championship that year.

Martin, a defensive end and offensive tackle in Cleveland, learned to kick from Lou "The Toe" Groza, the Browns' Hall of Fame booter. "I stayed with Groza after practice," Martin recalled. "I'd hold the ball for him, and after he kicked it, I'd bring it back. He showed me how to kick. Lou was a fine man."

After one year in Cleveland, Browns coach Paul Brown traded Martin to Detroit for a 1952 first-round draft choice that turned out to be defensive back Bert Rechichar.

"Brown was a great coach," Martin said. "But he just didn't like me. I don't think he liked Notre Dame guys."

Martin found his professional niche with the Lions, where he stayed for 11 years. "It was a great place to play," he said. "They had a bunch of hell-raisers. They were the wildest bunch you ever saw. We had parties after every game and every practice."

Martin picked up another nickname in Detroit, "Jungle Jim." He played on both ends of the line, plus linebacker, wherever he was needed. "I wanted to be the best," he recalled. "I was like a shield for the quarterback. I could block. That's what I liked."

Eventually Martin became the Lions' place-kicker. He scored 434 points in his career, which ended with Washington in 1964, when he was 40. After that, he was an assistant coach at Detroit, Denver and Idaho State.

Memories of a Gifted Athlete and a Time of Injustice

DAVE SUGIUCHI *Feb. 7, 1982*

Some kids you forget, even if you went to school with them a long time and you were friends. You open up the yearbook 20 years after graduation and you look at their pictures and you can't recall their names. Others, like Dave Sugiuchi, you remember all your life.

Sugiuchi (pronounced Sa-goo-chee) was a Japanese-American and was probably the most popular boy at East High from 1947–50. He was a straight-A student, served on the Student Council, played a scrappy infield in baseball and was the star quarterback in football, earning second-team All-Senate honors.

The good-natured, industrious Sugiuchi was a natural leader. There was something about him you had to respect. Even players on other teams seemed to single him out. Once, after a tough football loss to Benedictine, the Bengals filed past the East High bus. "Nice game, Sigooch," they called in affectionate abbreviation of Sugiuchi's name.

As a quarterback, he lofted long touchdown passes and took the hard tackles with the stoic toughness of a Samurai.

Sugiuchi was so popular that we didn't even think of him, in those days right after World War II, as the descendant of a country the United Sates had just fought in the worst holocaust in human history.

All this came back to me recently, during Congressional hearings on an old wound — the U.S. government's internment of Japanese-Americans during the war. I wondered if Sugiuchi had spent time in the detention camps. It had never occurred to me to ask him during the old school days, when our minds were only filled with baseball, football and girls.

So, across the chasm of 32 years, I phoned Sugiuchi in Hudson, where he works with troubled kids for the Cuyahoga County Department of Youth Services. For 20 years before that, he was in the mental health field, helping adults.

Sugiuchi said he had been incarcerated during the war. He was born in California and was living on a farm outside Long Beach, Calif., when the Japanese bombed Pearl Harbor on Dec. 7, 1941.

There was much American hatred of Japan. Many people feared a Japanese invasion of California and there was suspicion that Americans of Japanese heritage might cause sabotage. So there was no public outcry when the country put all Japanese-Americans in detention camps in early 1942.

The 10-year-old Sugiuchi, his parents, two brothers and two sisters were taken with thousands of others to Santa Anita racetrack, which had been closed. They were placed in horses' stables, with clean cots to sleep in. Their food was served in a large mess hall.

Sugiuchi said the parents were upset and discussed the situation among themselves. But they kept their complaints away from the children. As a result, Sugiuichi and the other kids had a minimum of psychological scars.

"There were a lot of kids to play with," recalled Sugiuchi. "Our playground was the Santa Anita grandstand."

After four months, the Sugiuchis were transferred to a camp in Jerome, Ark. Conditions there were about the same, with the addition of schooling. "Us kids played baseball and football," said Sugiuchi. "There were guards with guns in the turrets, but they never bothered us."

In 1944, with the war going well for the Allies, Sugiuchi's father was allowed to leave the camp to find work in Cleveland, to which a Japanese friend had relocated. He got a job in a basket factory, then sent for his family. The Sugiuchis moved into a house at W. 150th and Lorain, and Dave went to John Marshall Junior High.

There was still hatred toward Japan. Sugiuchi's schoolmates called him derogatory names and constantly referred to him as "Jap."

"I never really said much," said Sugiuchi. "At that point, who needed a fight?"

Then his father got a new job and the Sugiuchis moved to Perkins Ave., near E. 32nd St. The war ended in that summer of 1945 and Dave made many friends at Waring School playground. Most of them were pupils at Willson Junior High, where Dave enrolled. He never had any trouble after that, sailing through East. Later he graduated from Fenn College, then obtained a masters degree. He also was in the Army and is married with three grown children.

After all these years, I asked him how he felt about his incarceration. "It was an injustice," he said.

It has been suggested that those who endured the internment be given reparations of $25,000 each to assuage the humiliation. Sugiuchi was asked if he felt he deserved that.

"For myself, no," he said. "But if my parents were still alive, they should have been entitled to it. Their lives were really uprooted."

Once Upon a Time, Santa Wore Cleats

NICK SABADOSH *Dec. 23, 1984*

Some people say there is no Santa Claus. They are wrong. Nick Sabadosh has been a Santa for many years.

All year long we fill the sports pages with stories of great athletes. Often they are nice guys, but they are rewarded by fame and money, too. Many times the unknown guy reading their stories is more interesting than the honored jocks.

Sabadosh is like that. He was a teacher for 46 years, mostly at Lincoln High School. Generations of Lincoln graduates remember him as the freshman football coach.

When Sabadosh received the Golden Deeds Award from the Greater Cleveland Football Association this year, his sponsor, the veteran coach Vic Hanchuk, wrote:

"Sabadosh is an unsung hero of the coaching profession who has received very few honors and virtually no publicity for the dedication and determination that has positively influenced the lives of so many. It is a real honor to recommend him."

Sabadosh wasn't only a coach and teacher, "I made more visits to kids' homes than any teacher in the city," he said. "I brought them to my house. Once we had the whole football team there. My wife said she didn't realize our house was so big."

Many of the Lincoln pupils came from poor families. Sabadosh would go to flea markets and buy clothes and shoes for them with his own money.

"I'd buy whole racks of overalls, shirts, coats," he said. Remember, teachers weren't paid much then. Sabadosh never got an extra cent for coaching, either.

Sabadosh recalled the time an eighth grader was absent frequently. "I want you to do well in school," Sabadosh told him. "Why are you out so much?"

"I'm having stomach aches," the boy said.

Sabadosh went to his house. There was a bushel of potatoes in a corner. "That's all they were eating, potatoes for breakfast, potatoes for lunch and potatoes for supper," said the indignant Sabadosh. "And this was in the United States of America!"

Sabadosh helped them out, as he did many families. Until a few years ago, he and his son-in-law would buy 60 chickens with their own money and put together 15-20 baskets of food for Thanksgiving. For years, a kind-hearted farmer gave him 150 baskets full of apples. Sabadosh and his son-in-law gave everything to the needy.

A store owner said to him, "It must make you feel real good to do this for people."

Sabadosh replied, "No, it makes me feel terrible that people don't have enough to eat."

Once he took a poor boy's shoes to be repaired. When Sabadosh reached in his pocket to pay the shoemaker, he wouldn't take a cent. "You helped my son get into the hospital when they wouldn't admit him," explained the shoemaker.

The son, an army veteran of World War II, was living at home with his father, suffering from what was then called shell shock. But the hospital wouldn't take him until Sabadosh intervened.

"He had been in two or three invasions, including Normandy," said Sabadosh. "That was enough to crack up anybody with any sensitivity."

Sabadosh has been a lifelong pacifist. He feels war is stupid. He took part in one of the first protests against the Vietnam war, when 300 people marched in front of the Old Stone Church.

They were heckled by a small group of rednecks. One guy called Sabadosh a "dirty rat."

Sabadosh replied, "You punk. If you didn't have 10 buddies with you, I'd rap every tooth down your throat."

Contrary to the image that all liberals are limp-wristed quiche eaters, Sabadosh is a former Golden Gloves boxing champion. He also fought professionally under the name "Bulldog Drummond."

Once Sabadosh offered a challenge to a group of Lincoln roughnecks. One boy started after him, but another held him back, saying, "I wouldn't go after Mr. Sabadosh. He'll knock your head off."

Sabadosh doesn't live under the illusion that everybody wants to help his fellow man. He tells of the time he asked a store owner for some clothes and shoes for his pupils. He only wanted the articles that were discolored or irregular, stuff that wasn't going to be sold anyway.

The store owner had recently won an outstanding citizen award, so Sabadosh thought he would be a good bet to help out. He wasn't. "He didn't give us a single thing," he recalls.

Sabadosh also was active in school desegregation work and once spent four hours alone in front of the CEI building, protesting the Perry nuclear plant policy.

Even now, at 77, he is deeply involved in helping the Indians of the poverty-stricken Pine Ridge reservation in South Dakota. He puts the arm on institutions for hospital beds, heaters, blankets, etc. The baseball Indians gave him 50 used bats to send there.

Sabadosh's interest in the Native American may have begun about 25 years ago, when he saw an Indian standing on E. 9th St. shivering in the cold. Sabadosh bought him a beer and got him a job as a security guard.

Sabadosh and Audrey, his wife of 50 years, lived in Brecksville until a few months ago. They moved to Waverly, near Columbus, but are back in town for the holidays, visiting their daughter and grandchildren.

When Santa comes down their chimney tomorrow night, he will shake Sabadosh's hand.

Indians 1970s–'90s

He Reduces Baseball to a Simple Game

GAYLORD PERRY *Jun. 25, 1972*

My uncle Frank used to take two spiced ham and cheese sandwiches to work for lunch every day. The menu never varied. It was always two spiced ham and cheese sandwiches.

"Don't you ever get tired of spiced ham and cheese, Uncle Frank?" I asked him once.

"Why should I?" the gourmet answered. "There's nothing wrong with it."

Gaylord Perry, a pitcher for the Cleveland Indians, strikes me as being the same sort of person, uncomplicated and unimaginative and thus free of many of the demons that bedevil modern man.

I can't imagine him asking himself in tortured introspection if he went into the right line of work or married the right girl. I can't see him quitting a good safe job because he felt unfulfilled and I can't picture him running out on a wife and four brats because he was bored.

As I envision him, Gaylord Perry is not afraid of boredom. In fact, one might almost say that he is quite willing to be bored and, if necessary, to be boring. It's as though he feels it is the mark of a mature man to conquer monotony and learn to live happily with it.

But of course it would never occur to Perry to think that.

Let's just say that conversation isn't the long suit of the Perry clan that hails from farm country in North Carolina. I used to know Gaylord's older brother, Jim, in the faraway days when he pitched for the Indians, and he could be just as determinedly tedious as Gaylord.

I remember Jim Perry bending the ear of Barry Latman, an Indian teammate, one day. Latman was just the opposite of Perry, a sophisticate from Los Angeles who was at home in the best saloons in the American League.

After their conversation I asked Latman what Perry had been talking to him about. "Damned if I know," replied Latman. "I've been listening to him for two years and I haven't understood a word he's said yet."

So maybe the Perrys aren't talkers, but a smart talker has to know what not to say too, and nobody ever heard of Jim or Gaylord talking their way into trouble.

Gaylord had plenty of opportunity for that early this year, when his pitching for the Indians was burning up the league. He was being besieged for interviews from all sides.

This didn't faze him. An amiable sort, he was ready to chit-chat superficially with the reporters. But if they were looking for controversial material they weren't about to get it from him.

For example, let me tell you about a game the Indians played during the merry month of May. Gaylord pitched a shutout and afterward Dave Martin, a telecaster for Channel 8, placed Perry on camera as reward for being the contest's outstanding player.

Martin soon found he was overmatched. Perry had certain things he planned to say and By God He Was Going To Say Them, no matter what questions Martin asked. It is a fine art also shared by successful politicians.

Before Martin knew what was happening, the interview had deteriorated into a seminar on pitching.

"I just try to keep the ball down and let 'em hit it," chattered Perry, with practiced glibness. "I got eight good players behind me and I depend on them. Keep the ball low, inside, outside."

The interview proceeded along that path, with Martin bobbing his head up and down and trying to put the dialogue on a more provocative level.

When Perry finally paused in his baccalaureate to take a deep breath, Martin seized the opportunity and said, "Gaylord, I'm going to put you on the spot. Is the National League tougher than the American League?"

Well, now. Anybody who knows the difference between a touchdown and home run understands that the majority of baseball's distinguished players live in the N.L.

This is probably one of the reasons Perry, at the advanced baseball age of 33, got off to such a fast start. He won eight games by the end of May after coming to the Indians in the controversial trade for Sam McDowell

It was understandable. After sharpening his tools against the sluggers he faced constantly in the N.L., Perry must have felt as though he was in the Three-Eye League after coming to Cleveland.

But now he had to answer Martin's question. Was the National League tougher? He replied exactly as I knew he would.

"We've got some fine young players on our club," he said. "Fosse, Chambliss, Bell, Nettles, Johnson, Brohamer. Yessir, I think we'll be all right. I'm just gonna throw the ball up there and let 'em hit it."

Martin, eyes glazed, concluded his probing interview and went into the next commercial.

The only controversial issue surrounding Perry is his alleged use of the spitball and greaseball. Opposing managers and batters have been screaming for years that Gaylord has learned to accentuate the drop on his sinker by applying saliva to the ball. This is not only unsanitary, it is also illegal in baseball circles.

Perry does little to discourage speculation that he employs spit or grease, correctly figuring that, like a temptress, a pitcher operates best when he has added mystery to his repertoire.

If the batters want to believe Perry cheats, why that's all right with him. It just gives them a little bit more to worry about. And Perry coaxes them along into his web of deception, constantly making motions with his hand around the area of the facet and cap.

Then the ball comes swerving up to the batter, dipping and careening, and the old protest erupts.

"There it was, he threw it then," the foes yell and umpire goes running out to the mound leading a battery of Keystone Kops in an effort to locate Perry's reservoir of grease.

Because of this, Gaylord has had to submit to much indignity. How would you like to be frisked in full view of 50,000 people? The worst part comes when the umps make him take his cap off, for Gaylord's hairline is hell-bent for the back of his noggin. So far no umpire has asked him to remove his pants as happened once to another alleged greaseballer, Pedro Ramos. But you never can tell.

I asked Perry when it was that he was first accused of throwing a spitter or greaseball. "Oh, about six, seven years ago," he replied.

"Who accused you ?" I asked. "And against what team was it?"

"I don't remember," answered Gaylord. "It was so long ago."

I don't think he was trying to be evasive on that one. There was no point. I just think Gaylord lives in the present and that his memory isn't any too good anyway.

I asked him if he'd ever been in a fight in baseball and he said,

"Yep, just once. It was when I was in the minors and this team was beating us by 14 or 15 runs all the time so our manager told me I had to get tough out there.

"So this little second baseman came up and I threw the ball at his ribs to scare him and I hit him. He came running out at me and we tossed a few punches."

"Two years later I played winter ball and that little fella was my roommate. We got along just fine."

Perry's most recent excursion into violence came last season, when he was with the Giants. His great teammate, Juan Marichal, hit Billy Buckner of the Los Angeles Dodgers with a pitch and one of those typical baseball fights ensued. All the players ran out on the field and the net result of the combat was three scratches, four bites and a dozen dirty looks.

"I ran out like you're supposed to," said Perry. "and I went straight for Richie Allen. I wasn't going to hit him though. He's built this wide . . . I'd have to be crazy. Besides, Richie's a good friend of mine. So I ran up behind him and pinched him in the ass."

I suppose I ought to throw a little baseball into this right about here in case any of you sports fans are reading. Perry says that Marichal, a cinch for the Hall of Fame, is the most complete pitcher he ever saw and that he can throw a baseball through a doughnut. That's how good his control is.

But Sandy Koufax, he says, had the most stuff of any pitcher he's seen. "He didn't have to worry about control," says Gaylord admiringly. "All he had to do was throw the ball over the plate and they still couldn't hit it."

I asked him how he compared himself with McDowell.

"He has better stuff," said Gaylord. "But I have better control and endurance."

Perry has been compared to other pitchers before. In fact, his brother Jim once offered an immortal quote about him.

This happened away back in 1959 when Jim broke in with sensational style as a member of the Indians. Everybody wanted to know more about him and in the midst of one interview, Jim said:

"I got a baby brother back home who just signed a bonus contract with the Giants for $90,000. He got the money but I got all the talent."

I asked Gaylord about that quote and wondered if he resented it. Fingering his wallet, he said he didn't and he reflected on the fact that both he and his brother have had pretty good major league careers.

Both have won 20 or more games in a season a couple of times and by the time they're through they should both be near the 200-victory mark. Gaylord had 142 big league triumphs as this was written and Jim, now with Minnesota, was up around 165.

The Perrys have meshed well since boyhood, when Jim pitched the high school team to the North Carolina state title, with Gaylord playing third base.

The association continues. Last year they paired up on a razor blade commercial that was bouncing around the network TV screen all summer. It was a rather famous little spot, for in it Gaylord stumbled on the words.

"I was supposed to say 'Gillette Platinum Plus' and the first time I said it it came out 'Gillette pulinass plum' or something like that.

"So they filmed it about 70 times more and I said it right every time. But the one they used was the one where I goofed the words."

That's okay with Cleveland's baseball fans. They don't care how Gaylord sounds. All they ask is that he keep pitching the way he did early in the year, when he made them forget Sudden Sam.

Hitting, Not Hustle, Was Silent George's Style

GEORGE HENDRICK *Aug. 21, 2001*

George Hendrick was one of the all-time Indians mystery men. Some fans disliked him. But he also had a cult following that remembers him as its favorite player of the middle 1970s. Hendrick, chosen one of the Indians' top 100 players, had style. He looked good during his four years with the team. He was tall and lean. He could run like a lion and he hit the baseball long distances in elegant fashion.

He had appeal as a rebel against authority. He was above straining every muscle racing to first on a hopeless grounder to the infield, just to keep his managers happy.

No, sir. If George knew he was likely to be out, he simply trotted to first base.

As for cranking out quotes to please the writers, Hendrick disdained that, too. He hardly ever talked, earning the nickname of Silent George or Lonesome George.

"But he was always polite when he turned down an interviewer," recalled former teammate Rick Manning, 46, now an Indians sportscaster.

Hendrick preferred to let his bat make his speeches for him. He averaged 23 homers and 78 runs batted in from 1974 to 1976. That was excellent in those bleak days at the Wigwam.

His greatest day with the Indians came on June 19, 1973, when he hit three home runs and a ninth-inning game-winning single for an 8-7 victory over Detroit at the Stadium.

A tiny crowd of 3,485 saw the performance, in which Hendrick hit one homer to left and two to right, all against Woodie Fryman. He gave a major speech after the game. After vigorous encouragement, Hendrick cleared his throat and pronounced, "I was lucky. I've got nothing to say."

That was all. A photographer managed to take a picture of a smiling but protesting Hendrick.

"He stopped talking because he couldn't take criticism from the press," said ex-teammate Oscar Gamble, 51, of Montgomery, Ala.

Charlie Spikes, 50, of Bogalusa, La., was Hendrick's roommate. "He never liked to be interviewed because he didn't like anybody to know his business," said the Bogalusa Bomber. "He liked to spend a lot of his time with his family and we'd go to the movies."

Hendrick had other moments. In 1974 he broke up a no-hitter by Nolan Ryan of the California Angels with a towering two-run homer in the seventh inning that started the Indians on the way to a 7-2 victory. That same year he drove in four runs, including a three-run homer, in a 9-2 triumph over the first-place Red Sox. The Cleveland Press said he saved several games with his brilliant fielding and fine throwing arm.

Ken Aspromonte, 69, of Houston, was the Indians' manager in Hendrick's first two seasons in Cleveland, 1973-74. The two had a love-hate relationship.

"I managed against George in Class A in the minors and I always thought he had great potential," Aspromonte recalled. "He whipped the bat like Hank Aaron. Whenever I saw him I would tell him, 'You're going to make a lot of money.' I thought he would average 35 homers and 100 RBI."

When Hendrick came up with the championship Oakland club, he had trouble cracking the lineup. Aspromonte lobbied for a trade. The Indians sent catcher Ray Fosse and shortstop Jack Heidemann to Oakland for Hendrick and catcher Dave Duncan on March 24, 1973. But Hendrick's nonchalant trips down the first-base line on ground balls soon bothered Aspromonte, fans and media. Pitcher Gaylord Perry also jumped on Hendrick for passive outfield play, Aspromonte said.

The manager called Hendrick into his office and said, "'We're a young club and you've got to show the guys you want to play. If you keep trotting to first, it will reflect on me.'"

"He'd get mad at himself for hitting a grounder and put his head down," Aspromonte recalled.

"He sat there and said, 'I'll do better.' I fined him $1,000, but [General Manager] Phil Seghi rescinded the fine."

But there were occasions when Aspromonte could not say enough about Hendrick's play. "George has been outstanding for a month," the manager said in 1974. "He's done everything."

Ex-shortstop Frank Duffy, 61, of Tucson, Ariz., got along well with Hendrick. "I liked him a lot," Duffy said. "I felt he got a bum rap. Gaylord would bad-mouth him. Fans and players didn't think he tried hard, but I don't think he could have played any other way. He had that gliding style. He just wasn't aggressive. But he had incredible talent.

"That's what burned a lot of guys. They would say to themselves, 'If only I had that kind of talent.'"

The Indians traded Hendrick on Dec. 8, 1976, when Frank Robinson was manager. They sent him to San Diego for role players Johnny Grubb, Fred Kendall and Hector Torres. He hit .311 with 23 homers for the Padres in 1977."

I phoned him there and asked how the San Diego beat writers were treating him. Hendrick replied, "I don't like either one of them." The Padres sent him to St. Louis the next season for pitcher Eric Rasmussen. Hendrick spent the next six years with the Cardinals, hitting over .300 three times and twice batting in more than 100 runs.

"He improved with age," said Gamble. "He didn't play much in high school." Hendrick played 18 seasons in the majors, hitting 267 home runs and driving in 1,111 runs.

Hendrick coached for the Cardinals and Padres for four seasons, from 1996 to 1999.

"It shocked me that he became a coach," said Aspromonte. Coaches are usually former players who hustled and were aliens to controversy. Hendrick, now 50, didn't return phone calls for this story. He is still Silent George.

1977 Contract Still Haunts Pitcher

WAYNE GARLAND *Jan. 20, 1997*

Wayne Garland, one of the original high-priced free agents, is amazed at all the money baseball players are getting today. "How can they keep paying that much?" asked Garland in a phone interview from his home in Lakeland, Fla. "I don't know where all the money is coming from. I'm not the one to say, but it has to stop somewhere."

Twenty years ago, Garland, then 26, became a sensation when the Indians gave him a 10-year, $2.3million guaranteed contract, amounting to $230,000 a year. At that time, it made him by far the highest-paid player in club history.

The right-handed pitcher had won 20 games and lost seven for Baltimore the previous season, posting a 2.68 earned run average. "My father-in-law said I wasn't worth that much," said Garland, "and he was right. No pitcher is worth that based on one season. But if they offer it to you, naturally you're going to take it."

The stunning salary caused more of a furor than the $55 million, five-year contract Albert Belle recently signed with the Chicago White Sox. Garland's deal redefined baseball's salary structure. "Even today, you don't see players getting 10-year guaranteed contracts," Garland said.

After signing, he developed a sore arm that eventually ended his career. He was 28-48 with the Indians before they released him after the 1981 season.

"We had some great highs and lows, and then it all came crashing down," Garland said. "But I wouldn't give anything in exchange for that experience. It made me a different person. I had to grow up real quick."

Garland was a pitching coach in the Pittsburgh Pirates minor-league organization the last several years. He was in Class AAA Calgary in 1995, and in Class A Augusta, Ga., last season. The Pirates released him after the season.

He is at home recuperating from his third back operation in 16 months. "They inserted three screws in my back," he said. "I've had disk problems. I still want to get back into baseball. My ultimate goal is to be back with the Indians as a pitching coach. I think I'm good at what I do.

"I understand pitchers. I've been a hard thrower, a soft thrower, a sore-armed pitcher and a pitcher recovering from an operation. So, I know what they go through."

Garland is living in a rented house with his second wife, Kathi, whom he married in 1991. "Like everybody else, I've got my wants, but I've got my baseball pension," he said.

It is a far cry from the days when he lived in a $775,000 house in Hunting Valley with his first wife, Mary, and their children. The home had 13 rooms plus a swimming pool, tennis courts, horse stables and cottages, all on 22 acres.

Former Indians pitcher Dan Spillner, a teammate of Garland's, rented one of the cottages one summer. "The house was awesome," Spillner recalled. "It was really beautiful, massive, and the grounds were gorgeous."

The Orioles practically forced Garland into seeking employment elsewhere in those early days of free agency in 1976. He had gone 7-11, mostly as a sparsely used reliever, in the previous three seasons. He wanted a raise to $25,000 and a chance to start, but Baltimore cut his pay from $23,000 to $19,000. Garland's agent, Jerry Kapstein, advised him to play out his option and become a free agent.

At the time, Garland and his wife had two infant children and were sharing a two-bedroom apartment in Baltimore with teammate Mike Flanagan and his family. The Garlands' children were sleeping on a cot and in the playpen in the same room with their parents.

Garland got off to a great start with the Orioles in '76. With his record at 9-0, his pay was restored to $23,000. When he was at 10-1, the Orioles increased their offer to $40,000. Mary begged him to sign. "We had no money, just bills," she said. She was afraid he would get hurt and the offer would be withdrawn. But Garland, on the advice of Kapstein, still refused. He wasn't getting along with Orioles manager Earl Weaver anyway. When the season ended, the offers came pouring in. Mary was giving her youngest baby a bottle of milk when Kapstein called. "I couldn't get you a million," he told Garland. "I got you two million."

"I screamed," said Mary Garland, who is now a radio talk-show host in Nashville, Tenn. "I was so excited, I accidentally pushed the bottle into the baby's mouth, and he started crying." When Garland signed the contract, he said: "This is the greatest thing that ever happened to me and my wife. I'm looking forward to many happy days with the Indians. I don't see why we can't draw two million fans to the Stadium. We can win it all and be on top for a long time."

General Manager Phil Seghi, caught up in the euphoria, said: "We think we have one of the finer pitching staffs in baseball now. We have taken a large, large step forward." Dennis Eckersley, Rick Waits and Jim Bibby were the other starters.

Unfortunately, it didn't work out. Garland's arm began giving him trouble almost immediately and he went on to a record of 13-19 the first year. But he was better than those numbers indicate, throwing 21 complete games and working 283 innings. "He has a belly full of guts," Seghi said.

"I think I pitched better in 1977 than in 1976," Garland recalled. "The difference was I was pitching for a second-division team instead of a first-division team." The Indians finished in fifth place at 71-90.

Garland's salary was a constant source of discussion. "Frank Robinson [the manager] was always kidding me about it," Garland said. "It was all in fun."

When Indians teammate Don Hood accidentally picked up an equipment bag with Garland's name on it, Robinson quipped: "I see you've already got Hood carrying your money bags." When Garland noted that the whirlpool was not working, trainer Jim Warfield joked: "With your money you should be able to buy your own."

His number, 23, was another source of jest, for it reminded people of his $230,000 salary. When teammate Dave LaRoche was traded, Garland jumped at the chance to take his No. 17. Fans on the road would yell: "Who do you think you are?" Reggie Jackson and Catfish Hunter, both future Hall of Famers, were the only free agents with bigger contracts.

"He seldom let it get to him," Spillner said. "Occasionally, he'd come into the dugout and utter a cuss word. He just wanted to pitch. The players respected him for his competitiveness. By and large, the Cleveland fans were good."

The next year, Garland received a cortisone shot in his ailing arm in spring training. On May 1, 1978, the Tribe announced he needed surgery for a torn rotator cuff and that he was finished for the year.

"I feel like I got hit in the solar plexus," Seghi said. "They won't know until they go in if he'll ever pitch again."

In the meantime, the Garlands had bought their magnificent house. But on Jan. 18, 1979, after living there only two months, they sued the former owners and the real-estate company, charging breach of contract. The Garlands said that rugs and drapes in the house were missing. They also said they had been unable to rent the stables, as they had been led to believe would be the case. The Garlands asked that their $775,000 be returned, plus $572,000 in damages. The suit was settled out of court and the Garlands later sold the property. "We lost a little on it," Garland said. "I probably shouldn't have bought it."

"The house was like a dream," Mary Garland said. "At least we had some experience with that side of life." The Garlands owned two other houses in Chagrin Falls and Chesterland during their stay here.

"I still have great memories about those days," Mary Garland said. "We made some great friends. I still try to stop there at least once a year just to see them." Mary, who is not remarried, has been dating a lawyer in Nashville.

"Christmastime was such a great time in Chagrin Falls," Wayne Garland said. "It was like a little village. I remember the closeness and friendliness of the people."

By 1981, Garland had become the Indians player representative for the union. When the players' strike began that year, he took a job in a gas station. "I wasn't ashamed to be seen pumping gas and wiping windshields," Garland said.

Mary went to work as a weekend waitress at Landerhaven Country Club. "We can use the extra money," she said. "I can't sit around idle."

His arm was far from what it used to be. His friend and brother-in-law, Tom Sciarabba of Rochester, N.Y., used to catch him in the off-season. "He threw so hard he'd make my hand red as a pepper," Sciarabba said. "After the operation he couldn't break a pane of glass. We had great times together. He'd take me all over the American League, and I got to know all the players."

The tenacious Garland still had his moments. On July 3, 1980, he shut out the New York Yankees, 1-0, on a two-hitter in front of 73,096 in the Stadium. "That was a game I'll never forget," Spillner said. "He battled them all the way. He was very stubborn."

"It was one of those days when my arm felt great," Garland said. "Other times it was dead. There was nothing there." He also had a 1-0 win over Milwaukee in 1981, his last year in the majors.

After that, he was in a variety of occupations. He ran a batting cage franchise, got into the oil-well business, worked for Wal-Mart and served as a minor-league pitching coach. It rankles him that he never got another chance to prove he wasn't a one-season flash in the pan. But nobody wanted to take a chance on him at that salary. Mary Garland filed for divorce in 1983. "I try not to think about it," she said. "We had some problems. When I got married, I expected it to be forever. Wayne is a good guy, and we have four beautiful children, but life goes on."

Garland said: "It's hard to say what happened. There were a lot of things, being on the road so much."

He is resigned to the fact that he will always be identified with the 1977 contract. "No matter where I am, it still comes up," he said. "It will be that way until the day I die." As much as any player in big-league history, Garland was in the right place at the right time. His 20-victory season in his option season of 1976 was the only time he was over .500 in the majors.

Explosive Tenure Began with a Bang

FRANK ROBINSON *May 18, 1997*

Frank Robinson had no illusions when the Indians hired him to be the first black manager in major-league baseball history in 1975. "I'll probably be the first black manager to be fired, too," he said.

Robinson was right, of course. Almost all managers get fired. He was let go two stormy seasons later, but in between he had his moments. The apex came on his first day on the job, April 8, 1975, a chilly opening day in the Stadium. Player-manager Robinson hit a home run off Doc Medich in the first inning as the Indians beat the New York Yankees, 5-3.

It was probably the most spectacular managerial debut ever. Even winning pitcher Gaylord Perry, Robinson's chief adversary, ran to home plate to offer congratulations.

"Any homer is a thrill," Robinson recalled, "but I've got to admit this was more. Will miracles never cease to happen?" Indians first baseman Boog Powell said: "I got goose bumps when he hit it. I've never been involved in anything like that." Indians President Alva "Ted" Bonda, who hired Robinson, was sitting in a box with Robinson's wife and Rachel Robinson, widow of Jackie Robinson, the first black major-leaguer in the modern era. Rachel Robinson threw out the first ball for Frank Robinson's debut. "I couldn't believe he hit the homer," recalled Bonda, 80. "It was better than a movie script."

From that Hollywood start, Robinson went on to take a modestly talented Tribe team to a 79-80 record that first year and to an 81-78 mark the next, the first time they had finished over .500 in eight years. He was fired on June 19, 1977, with the Indians' record at 25-31.

A great slugger who had won Most Valuable Player awards in both leagues, he was the kind of person who inspired strong passions. Three books were written about him in his first two years here. Indians players Perry and Rico Carty disliked him intensely. But Duane Kuiper and Rick Manning cannot say enough good things about him.

"He was the best manager I ever played for," said Kuiper, 46, a second baseman who played for Robinson in Cleveland and San Francisco. "If you knew his ground rules and played hard, he'd encourage you and be your friend. He was always a step ahead of the other managers in the game."

Former Tribe center fielder Manning, 42, said: "I loved Frank Robinson. I'd run through a wall for that guy."

Bonda, a longtime civil rights activist, began thinking of Robinson as a manager when he signed him as a player in late 1974, when Ken Aspromonte was the Indians' pilot.

"I was very much impressed with Frank when I first met him," Bonda said. "I thought that having the first black manager could be a popular move in Cleveland. Attendance was important." The Indians were happy to draw a million fans in a season then.

"Critics said I did it just to have a black manager," Bonda said. "But I did it on merit."

The fiery Robinson had problems as soon as he joined the Indians as a player. Perry, who had won the Cy Young Award in 1972 and was the team leader, announced in the newspapers that he wanted a dollar more in salary than Robinson.

This infuriated Robinson. "Frank challenged Gaylord in the clubhouse," recalled Kuiper, now a broadcaster with the San Francisco Giants. "Gaylord was sitting on his stool and Frank stood over him. If he had tried to stand up, Frank would have punched him down. Gaylord was at a disadvantage. He never left the stool. It wasn't a racial thing. It was a dollars-and-cents thing."

Between seasons, Robinson replaced Aspromonte. The new leader was a big hit with the media, who found him to be cooperative and quotable, but the fireworks continued. When Robinson ordered his pitchers to run in spring training, Perry refused on the basis that he didn't need anyone to tell him how to get into condition. He was traded in May.

On May 17, Robinson was suspended for three days for bumping umpire Jerry Neudecker. On June 25, he called Oakland shortstop Bert Campaneris "a dirty little coward" after he hit the Tribe's Buddy Bell on the forehead with a throw. On June 30, in an exhibition game in Toledo, Robinson, playing as the designated hitter, punched pitcher Bob Reynolds, who had thrown a ball over his head. Reynolds was angry because Robinson had sent him to the minors in the spring.

Bonda said that Robinson was the victim of racism by some in the media and some players. "Everything he did was multiplied 12 times," he said. "It's easier for a black manager today. You have to remember the racial climate at the time."

Kuiper and Manning say they saw no signs of racism. "I would never call Gaylord a racist," Kuiper said. "He was the big chief. It was a matter of someone coming in and taking over his territory."

"I never heard people in the clubhouse talk about race," said Manning, analyst on the Indians games on SportsChannel. "When you're playing, color doesn't matter."

On July 19, catcher John Ellis became angry when Robinson pulled him for a pinch hitter. Ellis threw equipment around in the dugout and yelled at the manager.

"You're batting only .217," Robinson said. "You're lucky you're here."

"You're lucky you're here, too," Ellis retorted. Robinson vowed Ellis would not play for him any more. The next day Ellis apologized, but three weeks later he was traded. Late in the year, Robinson caused another flap when he issued a list of umpires he thought were good and bad.

Designated hitter Carty was Robinson's chief thorn in 1976. "Frank didn't like him and Rico didn't like Frank," Bonda said.

"One time in the dugout they started yelling at each other," recalled Kuiper. "We all thought, 'This is going to be a great fight between two big guys.' But somebody broke it up." More public problems followed in 1977.

On April 25, Carty made critical comments about Robinson, who was sitting next to him, in a speech to 600 people at the Wahoo Club. On May 21, Robinson fined infielder Larvell Blanks for failing to hustle. He also wanted to fine pitcher Al Fitzmorris for taking himself out of a game after one inning, but General Manager

Phil Seghi rescinded the fine. By that time the late Seghi was anti-Robinson, partly because he felt he wasn't putting himself in the lineup enough.

"Seghi had the ear of the media," Bonda said. On June 7, Robinson sent Carty home, charging he was a divisive influence. Carty called Robinson a "liar and a bully." Bell left the team for a day.

On June 12, Robinson said managing was a "pain in the derriere" and added he did not want to come back in 1978. When he was fired on June 19, he calmly said: "I'd like to manage again. I have no one to rip. I want to thank everybody—club, media, players and fans. It's been tough, but it's been an enjoyable two years."

"He was crucified," utility player Ron Pruitt said.

"I always regretted I fired him in mid season," Bonda said. "I caved in to pressure. Seghi wanted me to fire him the year before."

Robinson left Cleveland to coach with the California Angels and Baltimore. In 1980, he made news when he charged that baseball discriminated against blacks at the front office and managerial levels.

Robinson managed San Francisco from 1981–84, then took over at Baltimore from 1988–91. He was American League manager of the year in 1989, when the Orioles finished second with an 87-75 record. In his 11-year managerial career, he posted a 680-751 record, a .475 percentage.

Kuiper said the timing was difficult for Robinson. "He started managing when players were changing," he said. "The modern players want the managers to explain their situations to them. In Cleveland, he never called a player into his office. He thought that a player should approach him. In San Francisco, he softened up a little, but then it turned into a country club. Jack Clark, our best player, was a problem. He wanted to be patted on the back when he hit a three-run homer. Frank's approach was, 'That's what you're getting paid for.'

"I wish he'd been able to manage a little longer in Baltimore. By then, he understood modern players better and he had a lot of talent there."

After spending more time in Baltimore as a coach and personnel person, the Hall of Famer retired.

Two weeks ago, at 61, he was hired as director of baseball operations for the Arizona Fall League and as a consultant to acting Baseball Commissioner Bud Selig.

"I'm glad he's back," Manning said. "Baseball needs guys like that. He is baseball."

The Day 'Captain Kipe' Tripled His Way to Fame

DUANE KUIPER *Aug. 26, 2001*

Duane Kuiper holds two wildly different baseball records. He is honored once for muscle and another time for weakness. A good singles hitter in eight years with the Indians, the former second baseman hit one home run in 3,379 major-league at-bats. Of all the players who had at least 3,000 trips to the plate, he has the fewest homers.

But Kuiper also split his personality and slugged two bases-loaded triples in one game, a momentous feat that only two other players have accomplished since 1900. They are Elmer Valo of the Philadelphia Athletics in 1949, and Bill Bruton of the Milwaukee Braves in 1959.

Kuiper, 51, a broadcaster for the San Francisco Giants, remembers the day, July 27, 1978, when he tripled into the record book. "We were playing in New York and I got up at 5:30 in the morning for an appearance on the 'Today' TV show," Kuiper said. He was accompanying teammate Rick Waits, who was going to sing his mother's favorite song, "The Impossible Dream," on the program. "I went with him because I wanted to meet Jane Pauley, the anchor," said Kuiper. "Waits sang, but he forgot some of the words."

On the way back to the hotel, a couple of New Yorkers spotted Waits. "One said, 'I saw you sing on TV today. You were good.'" The other one, in typical merciless Gotham style, said, "Stick to pitching."

The Indians had a doubleheader that afternoon. Kuiper went 0-for-3 in an 11-0 loss to the Yankees in the opener. "I thought about not playing the second game," said Kuiper. "I didn't get a good night's sleep and I was tired. But I played and had more runs batted in than I did all month. . . . It's a great memory. I can't remember who the pitcher was, but I assume they released him after the game."

The Indians team captain, who was nicknamed "Captain Kipe," rapped both three-baggers off rookie Bob Kammeyer. Kuiper was wrong about the release, but not by much. Kammeyer was in only seven games that season and in one more the next before disappearing from the majors.

The starting pitcher for the Yankees was future Hall of Famer Jim "Catfish" Hunter, but he didn't have it that day and was gone by the time Kuiper, batting eighth, stepped into the box with Bernie Carbo, Tom Veryzer and Ted Cox on base in the first inning. Kuiper lined the ball deep into the right-center field gap for a 9-0 lead.

Kammeyer was still pitching in the fifth when Kuiper came up with Andre Thornton, Veryzer and Cox aboard. He lined another triple into the same gap, climaxing a five-run inning that put Cleveland ahead, 15-0.

Kuiper, recently chosen as one of the Indians' best 100 players, hit his home run off Clevelander Steve Stone in a 9-2 rout of the Chicago White Sox on Aug. 29, 1977.

A gathering of 6,236 at the Stadium saw him drive a fastball into the second row of seats in right, about 360 feet from home plate. It broke a string of 1,381 at-bats without a dinger for Kuiper. The Indians retrieved the historic ball for him and he brandished it before a crowd of reporters. "When I got back to the dugout I thought, 'Did I touch all the bases?'" Bob Sudyk of the Press quoted him as saying. "It was a big thrill."

Kuiper has the ball and bat from his homer in the office of his home in suburban San Francisco. "He also has the seat the ball hit," said his wife, Michelle. "When he was traded, the Indians gave him the seat and made a plaque out of it. The kids look at it all the time." The Kuipers have two children.

Kuiper was traded to San Francisco for pitcher Ed Whitson on Nov. 14, 1981. He had been with the Indians since 1974, forming a good double play combination with Frank Duffy and then Veryzer. He was an excellent fielder and hit .274 with Cleveland. On three occasions, he was the only Indian to get a hit in a game, against pitchers Nolan Ryan, Andy Hassler and Ron Guidry.

The popular Kuiper, who never took himself too seriously, has a standard line about his lack of home-run power: "I didn't want to hit more than one. Any more than that and people start expecting them."

In high school, he hit home runs "all the time," he said. He also had about 10 in the minor leagues.

He said he was the target of constant good-natured ribbing from his teammates before his first homer. "When I'd hit a triple somebody would say, 'You shouldn't stop at third,'" Kuiper recalled. "'Keep going until somebody tags you.'"

"It didn't bother me. I never heard it from guys on other teams, only my friends."

"He wasn't self-conscious about it," said ex-teammate Rick Manning, 46, an analyst on Indians telecasts on Fox Sports Net Ohio. "There weren't a lot of long-ball hitters in comparison to today. You could count the guys who hit 30 on one hand. Kipe's job was to get on base, move runners around and play good defense."

Kuiper stood about 6 feet and weighed 175 pounds at his peak. In those days, players did not do weight training. "We didn't have a weight room," said Manning. "Maybe we had three dumbbells under the trainer's table."

Kuiper never worried that lack of strength was the reason he did not hit the long ball. "I grew up on a farm and I had big, strong hands," he said. "But with the stroke I had, King Kong couldn't have hit home runs."

The left-handed-hitting Kuiper would slap the ball to left field. "He pulled fastballs that were mistakes," Manning said. His position at the bottom of the homer-hitters list does not bother Kuiper.

"We've all got to be remembered for something," he said.

Awful Baseball Fails to Discourage Him

GABE PAUL *Aug. 21, 1983*

Gabe Paul looks good, his face showing few signs of the depression and frustration he must feel in the debris of another appalling baseball season.

The 73-year-old Indians president knows that almost all Cleveland baseball fans regard him as Public Enemy No. 1.

But he faces his interrogator sitting upright, like a man in the electric chair, speaking with bravery and humor.

Talking about the barrage of criticism he has received this summer, the worst in his 55 years in baseball, Paul quipped, "I just changed my bullet proof vest and put sleeves in it."

"I'm not discouraged," he barked. "I'm mad at the way we're blowing ball games. You've got to win." A look of sadness almost imperceptibly fluttered across his face, perhaps at the thought of the Indians' 17 weak finishes in his 18 years here.

The big question was tossed at Paul. Is he going to retire from running the Indians? Nearly everyone in the Western World, including this scribbler, has suggested he should.

Paul replied, "It's crossed my mind. But I don't run from anything. I'm not going to leave under fire. That's not my nature. I'm not leaving under the present conditions."

Translated, the gallant old soldier wants to stay until the Indians achieve respectability, even if it takes until 1999. He doesn't want to go out a loser.

Paul attacks questions about his age as though they were a slur on his masculinity. "The people who say I should retire might be right," he said. "But I'll outwork most of them. I work 14-15 hours a day, seven days a week. Guys who say I should quit don't work that much."

That may be true, but productive work over a short time is preferable to unproductive work over a long time. But we didn't say that to him.

There have been accusations that Paul holds some kind of Svengali-like influence over Indians principal owner F. J. (Steve) O'Neill, 83, who permits him to keep control of the team despite its relentless losing.

Paul challenged that implication with vigorous obscenity. "Steve knows everything that's going on. He's sharp," he said.

How does O'Neill react to the unyielding disasters?

He tells me to keep my chin up," said Paul.

It has been suggested that Paul hire a younger man to run the club, perhaps Tal Smith, who revived the Houston team a few years ago before losing his job in a power play. Paul could stay on in a reduced role.

Paul smiled as though he had me there. "I tried to hire Tal Smith five minutes after he was let go by Houston," he said triumphantly. "I told him he could do anything he wanted here, run the whole show. I'd still have plenty to do. But he didn't take the job."

This indicates Paul would give up at least one rein if he found the right man.

Even though he has been thoroughly excoriated in the media, Paul says, surprisingly, that he has not received as large a volume of hate mail as he expected.

"I don't know if that's good or bad," he said. "It may be an indication of not enough interest in the team." Indifference is the harshest form of cruelty.

It would also mean fans instinctively feel sympathy for this decent man, who, save for winning, symbolizes all that is good and wholesome in baseball.

It is inevitable that time defeats all men. In our newspaper library, called the morgue, there are several old photographs of Paul, taken in the 1940s. He was a handsome devil, married to the former Mary Copps, a Florida beauty queen. He was working for the Cincinnati Reds as traveling secretary. "The best job in baseball," he often recalls in fond memory. He was on top of the planet.

The aristocratic Mary is still with him, the mother of their five children. But otherwise it has all changed. The promise of youth has surrendered to the carnage of age.

A man who has known Paul for a long time said, "It will be an injustice if Gabe doesn't die at the ballpark, going to a ballpark, or coming from a ballpark." Baseball is his life.

Charboneau Looking for One Last Chance

JOE CHARBONEAU *Jan. 2, 1984*

Only a thousand days ago he was the king of Cleveland baseball. He was rookie of the year. Indians fans loved him as they had loved no diamond hero since Rocky Colavito. A book was written about him. He bought a $150,000 Avon Lake house that had an indoor swimming pool.

As 1984 dawns, Joe Charboneau is living in Lockport, N.Y., outside Buffalo, paying a modest $250 monthly rent on another house. The glamorous one with the pool is gone, lost to foreclosure. The baseball career is gone too, but he is hoping for one last chance.

"I'm running six miles every day," said Charboneau, 28. "I'm working with weights and taking batting practice at the YMCA. I weigh 198 pounds and I feel great. The big thing is that somebody gives me the chance. There's no doubt in my mind I can hit the way I did."

Charboneau says Buffalo-based baseball scout Cy Williams has been trying to get him a trial with another club. "But teams are shying away from me because of all that happened to me when I was with the Indians," Super Joe said. "It's discouraging, but I know I can help a big league team.

"If nobody picks me up, I'll just give up and get a job. I've had some pretty good offers around here to work for the city. I can make a good living and support my family."

Charboneau and his wife, Cindy, have two children, 4 and 2.

They are living on their savings. "Cindy has a chance to get a job soon," he said. "I'm not sure where."

People who insist on complicating baseball say Charboneau failed because he was an eccentric, a guy who drank beer through his nose and indulged in other clubhouse nonsense.

Sure, Charboneau might have been a screwball, but baseball will gladly put up with screwballs as long as they perform well. Babe Ruth is the prime example of that. It is when you stop hitting that baseball people start questioning your character.

The true reason for Charboneau's demise was back trouble, resulting in two operations in which three discs were removed. If you have ever had back pain, you will understand why Charboneau stopped hitting. He says he didn't feel right until about three months ago.

It is not going to happen, but the Indians would be wise to give Charboneau a look. They hit the fewest home runs in the American League last year. Charboneau hit 23 homers and had 87 runs batted in in only 453 at-bats for the Tribe in 1980.

"The Indians would never take him back," said his former agent, Dan Donnelly of Lakewood. "He embarrassed them too much."

That figures. The woebegone Indians organization would probably prefer to finish a sedate sixth again with a corps of gentlemen.

As far as we know, Charboneau was never in any real trouble. There were no stories about him getting involved with the police. His image was that of a big, good-natured kid who needed special handling from managers, that he slept in clubhouses in the minor leagues, and once pulled out his own tooth.

Donnelly adds that Charboneau owes him $20,000. The agent made several $1,200 monthly mortgage payments on Charboneau's ostentatious house.

After his up-and-down life with the Indians, Charboneau was exiled. One reason might have been that he did not get along with former Tribe manager Dave Garcia. How could the zany Charboneau compete against the word of a baseball lifer like Garcia?

"I called every team in baseball," said Donnelly. "They didn't want any part of him."

But Charboneau is still young. Once a hitter, always a hitter. Some club just might make a smart move by giving him a last chance.

Postscript: Charboneau became a popular batting instructor in the Cleveland area.

Touched by Superstition

KEVIN RHOMBERG *May 14, 1984*

Superstitions flourish in baseball. Most of them are commonplace. A player will touch second base every time he goes to the outfield. Another will wear the same sweatshirt for a week because he is hitting well.

The Indians' Kevin Rhomberg wins the award for the most unusual superstition in diamond history.

If anybody touches him, he touches the person back.

"I don't know why I do it," said Rhomberg yesterday. "I've been doing it since I was a kid."

The idiosyncrasy has led to some hilarious situations. Once Rhomberg was in the clubhouse men's room. The Indians' Rick Sutcliffe reached under the door and touched his toe. Since the door was closed, Rhomberg could not tell who did it. So he ran out and touched everybody in the clubhouse.

Rhomberg's personal choice for the funniest episode occurred when he was playing winter ball in Venezuela. The fame of his superstitions has spread throughout baseball, you must understand.

Rhomberg was at bat and Danny Rohn of the Chicago Cubs ran up behind him and touched him on the back.

"I was going to chase him into the dugout and touch him, but I knew I couldn't," said Rhomberg, an otherwise normal 28-year-old. "I would have been mugged. Everybody in their dugout would have touched me and I would have had to touch everybody back."

Rhomberg got even by setting his alarm clock to wake him up at 3:30 a.m. that night. He was staying in the same hotel as Rohn and knocked on his door. When the sleepy Rohn opened the door, Rhomberg touched his hand and fled.

Rhomberg never forgets. He waited two months to get umpire John Hirschbeck, hiding near the umpires' room to do it. If anyone escapes, he sends him a card that reads, "This counts as a touch."

Tribe pitcher Bert Blyleven once sent Rhomberg a Christmas card full of thumbprints. On another occasion Blyleven touched Rhomberg while they were in a car, then ran outside. Rhomberg's wife, Denise, pleaded with Blyleven, "Let him touch you or he won't sleep all night."

The superstition has spread to his children. When Rhomberg is in bed in the morning the tots sing, "Touch him, touch him, drive him nuts, drive him nuts." When they tap him, Rhomberg springs out of bed and returns the favor.

"My wife gets mad sometimes," Rhomberg admitted.

Rhomberg has another original superstition. He never makes a right turn. This is because you always turn left when you are running the bases.

Rhomberg will go to any extreme to avoid turning right. If he steps off the team bus and is supposed to go in that direction, he will make a complete left turn before doing so.

His children have absorbed that one too. They have a routine when turning corners in a shopping mall. They are walking three abreast holding hands. When a right turn is forthcoming, Rhomberg yells, "Western roll," and the kids make a complicated series of spins, holding hands all the while, to negotiate the corner properly and keep the devil at bay.

The touch and right-turn superstitions are the most exotic in Rhomberg's repertoire, but he has many others. When he bats, he sets his helmet on the ground with the brim facing the pitcher. He will take the batting-weight donut off his bat and try to make it roll evenly before he steps in to hit. He believes in ghostly "little people" who position him in the field and dictate the game's actions.

The other Indians regard the utilityman with awe, feeling he is the undisputed superstition champ of baseball.

"He's the best I've ever seen," said Dan Spillner. "He'll chase people into the stands to touch them."

"He drives me crazy, but he's a good guy," said Mike Hargrove.

"He's psycho," said Neal Heaton. "If I throw my towel and it accidentally hits him, he'll come right over and touch me."

"He's not all there, but how many of us are," said Blyleven, admiringly.

The Enigma

JULIO FRANCO *Jul. 20, 1988*

It is about two hours before a baseball game at the stadium and Julio Franco is having fun.

The Indians' most controversial player is tossing the ball up and hitting ground balls to his buddy, Mel Hall, at third base. Hall, a lefthander and an outfielder, is not exactly the reincarnation of Brooks Robinson at the hot corner. Franco is insulting him noisily, challenging his prowess with a glove.

When he raps a hot grounder that flees past Hall, Franco shouts in glee and raises his hands high above his head as though he just accomplished a great feat. He struts toward the empty stands in imitation of a conqueror.

"I'd have it in my back pocket," he scolds Hall. "I catch the ball."

It is fascinating to watch. Here is a millionaire second baseman and yet, he is horsing around like a street urchin. It reminds you of Bob Lemon's famous dictum: "You've got to be a man to play big league ball. But you've got to have a lot of little boy in you, too."

Indians manager Doc Edwards is nearby, talking to a group of writers. He ignores Franco's ongoing capers. Later, he is asked if Franco's display bothered him, if it was too uninhibited just before a game.

"Not at all," Edwards says. "I want players to come to the park and be happy. You're supposed to enjoy this."

Franco amuses himself some more in the clubhouse. Walking by first baseman Willie Upshaw, who is being interviewed, he says, "How many times do I got to listen to that (expletive)?" Upshaw just smiles.

Contrary to his image, Franco gets along well with his comrades in the clubhouse, playing cards, trading jokes, sometimes sitting quietly in front of his locker.

He seems to be as popular as anyone else. He understands the length of the marathon season and the need to keep loose before the tension and frustration devour a player.

A smiling picture of Hall hangs above Franco's locker. Above Hall's locker is a smiling picture of Franco, with a note attached: "At this rate, you're going to hit three home runs all year."

You don't have to be a genius to guess who put it there. (Hall, in a long-ball drought, has hit only three homers, one inside the park.)

"Julio is like a brother to me," Hall said. "He's a free spirit, but he's a good person. He'll do anything for you.

Cy Buynak, the Tribe's clubhouse man agrees. "He would give you the shirt off his back," Buynak said. "The kids like him better than anybody. I coach a kids' basketball team, 10-11-12 years old, and when you ask them who their favorite is they all say Julio. He says hello to everybody."

Such is life around the enigmatic, talented Franco. He is the Indians' highest-paid player, a bona fide star. "I think he can lead the American League in hitting," said Edwards. "He has a ton of talent."

Said Hall: "If he ever decides to concentrate, there wouldn't be many like him."

Coach Johnny Goryl said, "Few players come along with the talent he has. If he ever learns to apply himself over 162 games, he could be as good as anybody."

There it is, those constant disclaimers: "If he ever decides to concentrate . . ." and "if he ever learns to apply himself . . ."

Perhaps they are asking too much. Franco is a fine player already. He is a .294 career hitter with hordes of stolen bases and good power. Currently he has a 16-game hitting streak, fitting nicely with the 21-gamer he had earlier this season.

Critics say his fielding range is limited. Yet, he leads American League second basemen in chances. They say he cannot turn the double play. But he is third in DPs in his first year on the job after switching from shortstop.

There is not much wrong with those numbers. That is why he will receive $2.2 million for this year and next.

There are signs Franco is finally winning over the fans with his ability and his refusal to complain or alibi. There are increasing chants of "Julio, Julio" in the Stadium when he comes to bat.

Still, the talk show lines burned up all winter from fans suggesting Franco be traded. It has been a long time since a first-rate player was criticized so often by Tribe fans.

Why do so many question him? "I hate him because he doesn't put his hands on his knees in the field before the pitch." says one fan, claiming Franco's looser pose lacked intensity. "My Little League coach told us to always do that." That is stretching criticism to the point of incredulity.

Others cannot forget Franco did not run out a couple of ground balls last year.

Catcher Andy Allanson, a good friend of Franco, comes to his defense on that. "Over the course of 600 at-bats who runs out every ground ball?" he said. "When he doesn't run it's only his frustration coming out."

Franco takes the raps calmly. "When you do good, the fans cheer," he shrugs. "When you do bad, they boo. I like Cleveland fans. I don't blame them for getting mad. I get mad too when we don't do good."

Another incident added to the Franco legend a few weeks ago. After he took himself out of a game with the flu, some unnamed teammates allegedly yelled at him in the shower, charging he could have continued to play.

It is nonsense to imply Franco is a gold-bricker. He is one of the American League's iron men, averaging 150 games a year during his first five seasons with the Indians. He has continued the pace this season, hardly ever missing a game.

Goryl is Franco's guru. "He has done more for me than anybody in baseball," Franco said. "We're so close, we fight all the time."

Goryl fully understands the fans' antagonism toward Franco. "There are times I would like to strangle him myself," old pro Goryl said. "We've had our moments. He divorced me two or three times, right Julio?"

Franco, standing by the batting cage, said, "Oh, yeah."

There is genuine affection between the white, ethnic Goryl, 54, and the black Hispanic Franco, 26. Franco sees him as a father figure. Perhaps Goryl looks at him with the wonder of a man who would have surrendered his molars to have possessed his pupil's gifts.

"It's a big compliment that he says I'm like his father," Goryl says. "But a father has to stay on his children's rear ends and make sure they go in the right direction. There are times when Julio gets discouraged. I try to keep his spirits up. He's a great kid."

Edwards has a good explanation for the fans' love-hate relationship with Franco. "He plays with a flair," the manager says. "It's in everything he does – his stance, the way he handles himself. He's more visible. When things are going wrong, you tend to pick out the most visible guy."

Ah, yes that stance. Franco curls the bat around his head as though he wants to be a matador and a dancer at the same time. Who did he copy that from?

"I don't copy from anybody," Franco says with a touch of pride and irritation. "Nobody batted like that before."

The artist does not simply want to do things well. He must look good doing them.

His batting philosophy is simple: "Hit the ball and run like hell."

Franco has developed a style with the media. It is difficult to get him to sit still and talk about himself. You get the feeling he thinks he has done enough of that and that it is all baloney.

In 50 years who will care what sort of person he was? All that will remain are the statistics in black and white.

When he is interviewed now, he gives answers in clipped, street-wise style. When he knows reporters will be coming to him for a story, he often starts answering before he is asked a question.

When he was snubbed for the All-Star team a few weeks ago, Franco noticed a writer talking to utility man Ron Washington at the next locker and shouted, "I don't care if I don't make the All-Star team. Right, neighbor? All I want is a World Series ring on my finger.

"I know a lot of superstars who don't have the World Series ring. Right, neighbor? If I don't get picked for the All-Star team, then I guess I'm not good enough. Right, neighbor?" That served as his interview on the subject.

But he is good enough to make a million dollars a year. "I save all of it," he said. He adds he bought land and houses for his two brothers who live in the Dominican Republic.

His mother spent much of the season living with Franco in Cleveland before going home. He often took her on trips with the team, a surprising departure from the norm. The average hedonistic ballplayer has as much use for dear old mom on a trip as he would for a bottle of milk and a box of crackers.

"She had a good time," said Franco of his mother, who does not speak English. "She knows baseball."

Joe Maenza, Franco's agent, said the ballplayer and his wife are going through a divorce. Franco says proceedings have not been completed. Asked if he and his wife might reunite, he said, "I don't know." Pressed further, Franco cuts short the subject, snapping, "Do you want to talk about my private life or baseball?"

Franco spends the off season in his home in Boca Raton, Fla. "It's a contemporary made of stone and stucco," says Maenza. "It's between 3,000 and 4,000 square feet. It's a beautiful home with a big screened-in pool and a Jacuzzi. Not bad for a person who grew up in a one-room house in the Dominican."

Maenza visits Franco often during the winter. "He's a superstar, but doesn't act like one," the agent says. "Most of the time, we just sit around talking and watching TV. He likes to watch NBA basketball. It's his second favorite sport."

Said Franco, "I'm a good basketball player. If I wasn't playing baseball, I'd be a basketball player. Ask Andy Allanson."

Said the catcher, "We played in spring training. He can slam dunk. He's also a great meringue dancer."

Franco agreed, but said, "Everybody in the Dominican can dance the meringue. It's the national dance."

Filtered through all this are Franco's off-field adventures. In New York in 1985 he missed a game under mysterious circumstances. In 1986 he missed another game in Cleveland. These defections have never been explained. Even Goryl says he does not know what happened.

"Everybody in life makes mistakes," Goryl said. "I don't think he was very proud of himself when it happened. I don't think it will happen again. If it does, I'll be extremely disappointed in him as a man."

As he approaches his peak, Franco is adamant that his shortstopping days are over. "I'll never go back," he says.

He continues to live with the expectations of people who want him to be better and better. Maybe it is unfair. Maybe he has already reached his loftiest level, which is higher than 95% of ballplayers ever get.

Goryl disagrees. "I think that if we are in the race in August and September, you will see a Julio Franco you have never seen," he says. "A new part of Franco will surface."

In the meantime, the current Franco is plenty good. Put nine guys like him on the field, as the saying goes, and you win a pennant.

Peaceful Manager Showed Fire as Player

MIKE HARGROVE *Jul. 12, 1991*

We all know what Mike Hargrove is like. Nice guy. Solid family man. Never makes any trouble. He'd be a good neighbor to sit with on the deck and talk about getting the weeds out of the lawn. But the new Indians manager was not always that peaceful. In fact, he could be downright ornery when the right buttons were pressed. He got into a surprising number of scuffles in his youth, according to his old friends. They paint a picture of Hargrove as being a physical, competitive man, completely different from the image he projects with his broad-beamed, managerial walk.

It wasn't that he was looking for trouble as a young man. He was just intense. His old buddies say this competitive nature will be a strength as he undertakes the role of managing in the big leagues for the first time.

49. Harrison Dillard followed his idol Jesse Owens to the Olympics and won gold, too. *Page 174* (CSU)

CSU - Courtesty of the Cleveland Press Collection, Cleveland State University Archive.

50. Tommy "Red" Williams, the Barons' cult hero, almost never took a shot. *Page 168* (CSU)

51. Jesse Owens showed up Hitler at the 1936 Olympics, won fame and gold medals, but never cashed in. *Page 170* (CSU)

52. Mike Medich, celebrated prep basketball star, put Benedictine in the spotlight. *Page 183* (Courtesy of Benedictine High School)

53. Nick Sabadosh: coach, teacher, unsung hero. *Page 194* (Courtesy Diane Fuller)

54. Sam Jethroe, former Cleveland Buckeyes star and major leaguer, still batting. *Page 180* (CSU)

86. A young, chubby-cheeked Bob Feller (right) and family: from left, Feller's mother, Lena, his sister, Marguerite, and his father, William. *Page 290* (CSU)

87. Johnny Allen had a flaming fastball and a temper to match. He hated umpires . . . but later became one himself. *Page 293* (CSU)

88. Jeff Heath, one of the lead "Crybabies" who led the revolt against unpopular manager Oscar Vitt. *Page 295* (CSU)

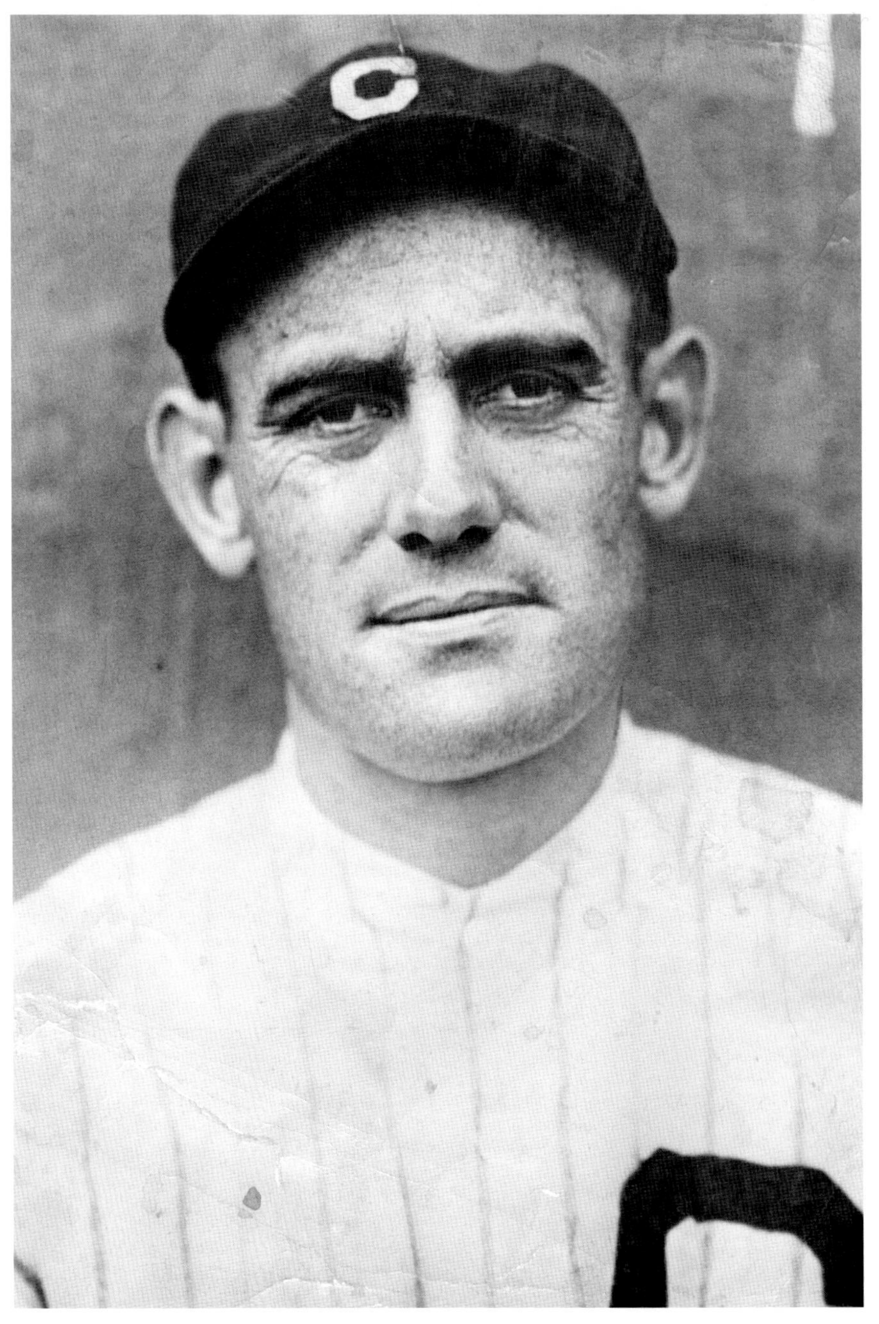

89. The tragic Ray Chapman. One of the most popular players in the American League, he died after being hit by a pitch on August 16, 1920. *Page 303* (CSU)

90. Al Milnar, a lefty with smoke. Like most players of his era, when he retired from baseball he had to get a real job. He became a security guard at Fisher Body. *Page 298* (CSU)

91. Mel Harder was in the money on Mel Harder Day. He spent 36 years in an Indians uniform as player and coach. *Page 301* (CSU)

92. Indians press box denizens at the Stadium in 1963. From left: Nate Walleck, Tribe publicist; Eddie Katz and Bob Dolgan, Plain Dealer; Tom Breuning, Associated Press; Herman Goldstein, retired Cleveland News sportswriter. (Author's collection)

Cecil Perkins, Hargrove's baseball coach at Northwestern Oklahoma State University, recalls the time a runner stepped on Hargrove's foot at first base. "Mike started fighting him before the guy turned around," Perkins said.

"Mike had the guy down," said Steve Hildebrand, a teammate. "He didn't put up with much."

Mike Moore, Hargrove's college roommate, recalled a basketball game against Langston University in which Hargrove tangled with an opponent who had been elbowing him. "If I was walking down a dark alley, I'd want Mike with me," said Moore. Hargrove was a guard who averaged about 10 points a game.

Moore and Hargrove were also on the football team, with Hargrove punting and playing defensive back. "In one scrimmage, I told him I was going to knock him on his can," said Moore, who was the center. "But when the ball was snapped, he came over the top of the pile and leveled me, knocked me cold. He could really stick it." Hargrove's college escapades were not confined to fighting. Once he and Moore rode a Shetland pony onto a dance floor at a college hangout, whereupon the owner requested they leave. Rich Donnelly, Hargrove's manager in his first full minor-league season at Gastonia, N.C., remembers his first baseman's inclination for boxing.

"Mike quickly became our team leader," said Donnelly, now a Pittsburgh Pirates coach. "On nights after games, he'd set up boxing tournaments with his teammates at their apartment complex. They'd be out there on the grass in their shorts at 1 a.m. He especially would like to box guys he didn't like. He'd get on them if he thought they were loafing."

Donnelly says Hargrove would have made a perfect Wild West sheriff. "He spoke soft, but he was like Matt Dillon," Donnelly said. "Once we were in a country-western place and a guy we didn't know was tearing some paneling off the wall. Mike told him to stop. The guy told him to go to hell. So Mike took him outside and beat him to a pulp. Then he bought him a drink."

The same inclination to forgive and forget comes up repeatedly in conversations with people who know Hargrove best. Jeff Shaw, the Indians' pitcher who played for Hargrove when he was managing at Williamsport in the Class AA Eastern League, said he would chew players out and be their best friend five minutes later. Perkins, now the athletic director at Southwestern Oklahoma State, is not surprised Hargrove has risen to the demanding job of major-league manager, where he must handle 25 personalities. "His people skills were always excellent," Perkins said. "His values are good. We're all tickled to death for him."

"You have to handle each guy differently," Hargrove said. "Some guys you have to yell at and other guys you have to pat on the back. Other guys you have to yell at and then pat on the back. You have to keep repeating the message and not always in the same way, or they quit listening."

Hargrove will talk cordially to almost anybody. Maybe that comes from his background. He and his wife, Sharon, both grew up in the small farming community of Perryton, Texas, and still live there in the off-season, surrounded by their parents, relatives and friends. When you have that kind of cocoon for a base, friendship comes easily.

"Every Christmas and Thanksgiving they have a party at their house for 200 or 300 people," said Donnelly.

The only time Hargrove ever had trouble returning to Perryton was in 1986, when his 12-year major-league career came to an end when he was released by the Oakland A's.

"He felt like a failure," said Sharon. "He didn't want to go home. But I told him he had played 12 years and there was nothing to be ashamed of."

One of Hargrove's strengths is in his marriage, which has produced five children, ages 16 to 2. Everyone says Sharon is the perfect baseball wife. "She's been instrumental in Mike's success," Perkins said. "Some women fight their husbands. She supports him." The two have been together since their first date when she was 14, when they went to the eighth-grade prom in Perryton.

"My dad told me I couldn't go if Mike honked the car horn," said Sharon. He had to come to the door. It was a double date and the car got a flat tire and went into a ditch. From that inauspicious beginning, Mike and Sharon got along famously. They went to college together and have been married 20 years.

In Hargrove's rookie year at Gastonia, the players were paid so little that their wives had to get jobs to help support them. Most of the wives were waitresses, but one day Sharon noticed a laundry truck pull up outside the ballpark. Realizing the players' uniforms had to be cleaned regularly, she went to the general manager and said, "I'll do the uniforms for half of whatever you're paying." She got the job, doing the uniforms for 50 cents each and the towels for five cents each on her washer and dryer. Hargrove would help bring the uniforms in and out of the clubhouse. "That saved us," she said. "I think I was making more money than Mike." She still maintains that economical bent. She and the family go to every Indians home game and usually she makes her own sandwiches for the entire brood.

Sharon says she loves the gypsy life of baseball. "We stay in touch with everybody we've ever met," she said. "I send out 350 Christmas cards every year. When Mike was hired as manager, we got tons of calls from around the country. It's fun to see people are as happy as you are."

Lee Anthony of LeRoy, Kan., is the scout who signed Hargrove to his first professional contract, back in 1972. "I've signed 55 players and he's the only who still sends me a Christmas card every year," said the retired Anthony. "A couple of years ago he sent me a diamond-studded wristwatch. He and Sharon are great people." Mostly because he played at an obscure college, Hargrove wasn't drafted by the Texas Rangers until the 25th round in 1972. His rise was rapid. He jumped from Class A to Texas in 1974, where he hit .323 and was named rookie of the year. He was traded to San Diego in 1979, then came to Cleveland the same year for Paul Dade, in one of the Indians' best trades ever. He hit .292 in seven years with the Tribe and was man of the year twice.

Along the way, he picked up some fussy mannerisms at bat that caused him to be nicknamed The Human Rain Delay by a Toronto sports writer. He would pull up his batting gloves, touch his shoulders and look like he was screwing his thumb into his hand before each pitch. "Earl Weaver (Baltimore manager) used to scream and holler at me," recalled Hargrove. "I ignored him. Dave Stieb (Toronto pitcher) would scream too. I didn't do it to bother anybody. But if I knew it bothered anybody, I could make it last a little longer than necessary."

Hargrove said the mannerism was an outgrowth of a thumb injury. He put a pad on his thumb and had to pull on his batting gloves to get the creases out.

Hargrove's habit became nationally famous. When he was named manager last week a CNN commentator expressed the hope he would be quicker taking his lineup card to the plate than he was getting ready to hit.

"It's good to be remembered for something," Hargrove said. After his playing days, Hargrove became a manager, starting in the low minors. The family went with him. "I think he felt guilty dragging us through it again, but there is something so refreshing in the minors," said Sharon. "Everybody is enthusiastic and nobody has anything."

From all accounts, he was popular with players and the media wherever he went. The only people he had trouble with were the umpires. He was ejected 10 times in his rookie year at Kinston and led the Pacific Coast League in fines in 1989 when he managed at Colorado Springs. Considering his fiery nature as a youth, it is understandable.

Hargrove said he is still learning how to argue without arousing the enmity of the umpires.

The Hargroves take a realistic view of managing. "Mike knows that every manager gets fired," said Sharon. "It will happen to us too. But Mike says he's going to enjoy managing today and not look over his shoulder. My goal is for him to keep managing the Indians at least until 1994, when Gateway opens. He can start fresh if we get to Gateway."

Postscript: Hargrove went on to the Indians to American League pennants in 1995 and 1997. His 721 victories are second in team managerial history to Lou Boudreau, who had 728.

Unique Feat Highlights Baerga's Strange Career

CARLOS BAERGA *Sep. 11, 2001*

There was not much time between Carlos Baerga's best and worst days in baseball—only 1,208 days.

On April 8, 1993, the Indians second baseman hit a home run while batting right-handed. Then he turned around and hit another homer left-handed.

It wasn't just in the same game.

It was the same inning.

It is the only time in Major League Baseball history that a switch-hitter has hit homers in the same inning from both sides of the plate, and that includes the caveman era of the 19th century when pitchers were throwing underhand from 50 feet.

"That was a day I'll never forget," Baerga recalled, quoting the exact date of the game. "Baseball has had a lot of great switch-hitters, and to think I'm the only one to do that is really special. The bat is in the Hall of Fame."

Baerga's career seemed to be careening toward unknown heights then. His batting statistics were being compared to those of the great Rogers Hornsby.

He was only 24 years old.

Scarcely three years later Baerga was through in Cleveland. His batwork slipping, he was traded to the New York Mets on July 29, 1996. It is still one of the most baffling stories in Indians history. "I can't put a finger on what happened," said John Hart, the Indians general manager who risked the wrath of the fans when he traded Baerga.

An airplane circled Jacobs Field the next day carrying the sign, "Trade Hart, Not Carlos." But it turned out he made the right decision.

Baerga, who had been batting third in the best lineup in baseball and had not yet reached the age when players are at their peak, never again hit with his old authority. Today he is playing second base in Korea for the Samsung Lions.

"He was a great guy, probably the most exuberant Indians player in my tenure here," Hart said.

"It was heartbreaking," said Jeff Sipos, Indians manager of equipment. "He loved the game and we all loved him."

It is better to remember Baerga as he was on the day he crashed the record book in a 15-5 victory over the New York Yankees at Cleveland Municipal Stadium.

When he came up in the seventh inning, the Indians were leading, 6-5, and had one man on. Batting right handed, Baerga hit a 3-2 pitch by Steve Howe over the left-field fence.

The Indians batted around and Baerga came up again with Steve Farr on the mound. Alvaro Espinoza had just hit a three-run homer. "Farr knocked me down with his first pitch," Baerga remembered in a phone conversation from Samsung. "He was mad because we were scoring so many runs." Batting lefty he hit a 2-0 pitch over the right-field fence. He is the only Cleveland player to hit two homers in the same inning, switch-hitting or not.

Only good things were happening to Baerga in those days. "For four years, he had Hall of Fame numbers," Hart recalled. In 1992, he became the first AL second baseman to hit .300, get 200 hits, 20 homers and 100 RBI in the same season. In 1993, he did it again.

Hornsby, the National League Hall of Famer from the Roaring Twenties, was the only other second baseman to accomplish the feat, doing it four times.

In 1995, Baerga outpolled Roberto Alomar, who was with

Toronto, in the All-Star vote, then went 3-for-3 in the All-Star Game. That same season, the Sporting News chose him as baseball's best second baseman.

The Puerto Rican was the acknowledged leader of the team, always jolly, always cheering for teammates. He was the unofficial team captain, the man the others gathered around. By age 23, the Cleveland baseball writers had twice voted him the team's man of the year, a rare tribute.

The handsome Baerga was always proud of his appearance. Cy Buynak, longtime Indians clubhouse man who is now in charge of the visitors' quarters, recalled how Baerga would comb his hair before the large mirror in the old Stadium clubhouse prior to games. "He'd work on it for 15 or 20 minutes to make sure it was perfect," Buynak said. "Then he'd put his helmet over it."

"At the end of the summer, the mirror breathed a sigh of relief," joked Sipos.

Baerga led the move to wear blue tops on team uniforms instead of the traditional white, feeling it made his 5-9 body, which once ballooned to 228 pounds, look taller.

Nobody minded his vanity because Baerga was so friendly and such a splendid player.

So what happened? Why is he playing in Samsung today when he is still young enough to be hitting fences in Jacobs Field? At 32, he is a year younger than Alomar, for crying out loud. "He was not a drinker or drug abuser, but he kept late hours," said Hart, searching for the answer. "But a lot of guys are like that and it doesn't affect them."

In midseason of 1996, he was hitting .267 with 10 homers and 55 RBI. He was still on his way to a 90 RBI season, but he was not what he had been.

"I never saw a guy break as many bats as he did when he started to go down," Sipos recalled. "He was getting jammed because he wasn't getting around on the ball."

Hart sent Baerga and Espinoza to the New York Mets for Jeff Kent (NL Most Valuable Player last year with San Francisco) and Jose Vizcaino.

Baerga was shaken when the stunning deal occurred. "I never thought this day would come," he said in a story that was bannered across the top of The Plain Dealer. "I thought I would spend the rest of my career with Cleveland." He seemed near tears. He and Buynak were pictured in a sad embrace.

Then the spirit returned. "Next year, the All-Star Game is in

Cleveland," he said. "I'll be here in the National League lineup."

It never happened. But Baerga has not given up. He sounds as buoyant as ever. He loves playing in Korea, where he is hitting .300 with three homers since joining the team in late July. His salary is over $200,000. Samsung signed him out of an independent league where he was hitting .335 for the Long Island (N.Y.) Ducks. "I had a great year in the independent league," he said.

Baerga denies his big-league career was cut short by carousing. "Injuries [ankle, groin, rib] were my problem," he said. Now he says he is finally healthy again.

Baerga has his wife and two children with him in Samsung, which has a 15,000-seat stadium. "This is good baseball," he said. "A lot of guys in the league could play in the majors. I'm set financially, but I'm playing because I love baseball. I want to get back into the major leagues. Tell the people in Cleveland I still love them."

Belle Produced Summers of Fire, Fury

ALBERT BELLE *Sep. 25, 2001*

Cleveland baseball fans will never forget the season of 1995, when Jacobs Field was 2 years old, Albert Belle was at his marvelous hitting ceiling and the Indians gave the city its first American League pennant in 41 years.

"We were a team with a swagger," recalled General Manager John Hart. "Albert's presence in the cleanup spot translated the feeling. He was an enormous talent, arguably the best Cleveland player in modern times."

Belle could do little wrong that year. He led the league in home runs, slugging, runs, total bases, doubles, and shared the RBI crown with Boston's Mo Vaughn. He had 50 homers and 52 doubles, becoming only the eighth player to achieve 100 long hits in a season, and the first since Stan Musial in 1948. The Sporting News named him Player of the Year.

Mike Hargrove was the Indians' manager that season. "I remember all the ringing bells when Albert went to bat," said Hargrove's wife, Sharon. "Every time he came up everybody felt he had a chance to hit the ball out. We had so much fun that year."

Belle, batting out of a menacing crouch, wiggling the bat low before each pitch, produced a treasure chest of memories. He hit a grand slam with two outs in the ninth inning off Lee Smith to overcome a two-run deficit. He hit extra-inning, game-ending homers on consecutive nights. He belted an amazing 31 homers after Aug. 1 and had five in two days.

That is only Chapter One in the story. Chapter Two revolves around his behavior, among the most bizarre in baseball history.

"I loved him from 7 to 10 p.m.," said Hart, referring to the approximate time of games. "But he could suck all the joy out of a franchise."

"He was an equal opportunity discriminator," said a former associate. "It didn't matter if you were black, white, man or woman, he was miserable to everybody. But his bark was mostly mouth. If you stood up to him, he'd back down."

Early in his career with the Indians, Belle jogged after a fly ball and then made a lazy throw that cost a game. Hargrove, who knew how to handle his fists, was livid. He called Belle into his office at the Stadium and told coach Jeff Newman, "I'll leave the door open a crack. If it gets quiet in there, come in and get me. I can hold him for a while, but I don't know for how long."

When Belle came in, Hargrove attacked him verbally.

"I said things to him I've never said to any other man," Hargrove recalled. "He reacted like he knew he was wrong. I think that was the turning point in our relationship." From then on, Belle respected Hargrove and ran hard enough to keep him off his back.

Belle's weird actions were rooted in a desire to do well. He became frustrated and angry when he failed. "He wanted to hit 2.000, not 1.000," said Jeff Sipos, a longtime Indians clubhouse employee.

He would knock a table full of snacks and food on the floor with his bat, usually after a bad game or even a bad batting practice. Belle wanted the temperature cold in the clubhouse.

"It was so cold you could hang meat in there," Sipos said. "That's why they called him, 'Mr. Freeze.'" In the old Stadium, the thermostat was controlled by hand. Belle would turn the heat down; others would turn it up. At Jacobs Field, Belle smashed the automatic thermostat with a bat.

By all accounts, Belle was fairly popular with teammates. He would exchange angry, profane words sometimes, but never to the point of fisticuffs. Primarily, he was a loner.

Another clubhouse aide played golf with Belle. "He shot about

80 and hit a long ball," the aide said. "He liked video games and thought he could sing. He was nice away from baseball. The only time I ever saw him get upset was in baseball."

Turner Ward played alongside Belle for years, both in the minors and with the Indians. Ward suggested he trot to first base after a base on balls instead of walking. "Why do you think they call it a walk?" Belle said, continuing to stroll.

When Belle was in the minors at Canton, he played chess with teammates and gave interviews. But when he came to the major leagues, he suddenly changed.

Belle was a tyrant with the media, either ignoring or insulting reporters in brutal terms. His vicious behavior cost him the 1995 Most Valuable Player award, which the writers voted to Vaughn by eight points. "I don't even think Vaughn should be the MVP of the Red Sox," said an angry Belle. "I think it should be [pitcher] Tim Wakefield."

At the start of each spring training, Belle would strike a lukewarm truce with the writers, saying he would be more available. That always changed in a few days.

The definitive episode occurred with NBC sportscaster Hannah Storm. Seeing her conducting a dugout interview during the 1995 World Series, he yelled at her in the most churlish terms. He was fined $50,000.

The incident sickened Hart.

"We had a great team," he said. "We had the eyes of the world on us. We should have been a feel-good story, but we weren't because of Albert."

Belle wasn't even impressed by the man who signed his paychecks, owner Dick Jacobs. Other players, who liked the owner, shook Jacobs' hand during spring-training visits to batting practice. But Belle grumbled and made a coarse remark.

"Dick just laughed it off," Hart said.

Hart grew tired of Belle's behavior. "Fans would call complaining that he cursed their son," he recalled. In 1991, he had thrown a ball at a fan sitting in the third row at the Stadium, hitting him. In 1996, he hit Cleveland photographer Tony Tomsic with a ball. Both episodes cost him money.

"It went on and on," Hart said. "Trouble made him tick."

He seemed to hit at his best when he was in some kind of controversy.

After another great season in 1996, Belle became a free agent and signed with the Chicago White Sox, getting a five-year contract for $55 million. The Indians had offered him about $32 million for four years.

"He laughed at us," recalled Hart. "But he made a big mistake by leaving. He was loved here by the fans. He was their bad guy."

He never again was on a team that made the playoffs.

When Belle faced the Indians for the first time in 1997, he was booed unmercifully. The fans scornfully threw dollar bills at him.

"His parents were at the game," recalled Sharon Hargrove. "I felt so bad for them. I went over and gave his mother a hug. They were very nice people. It was sad, after all the great years in Cleveland."

True to his nature, Belle rose above the uproar and hit a three-run homer and two doubles. He ended the game with an obscene gesture that cost him $5,000.

He was with the White Sox for two years, then went to Baltimore, where he was reunited with Hargrove in 2000. A degenerative hip forced his retirement last spring. He is only 35 and living in Arizona. He could not be reached for this story.

"I feel real sad for him," said Sharon Hargrove. "His life was baseball."

"Retirement must be killing him," Sipos said.

Hart feels he did not play long enough or hit enough homers (381) to make the Hall of Fame.

At first, Hargrove agreed, then said, "He's probably on the bubble for the Hall."

"He was a fine player, but he never enjoyed his great fortune," Hart said. "It still bothers me to think a man so gifted could be so miserable."

Thome Aims at History with Every Mighty Swing

JIM THOME *Sep. 18, 2001*

When Jim Thome was 8 years old, he strode into the kitchen of his home in suburban Peoria, Ill., and announced to his mother, "I'm never going to work. I'm going to play big-league baseball." The boy was crazy about the sport. His father, Chuck, 66, recalled that he would walk all over the neighborhood rounding up friends for a game. At other times, he would stand in the driveway of his home for hours, tossing up rocks and batting them into a field across the street.

"I honestly think my two older sons, Chuck Jr. and Randy, who were both all-state, had a better chance to make it in baseball than Jim did," said the father. "But they didn't want it as bad as he did. Jim's living his dream. I'm awful proud of the things I've seen him do."

Thome, the Indians' first baseman, is having his greatest season, with 47 homers and 118 runs batted in. He became the team's career leader in home runs and bases on balls this season. He needs 281 runs batted in to break Earl Averill's club record. As manager Charlie Manuel said, "By the time he retires, he could have most of the club records."

At age 31, he has plenty of time to break Averill's club marks of 1,154 runs and 724 extra-base hits.

"When I came up I never thought I'd be the team's all-time home run leader," Thome said. "Right now I'm hoping I can play eight or nine more years, or even longer. I'd like to play my whole career in Cleveland." His contract expires at the close of 2002.

When the lefty hitter started with the Indians in 1991, he rapped almost everything to left field. He weighed about 205 pounds. Now he has grown into a 6-4, 240-pound powerhouse who can pull. He struck the longest homer in Jacobs Field history, a clout of 511 feet in 1999.

One thing he has not been able to do is cut down his strikeouts. He led the league with 171 two years ago and is on top again this year with 163.

"I'm not a perfect player or claim to be," Thome said. "They're few and far between. My flaw is I swing and miss. If I struck out as much as I do and never walked I'd be concerned. Walks help your team win. One hundred walks are like 100 hits." He leads the team in on-base percentage at .418 this season and is .409 for his career.

Thome, who is married to a beautiful former TV anchor, Andrea (Pacione), says his father was his biggest baseball influence as a youth.

"Dad made me tough," he said. "He told me not to show a lot of emotion and said, 'When you're struggling, don't let people see you're struggling.' Charlie Manuel was very similar. He taught me to show up to work early and want to be in the lineup every day." Thome has been on the disabled list only once in his big-league career, with a broken hand in 1998.

Jim has a twin sister, Jennifer, who is three minutes older. "Jim's the baby," recalled his father, a retired foreman at Caterpillar Co. "He relied on her. She got him through kindergarten." When Jim went off to play minor-league baseball, Jennifer, who was working in a bank, called home and said, "Did anything happen to Jim today? My ankle started hurting." A couple of hours later Thome called and said he hurt his ankle.

As a boy, Thome worshipped the Chicago Cubs and slugger Dave Kingman. When he was about 9, he and his father drove 150 miles to Wrigley Field to see the Cubs play. They had good seats near the dugout and Jim asked Kingman to autograph a ball during batting practice. His hero ignored him.

"Jim had a tear in his eye," recalled Chuck. "But he said, 'I'm still going to get it.' Next thing I know he's gone. He had jumped into the Cubs' dugout. He went in there with one ball and came out with two. A coach got Kingman's autograph for him."

Chuck feels the incident had an impact on Thome, who is courteous to everybody. He has never been ejected for arguing with an umpire. "The call's not going to change," he said. "I get mad, absolutely, but the umpire is trying just as much as I am. I make mistakes too."

Jim's oldest brother, Chuck Jr., who stands 6-5, was a huge star in high school sports. "Jim wanted to live up to him," said the father. "Chuck once got 30 rebounds in a game. Jim couldn't believe anybody could get 30 rebounds. But Jim tried and got 23 once." The brother now runs Thome's 90-acre Illinois ranch and log cabin lodge, where family and friends such as Travis Fryman, Bob Wickman and David Wells come to hunt.

Thome was an excellent high school off-guard in basketball. In the conference title game, he was in a close race with another boy for the scoring championship. "I scored 36 points and he beat me with 37," Thome recalled. "But we won in triple overtime." In baseball, he was a 6-2, 175-pound shortstop. The Cincinnati Reds were interested but never drafted him. So Thome enrolled at Illinois Central College, where he played baseball and basketball. The Indians drafted him in the 13th round in 1989, one of the smartest selections they ever made.

Thome's feelings were not hurt because he was chosen so late. "I never thought I'd be drafted," he recalled. "I was happy. I wanted to play baseball."

When Thome left for the minors, he slyly said to his father, "Who's going to cut the grass now?"

"He never cut the grass once," said his father. "But he was a good kid. The only time I had to discipline him was when he broke a neighbor's mailbox playing baseball."

Thome's crafty sense of humor again showed up a few weeks ago, when the Indians got their first look at the new Millennium Center, soaring behind Boston's Fenway Park. "That must be Manny Ramirez's new penthouse," Thome quipped. (Ramirez had deserted the Indians for more money from the Red Sox.)

Thome's beloved Wrigley Field is never far from his mind. Behind the wall in Wrigley there was a sign sponsored by a car dealer named Turco. Only the longest hitters could reach that sign. When Jim pounds a long one now he invariably says to his dad, "Was that a Turco homer?"

When the Indians play in Chicago, Thome always takes a nostalgic ride around the park.

Ken Harrelson, the Chicago White Sox announcer, recently said, "This guy could end up in the Hall of Fame someday." "The hair on the back of my neck stood up when I heard that," Chuck Thome said.

More Variety

Boxing, Horse Racing, Miscellaneous

Colorful Promoter Ruled Cleveland Boxing

LARRY ATKINS *Mar. 28, 1979*

Larry Atkins, the colorful boxing promoter from Cleveland's gilded ring era, sat in his efficiency apartment on the far East Side.

He was eating breakfast, some cakes that had been delivered by a nice young fellow who also stayed to clean up the place a little. A quiz show blared from the TV set. "If it wasn't for that thing and my reading I'd be dead," said Atkins. "I follow the sports news and I like detective magazines.

"You caught me on a good day," the 77-year-old continued. "Sometimes I don't even get out of bed. But I'm very lucky. I beat spinal meningitis when I was 24. I had throat cancer eight years ago and I beat that. And I've had three strokes and I've just about beaten them."

The setting was a far cry from the rollicking days of the 1940s, when Atkins was among the most prominent men in Cleveland sports, the promoter of boxing shows that equaled those staged anywhere in the country.

Atkins lived high off the shelf in those days. Everything was the best, from the liquor to the laughs. He was a member of the Jolly Set, that celebrated band of midnight adventurers that included sportswriters, baseball's Bill Veeck and racketeer Shondor Birns.

But those times are long gone. "Never look back," Atkins said. "That's my motto."

On this day he was preparing to take a taxi to Diamond's restaurant in Severance Center, where he gets together with some old cronies every Tuesday. "We kill the afternoon," he said.

The phone rang. It was his daughter, Marcy, calling from her home in Fort Lauderdale, Fla. She is married to a lawyer and they have two children. Atkins had sent her to Finch College, from which she was graduated cum laude.

"I'm better, sweetheart," Atkins barked into the phone. "I just walked downtown and back. No, you know I'm kidding. My left arm and left leg are weak, but I don't have to use the walker no more, I use a cane when I go outside.

"I'm looking at a picture of my grandchildren on top of the TV. That's all I got now. How's your husband? Tell him I'm still better looking than he is. Gotta go now honey. Being interviewed."

Atkins, whose real name is Nussbaum, made a lot of money in the boxing business. "Yeah, but I didn't keep it," he said. "Thank God for Roosevelt and Social Security."

He is still a wisecracker. Noting that he grew up on E. 31st and Scovill, he said, "They got a college there now in my honor." He was jokingly referring to Cuyahoga Community College, of course.

Atkins was pressed into some reminiscing. The most memorable fight he put on, he said, was between Sugar Ray Robinson and Artie Levine at the old Arena on Nov. 6, 1946. A packed house saw Levine, a Brooklyn, N.Y., slugger, floor the great Robinson in the fourth round, then get knocked out with ten seconds left in the tenth.

"Robinson would never fight Levine again," said Atkins. "Artie's an insurance man now. He was here last summer and looked me up. He's got all of his buttons."

Atkins' biggest thrill came in 1927, when Jack Dempsey knocked down Gene Tunney in the famous Long Count fight.

"I was Jack's press agent for that fight," said Atkins. "He was my idol and always will be. He could fight. I'd like to have the money peopled owed him. He'd give money away to anybody. He'd give a guy something and then ask me, 'Who is that guy anyway?' He's a very sick man now."

But Atkins' choice as the greatest fighter, pound for pound, will surprise many people. He gives that accolade to Lloyd Marshall, a light heavyweight who starred on several of Atkins' cards here in the 1940s.

For what it's worth, Honest Yockim, the legendary gambler and sage of Short Vincent, also told me once that he considered Marshall to be the top fighter he'd ever seen.

"Marshall was actually a middleweight," said Atkins. "He couldn't get fights because he was too good. So he had to lose fights deliberately. He told me he did it because he had to make a living."

"He was already in his late 30s when I brought him to Cleveland. I made him an honest fighter. I sat down with him on a bench in the Terminal Tower when he came in and told him that if he fought here he'd have to fight honest.

"He was a beautiful fighter. He'd hold his hands down at his side and he could counter punch better than anybody who ever lived.

"I started him out against Ezzard Charles, a heavyweight, and Lloyd knocked him out. Then he gave Jake Lamotta the worst beating you ever saw. He knocked down Jimmy Bivins and he beat Anton Christoforidis when Christo was really good."

For the moment, the realities of the present faded into the memories of the past. Soon though, it was time to go. "Goodbye, kid," said Atkins.

He Wasn't Afraid of Joe Louis

EDDIE SIMMS *Sep. 6, 1978*

To a lot of Americans who lived through the 1930s, there were two standout personalities – President Roosevelt and Joe Louis, the heavyweight boxing champion. So it is understandable that a new book is out on the fighter's life.

The book tells about the only fight Louis had in Cleveland, in which he knocked out Eddie Simms in 26 seconds of the first round at Public Hall on Dec. 14, 1936.

This is the one of the most storied fights in Cleveland history. It is particularly interesting to me because Simms came from my old neighborhood around Norwood and St. Clair Avenue. I was brought up on tales about the bout.

Numerous old-timers told me that Simms, a neighborhood hero and character, strolled around the community's pubs in the days before the match, playing his accordion and telling people how he would handle Louis.

"I paid five dollars for a ringside seat," a veteran raconteur told me once. "When the bell rang, I strike a match on the floor to light my cigar and when I look up Eddie is on the floor."

My late father, who was a good friend of the jolly Simms, asked what happened on the day after the knockout. "When Louis took off his robe in the ring he looked like he was made of steel," my dad always quoted Simms as saying. "So I just laid down for the $4,000." I'm sure he felt he quoted Simms accurately.

But Simms denied it when I phoned him at his home in Las Vegas the other day.

"Your dad was a great guy, but he got that mixed up," said Simms. "I never said that about Louis. The guy who was built like steel was my brother Frankie. When Frankie hit you on the shoulder he'd break your toenails, he could hit so hard. He looked like he'd live to be a thousand, but he dropped dead when he was 60. He wound up a beautician, you know.

"No, I wasn't afraid of Louis," the 70-year-old Simms continued. He just hit me with a left hook and I couldn't see. I was 28 and he was 22 when we fought. Maybe it would have been different if I was 22 and he was 28."

After the fight, Simms dropped in at the office of Al Sutphin, the builder of the Arena. He was expecting a big payday, for a full house of 10,000 had attended and he was getting 37% of the gate. Instead, he says, Sutphin gave him $71.

Simms demanded an explanation and Sutphin said, "We have 5,000 stockholders in the Arena and each one came and brought a friend. So there were 10,000 deadheads in the house. We only had 400 paid admissions.

Simms can afford to laugh at that now. Always a shrewd man with a buck, he saved his money from his ring earnings and parlayed his bluff personality into a movie career in which he played numerous bit parts. After that he worked as a steamfitter for about 20 years. Seven years ago he sold his home in Long Beach, Calif., for $88,000 and retired to Vegas, where he and his second wife live in an apartment.

He is still a tourist attraction to older Clevelanders who visit Vegas and know him from his boxing days here. They invariably phone him when they get to Vegas and I hear he is always hospitable.

"I get my accordion out and show people around town," said Simms, a great accordion player. "I take 'em to all the lounges and we have fun. The other day I was kicking it up in a lounge and the bandleader invited me up to play with the regular band. I did so good that he wanted me to join his band for $385 a week. But I don't want to work steady. I don't need it."

Simms' old adversary, Louis, also lives in Vegas, where he is the greeter in Caesars Palace. "I talk to him a lotta times," said Simms. "He's a nice guy, but he's in pretty bad shape. He's in a wheelchair.

"Am I better off now than Joe? Absolutely, I've got my health."

Ex-fighter Wins Struggle to Earn His College Degree

SUGAR COSTNER *Aug. 27, 1979*

It was May 9, 1949, in Philadelphia. George (Sugar) Costner, a 26-year-old nationally ranked welterweight boxer, was drubbing tough Chico Varona. In the sixth round, however, Verona landed a left hook to Costner's right eye.

"All of a sudden I saw the brightest light in the world," Costner recalled the other day. "It felt like a ball of fire. I didn't know it then, but I had suffered a detached retina. It didn't bother me that much. I thought it was a broken blood vessel."

Costner went on to knock out Varona, but he never forgot that punch. It was the beginning of a 30-year odyssey that will have its finest chapter Thursday night when Costner receives his B.A. at Cleveland State University.

Costner not only deserves a diploma, he deserves a medal for courage and fortitude.

Costner, 56 now, is blind. "I'm happy to finally be finished," he said, talking about the hardships endured on the way to the treasured sheepskin. "It's been a very difficult four years."

Transportation, for example, was a constant problem. Every morning, at about 6:30, he would stand in front of his apartment on Cleveland's northeast side, waiting for the first of four busses he needed to go back and forth to CSU each day.

"We've had some bad winters lately," Costner said, followed by a laugh. "I almost froze a couple of times. Sometimes I got so cold I would get on the wrong bus deliberately so I wouldn't freeze." Despite all that, he missed only three classes in four years.

Costner could not take notes during class lectures, so he used a tape recorder. When a tape would run out, the professors would stop talking and give him time to slip in a fresh cassette.

Since he could not read, Costner got tapes of entire books from the New York public library system and from the Sight Center in Cleveland. Tests were given to him verbally. He did well; he will graduate with better than a B average.

Costner paid his college tuition almost unaided, relying on a small nest egg and the meager disability pension he receives from Social Security.

"George is one of the most highly-motivated students I have every seen," said Michael Zuccaro, CSU coordinator of services for the physically handicapped. "He ran into considerable difficulty paying his tuition. The average guy would rather use the money from Social Security to eat, not for an education.

"He applied for more money from the state but he was turned down. He was told that, at his age, he probably wouldn't finish college and if he did he probably wouldn't be able to get a job anyway."

Through all this Costner, who is divorced, pursued the usual household duties – cooking, cleaning and shopping for himself.

Bernart Offerman, a CSU professor, taught Costner in a labor course. "He's a tremendous man," said Offerman. "As a student, he had the courage of a fighter. It was beautiful to see him progress, the way he'd participate in class. He is so youthful in spirit, yet a man of infinite patience. It was an honor to have him in my class."

"The professors and students were all beautiful," said Costner, a six-footer who speaks in the tones and cadences of a streetwise survivor. "They all helped me. It was good to be associated with young people. I helped a lot of them, too. They'd get discouraged and I'd talk them out of quitting."

Costner began his college career at age 52, a time when many men don't care about much more than the TV set and a can of beer. He started at Cuyahoga Community College's metro campus. Why did he go to school?

"I couldn't make a good living," replied Costner. "I was sick and tried of living on Social Security and working part-time jobs (most often as a masseur). I'm still a healthy, active man and I felt I had a long time to live. I figured there was only one thing to do – go to school."

Costner's next step is to get a job. He is moving back to Cincinnati, his hometown, to be near his 90-year-old mother and old friends. With his degree in management and labor relations, he is hoping to get a government job. He would especially enjoy a post with the National Labor Relations Board.

"I think he can land a job," said Zuccaro. "He presents himself well and can talk to just about anyone. People like him almost immediately. The only thing against him is his age."

Costner was familiar to sports fans in the 1940s, when he was one of the top welterweights in the nation. He had 91 fights, winning 48 by knockouts and 29 others by decision. A lethal left hooker, he lost only eight bouts. Two of them were one-round knockouts to the great Sugar Ray Robinson.

Costner kept fighting after the ill-fated Varona bout, whipping a succession of opponents. But by the time he was matched for the second time against Robinson on March 22, 1950, the vision in his right eye was pretty much gone.

"The doctors couldn't tell anything was wrong and I wanted to fight Robinson," Costner recalled.

The pay was $12,000, good money in those days.

About five days before the fight, Costner found he couldn't see punches coming from the right side. That was a big handicap against any fighter. Against a boxer of Robinson's caliber, it was suicidal.

Costner decided to try to knock out Robinson with an early punch. If it failed, he would lie down and live to fight another day. When his initial flurry failed, Costner took the count after Robinson's first attack.

"I felt guilty about it then and I feel guilty today," said Costner. "It was the only fight I ever gave up in."

Amazingly, Costner, fighting with only one eye, won his last three bouts, all against prominent boxers. He beat Kid Gavilan on May 8, 1950; Charley Cotton on June 12, 1950, and administered a fearful beating to lightweight champ Ike Williams in a non-title match on July 12, 1950. It was his last fight. The doctors took away his boxing license.

Between 1951 and 1958, Costner underwent six eye operations. Cataracts developed. "They took out a cataract that was the size of a shirt button," he said. "The next day I could see real good. But a couple of days later I couldn't see anything. I haven't seen anything since. For a while the shadows would come and go. Now there's nothing."

What did it feel like to go blind at such a young age? "I was lost," said Costner. "I didn't know what to do. My friends in Cincinnati were very kind to me. I'd be walking down the street by myself and they'd yell. 'C'mon, Sugar, lets go see the Reds play.'

"I said to myself, 'I can't just lay down and die like this.' I went to politicians for jobs but I couldn't get anything. Then I went to a rehabilitation center for aptitude tests and they put me in a room with some other people.

"I didn't know where I was or who I was with. Then I sensed there was something wrong with the other people there. It turned out they were mentally retarded. I started doing things for them.

"I was asked if I wanted to work with the retarded on a trial basis. My only pay would be carfare and lunch. I said yes. I was desperate. When I passed the tryout, I not only got lunch and carfare, but $50 a week."

Costner said he worked with the retarded at a Goodwill Industries Sheltered Workshop for three years. "I loved it," he said. "It was very rewarding."

He came to Cleveland in 1966 to attend Charlton College of Physical Medicine, earning a license as a physical therapist. He became a masseur at Jewish Community Center and other places.

College changed his life. Thursday will be a great day. His friends and three grown children will be in the CSU commencement audience as the old fighter walks across the stage for his treasured diploma. Even his mother might be there. They will applaud. Later there will be embraces and handshakes and laughter.

"This has to be the milestone of my life," said Costner. "I feel like I won the championship. I don't see how I could feel any better if I won the welterweight title."

Legendary Boxer Battles Back from Heart Attack

JOEY MAXIM *Mar. 16, 2001*

Boxing Hall of Famer Joey Maxim, former light-heavyweight champion of the world, is putting up a good fight against Old Man Time in the Veterans Hospital at E. 105th St.

"He has his ups and downs," said Charlene Bagnall, Maxim's daughter, who is constantly at his side in the hospital. "Today [Wednesday] he was doing real good. I got him to do some arm and leg exercises and he told me I was a pest. We had a good time. But he's got a long way to go."

Maxim, 78, one of only two Clevelanders to win world ring titles, was admitted four weeks ago with a mild heart attack. He has also had some mild strokes.

He is not walking and has trouble speaking. Jimmy Bivins, the fine Cleveland heavyweight who split two professional fights with Maxim, visited him the other day.

Maxim has his large Italian family around him, including his mother, Henrietta Berardinelli, 96. Maxim has lived in the spry old lady's house in Euclid for most of the last five years. Three brothers and a sister are also in the Cleveland area to give constant support. Bagnall and her husband, Scott, are hoping to take Maxim to live with them in Fort Lauderdale, Fla., when he is able. "He likes the warm weather," Bagnall said.

Maxim, whose real name is Giuseppe Antonio Berardinelli, won the championship with a 10th-round knockout of Freddie Mills in London in 1950. The only other Clevelander to win a world title was featherweight Johnny Kilbane, who ruled from 1912–23.

Maxim fought nine men who were champions at one time or another—Mills, Jersey Joe Walcott, Ezzard Charles, Gus Lesnevich, Sugar Ray Robinson, Archie Moore, Floyd Patterson, Bobo Olson and Willie Pastrano. He fought for the heavyweight crown in 1951, losing to Charles. His career record was 82-29-4 with 21 knockouts.

Emmanuel (Manny) Berardinelli, 80, saw many of his brother's fights, going back to when he won the national Golden Gloves championship in Chicago in 1939.

"My mother was always against him fighting," said Manny. "So was my father. He never saw him fight."

Manny says that Maxim's finest fight was against tough Irish Bob Murphy in Chicago on Aug. 22, 1951. "The papers were saying he wouldn't last four rounds," Manny recalled. "He was a big underdog. But Joe beat the living heck out of him."

Maxim, named after the old machine gun, was a master boxer. "He had a tremendous jab," said Manny. "He was a will-o'-the-wisp. You thought you hit him and you didn't." He was knocked out only once in his 18-year pro career, by heavyweight Curtis "Hatchet Man" Sheppard. But Maxim beat Sheppard two out of three.

Maxim's most famous fight was against the brilliant Robinson, often called the greatest fighter, pound-for-pound, of all time. The match was on June 25, 1952, with Maxim defending his light-heavy crown against middleweight champ Robinson before 47,933 in Yankee Stadium. The ringside temperature was more than 100 degrees. Referee Ruby Goldstein fainted after 10 rounds and had to be replaced.

Robinson was winning on points when the heat got to him. He could not come out for the 14th round and Maxim was declared the winner.

Of the charge that he won on a fluke, Maxim would always say, "Did you think I had an air conditioner? It was hot for me, too." He had his biggest payday in that fight, taking home $80,000.

Maxim lost his title to Moore in St. Louis on a 15-round decision on Dec. 17, 1952. On June 7, 1954, he handed future heavyweight champ Floyd Patterson his first defeat, taking an eight-round decision. Maxim retired in 1958.

He worked as a greeter in various Las Vegas hotels for 20 years. "Uncle Joe was in tremendous shape until he was about 73," said Gene Berardinelli, Maxim's nephew. "Then he had a mild stroke and lost some of his memory. But he always had that great personality. He was always well-liked. A very confident man."

Trouble Loomed for Extravagent Boxer

MICHAEL DOKES *Oct. 11, 1986*

You could almost have bet that Michael Dokes, the fighter, would some day get into trouble with the law.

It's not that Dokes is a bad fellow. In fact, he is extremely personable. But he was always so extravagant, so unrealistic.

Boxing people recall him when he was a fledgling pugilist at Estabrook Recreation Center on the West Side, wearing elegant white suits on the street. How can anybody wear a white suit in Cleveland? It gets dirty by the time you tie your shoelaces.

During his heyday as a professional, Dokes would enter the ring behaving more like a fop than a gladiator. He would blow kisses to the women at ringside. He would throw them flowers, sometimes roses, sometimes lilies of the valley.

He obviously was a man looking for something extraordinary out of life, maybe more than is there. He was living dangerously close to fantasy. Anytime you start flirting with dreamland, you are looking for trouble.

Dokes, a native of Akron, found trouble the other day. The former heavyweight champion was arrested in Las Vegas, Nev., where police allegedly found 11 ounces of cocaine in his home.

That is enough snow to start a blizzard.

Clevelander Rich Giachetti, who trained Dokes in his early days as a professional, is not surprised. "He's a night man, loves to party," said Giachetti. "It was the biggest problem in his career."

For a while, that career was a study in perfection. Dokes was undefeated when he knocked out Mike Weaver in 1982 to win the World Boxing Association's version of the heavyweight title.

But he lost the crown the next year when Gerrie Coetzee knocked him out in the 10th round at the Coliseum. "He never recovered from losing the title," Giachetti said.

Dokes kind of went into hibernation after that loss. He and powerful boxing promoter Don King, who guided his career, split up. He has had only a few inconsequential bouts since.

His most recent one was in March, when he was given a technical decision after journeyman Tex Cobb was disqualified in the fourth round for butting him and opening a cut.

"Cobb was beating him," Giachetti said. "Dokes had all that stuff coming out of his nose."

There have been persistent rumors Dokes was living high, in that misty world where worry and fear never exist.

"He had three title fights, so he must have made three or four million in the ring," said Giachetti, who also trained champion Larry Holmes.

"After taxes, he'd still have a million, a million and a half. He has money."

"I heard he was advised well in investments," said Ray Jefferson, a veteran Cleveland trainer. "He had oil ventures, a heck of a portfolio."

Chances are that Dokes' riches, combined with his large amount of idle time and penchant for drama, put him in the gilded lane toward disaster.

Jefferson speaks warmly of Dokes. "He was a beautiful person," he said. "Nobody who knows Michael can ever say anything bad about him. He was always Michael. Never got a big head."

Once, when Dokes was the champion, he was at Public Hall to watch a fight. He was being interviewed on TV when he saw Jefferson standing and watching, about 15 feet away. Jefferson's infant son was sitting on his shoulders.

"As soon as he saw me, he broke off the interview and came over and picked my boy off my shoulders," said Jefferson. "He really liked my boy."

"But there were some people around him I didn't care for. They were parasites. Some of them had class. But you can have class and still be a parasite."

"I used to throw them out of the gym," recalled Giachetti of the unemployed opportunists who often attach themselves to boxers and other celebrities. "I don't know why some fighters need an entourage. They like that fanfare. They're starving for something.

When Michael slipped, he needed a crutch and didn't have anybody to go to."

Another of Giachetti's fighters, the great Aaron Pryor, former junior lightweight champ, has had drug problems. "Fighters should have to take drug tests," said Giachetti. "It's getting to be too much."

Despite his recent travail, Dokes still has lost only one of 32 fights. He is 29, young enough to come back if he is not buried in jail.

Can he do it? "He'll come back," said Jefferson. "I remember when he fought his first main event. We were talking about the fight, which was a few days away, and he pointed to a car on the street.

"He said, 'See that car? I've never had the money to buy anything like that in my life. Before I lose this fight, they'll have to kill me.' He's got character."

Giachetti agreed. "He hurt his shoulder bad once," he recalled. "It almost finished him. But he lifted weights, did a lot of hard work and overcame it. It took character. I never give up on anybody."

Postscript: In January 2000 Dokes was sentenced to four to 15 years in prison for assault of his longtime girlfriend. She said drugs and alcohol made him violent.

The Old Pro Still Winning at the Races

DANNY WEILER *Apr. 4, 1980*

Danny Weiler, the splendid Thistledown jockey, has been riding horses for a long time. He brought in his first winner, Speed Wrinkles, at old Ascot Park on June 13, 1950.

That was another era. To put it into perspective, wonder jockey Steve Cauthen wasn't even alive then. Football player Brian Sipe was in the third grade. Star baseball players earned $20,000 a year and were glad to have it.

Twenty-two years later, Weiler, 43, is still at it, with nine victories in the infant Thistledown season so far, including one on his only mount yesterday.

His goal is to keep riding at least until he gets 3,000 winners, which is comparable to a baseball pitcher winning 200 games. Only 26 jockeys in the history of American racing, according to the last available figures, have reached 3,000. Weiler has 2,682.

"I'd like to keep riding as long as I can," said Weiler. "Fear of riding or excess weight usually finishes jockeys. I'm not overweight (108 pounds) and I've never been afraid. If the day comes when I'm always thinking of getting hurt, I'll quit. Funny thing, though, I quit playing baseball when I was a kid because the ball scared the hell out of me."

Weiler, like all jockeys, has had his share of injuries. The worst came at Ascot, when his steed fell and he was kicked by a trailing horse. It was such a bad spill that a radio station reported that Weiler was dead.

"I had a fractured skull and there was blood coming out of my nose, mouth, and ears," he recalled. "If I had died at the time, I wouldn't have cared. I was off the track for two months."

The only concession Weiler makes to age is that he doesn't take as many mounts. "I used to be able to ride eight or nine a day, but now I stay around four or five," he said.

The public generally doesn't realize that jockeys need a lot of strength to control a horse. That's why the average rider has surprisingly muscular arms and a powerful chest.

"For the one minute you ride, you use more energy than in any other sport I ever played," said Weiler, who was a second baseman for the Cleveland Heights High School baseball team.

Weiler's biggest day came when he rode winners in six straight races at Thistledown on August 12, 1961. He has won a record 13 riding championships at the Big T. His top year was 1973, when he had 221 winners.

His philosophy at Thistledown is simple. He likes to get his horses in front, or as close to the lead as possible. "You have to do that here," he said, "because Thistledown has a comparatively short stretch, only about 900 feet. At a track like Churchill Downs, it's 1,300 feet.

"But I don't ride that way at every track. I went to Chicago one year and in two weeks I got a reputation as a come-from-behind rider because the stretch was longer."

A twinge of regret comes into Weiler's voice when he says, "I've ridden a lot of stakes winners, but I never rode a really great horse. I had three chances to ride in the Kentucky Derby, but I turned them all down because I didn't think the horses had a chance to win."

Weiler has spent almost his entire career on Cleveland tracks and there are those that say he is the greatest rider this town has ever produced, with Tony Rini next.

"I rode a few seasons in Chicago and did all right, but after I got married 15 years ago, I didn't want to travel anymore," said Weiler.

Now Weiler, who earns about $60,000 a year, spends the summer at Thistledown and rides at Florida Downs in the winter. He and his wife live on a 30-acre farm outside Chardon.

Weiler always was interested in racing. "We used to go to Thistledown and bet when we were in high school," he said. "We'd jump the fence to get in and the cops would chase us until we got lost in the crowd."

After a semester at Kent State, he and a friend went west. He learned to gallop horses at LaMesa Park in New Mexico. "All they did out there was drink and fight," he said. "I had plenty of fights. When I came back here I thought I could lick anybody in the world."

Stories of jockey fights after races are legend. They're like traffic arguments. "I've had about ten fights," said the five-foot, four-inch Weiler. "You have to establish your territory. It's better to have a fight with a guy and get it over with than to take a feud out to the track."

Weiler says Thistledown is loaded with excellent riders. "We have ten guys here who are better than anybody they have at Beulah in Columbus," he said. "We have better riders than they have in Chicago. I think good jockeys like to come here because of the long season. They don't have to move around.

"It's a very competitive business. You have to keep proving yourself. I feel just as much pressure as when I started. I worry every day. I have all my life."

Some Say Trainer Died of Broken Heart

JOHN RUTHERFORD *Sep. 13, 1986*

The official cause of John Rutherford's death was cancer. But many people say he died of a broken heart.

Rutherford was a wonderful old trainer at Thistledown racetrack. His greatest achievement came last season when he guided Glacial Princess to Ohio Horse-of-the Year honors.

Rutherford was a big man, 6-3 and 200 pounds. Oldtimers recall him working at forgotten tracks like Pitt Park decades ago. Nobody knew much about his past, but the death certificate shows he was born in Arizona in 1916 and that he had a former wife living in New Orleans.

He was a gregarious man who could enthrall a company with his tall tales about the turf. Yet, others call him a loner. He could be irascible. "He was a yeller and a screamer," said jockey Donald Stover. "But he was my friend."

"A lot of people didn't like him," said groom Floyd Roberts. "But he was his own man."

At horsemen's meetings, Rutherford would expound at length, like an orator. "John read a lot," said trainer Gary King. "He had so much information, he could tell you anything and you'd believe him. He loved to argue about horses, politics, anything. He was a great guy."

Rutherford lived in a Thistledown tackroom furnished with a cot and TV set. "Money didn't mean a thing to him," said Roberts. "But if you worked for him, the first thing he'd ask was if you had enough to eat. He'd buy you meals if you were broke."

Most of Rutherford's teeth were missing. Bill Blass would not have approved of his wardrobe. Vidal Sassoon would have winced at his grooming.

But at age 70, he was still an impressive figure, brimming with independence and self-respect. Here was a man who had done just about everything, even if he hadn't trained horses for movie comics Abbott and Costello or played football for the Chicago Bears, as he liked to tell wide-eyed romantics.

Rutherford's horses were his family "He nicknamed every horse he had," said Roberts. "He called Glacial Princess 'Mean Shank.' He'd take her on the track in the morning before a race and say to her, 'Mean Shank, there are a lot of tough girls coming in to try to beat you today and you have to be ready for them.' He talked to all of his horses. It sounds crazy, but they seemed to respond."

"He'd say that you had to get inside a horse's head before he'd run for you," said Al Asmundy, a friend. "He said you had to make a horse trust you. He treated his horses like children, said goodnight to each one."

After a lifetime of knocking about, Rutherford finally hit it big with Glacial Princess. He trained her for Equinall Stable, owned by Columbus orthodontist Dr. John Graver and Bill Fouss of Delaware. At first, she would get in front and blow leads. Rutherford suspected she had a breathing problem and put her on Lasix, a medicine. He would put her feet in ice.

"After she got Lasix, she reeled off nine victories in a row," said Roberts. She became Ohio horse of the year in 1985, winning $227,000.

Just when he had his big horse, life became cruel to Rutherford. He was hit by cancer last winter. "He kept it to himself," said Roberts. "He never went to a doctor. The doctor would go broke waiting for him."

Rutherford kept plugging away, a study in valor, handling the 15-horse Equinall stable. Asbundy recalls Rutherford did not have the strength to tighten a horse's girth toward the end. Last spring, nevertheless, Glacial Princess won her first three races.

Then Graver and Fouss fired him over a difference in policy. "He was no yes man," said Roberts.

On his final day on the job, Rutherford won the $56,000 Imp Handicap with Glacial Princess. The crowd at the winners' circle shouted congratulations and words of encouragement to the dismissed trainer.

"I don't need you, you need me," the old battler yelled to Graver. "I'll get another champion. I'll make one. I made her, didn't I?"

Despite his bravado, Rutherford slipped quickly after the firing. Only 10 days later, he entered Brentwood Hospital.

"It killed him when they took the mare away from him," said Stover.

"He became despondent, took it very bad," said a Thistledown official. "He went downhill fast."

Stover and his girlfriend, trainer Nancy Zagin, visited Rutherford almost daily. Stover would bring him the Racing Form and Zagin would give him chocolates.

Graver and Fouss visited him, too. "My kids were raised around John, listening to his stories," said Graver.

"I'm a believer in that what goes 'round comes 'round," said Stover. "Since she left John, the horse hasn't been doing that good. She finished last in her last race by 42 lengths and she was disqualified from a $147,000 victory and placed third. That cost them $72,000."

When Rutherford died, his former wife asked that his ashes be sent to her. A sermon was read in the racetrack chapel. There is not much else you can do for a broken heart.

The Queen Reigns as Husband Reins

BARBARA TURCOTTE *Feb. 11, 1984*

Barbara Turcotte, a spectacular blonde, is the queen of Northfield Harness. She is in the clubhouse every night. Everybody knows her. She hasn't missed a race since 1975. She is generous. She is a wise-cracker. She bets and she owns horses.

The other night Barbara was talking at her table on the finish line. Eight horsemen were there, five of them women. She recalled her days as a Playboy bunny in her native Chicago. She talked of her mother's muscular dystrophy, her father's master work in wood inlay. She said she was writing a harness-racing novel.

"It's about five drivers," she said. "Who knows? I might be the next Jacqueline Susann. It's a romantic book, not dirty. It's gonna tell it the way it is."

She has written about 400 pages. "Longhand or typed?"

She laughed. "Longhand. If I knew how to type I wouldn't have been a Playboy bunny."

Barbara's image is that she is the wise woman who gives tips to bettors. After all, her husband is driver Mel Turcotte. "If I knew everything that was going on, I'd be driving a Mercedes," she protested. She settles for a 1984 Park Avenue Buick.

She admits she has won many trifecta bets, however. "But it's not because I have any inside information," she said. "Women are lucky. I like to play long shots and I play the same numbers in every trifecta. And I'm a good handicapper."

Barbara, who neither drinks nor smokes, bought drinks for everyone at the table. A plump, cheerful lady, about 50, approached. She was selling raffle tickets for a church charity for $5. Barbara bought five tickets.

"I just went to confession today because it was First Friday," said Barbara. "I'm very religious. So is Mel. A lot of the drivers are. They say they ride with Jesus. Harness racing is a dangerous sport. They never know what's going to happen."

Barbara asked the raffle seller if she would like a drink. "Yes, a beer," she said with a lovely smile. After she downed it, she said to Barbara, "Thanks for the beer." Then she left to sell more tickets.

Barbara and Turcotte met when she was a barmaid at DeMarco's restaurant. Turcotte had been admiring a painting of a blonde running through a field of horses. A friend told him, "If you want to see a prettier blonde, come with me." He introduced them.

The courtship was long. They were engaged for about eight years. Turcotte first brought her to the track in 1975 and bought her a $1,700 horse, Mohican Gold, as a Christmas present. Until then, she knew nothing about racing.

"Mohican Gold was a nice old claimer," said Barbara. "He had arthritis, but show him the gate and he'd take off."

The best horse Barbara ever owned was Catamaran D., who cost $4,300 and won $185,000 before being hurt. "We had to put him to sleep," she said.

Barbara and Turcotte were married last Dec. 2 at St. John's Cathedral. "It was the most beautiful ceremony I have ever seen," said an aristocratic lady in clipped tones. "It was a very intimate, small chapel and the bride and groom looked very handsome. I cried through the whole wedding."

"Yes, and her husband slept," cracked Barbara.

The reception was held at the Taverne of Richfield, after which Barbara and Turcotte went to Northfield for the races.

"Mel was in six races and he lost them all," said Barbara. "He had bridegroom jitters. I told him I'd never marry him again."

Farewell to the Honest Bookie

HONEST YOCKIM *Feb. 10, 2001*

Honest Yockim, the last of the legendary sports gamblers who inhabited downtown Cleveland's Short Vincent St., died the other day at age 93.

It was a good time for Yockim to cash in. All of his old buddies are gone, men like Fuzzy Lakis, Hymie Mintz, Shoes Rosen, Joe Lombardo and Shondor Birns.

They were a gregarious bunch that congregated around the old Theatrical Grille, Kornman's Back Room, The Three O'Clock

Club, Mickey's and the Frolics, making bets, taking bets and talking sports.

When they saw a Damon Runyon movie, they were looking at themselves. Their turf was Vincent St., called Short Vincent because it ran for about 75 yards, and still does, between E. 9th and E. 6th, north of Euclid Ave.

Now it is full of parking lots. In its heyday, from the 1930s to the 1970s, the street was the city's center of entertainment, where captains of industry and politicians mingled with sports figures, journalists, entertainers and bookmakers.

Yockim, whose real name was Abe Rabinovitz, was not as flashy as Lakis, who had a standing $50 bet that nobody could throw an orange to the top of the nearby eight-story Gillsey Hotel and brazenly hawked bets in the corridors at fights, right in front of the cops. Nor was he as notorious as the convivial Birns, the reputed numbers king of the city who was killed in a car bombing. But Yockim might have been the most respected of the bookies. Plain Dealer sports columnist James E. Doyle, who nicknamed Yockim and called him "The Short Sage of Short Vincent," was always quoting him in his column.

The 5-foot, 2-inch Yockim was a likable fellow who never smoked or drank. He walked around Vincent as though he were a public relations man, offering opinions to the journalists and hobnobbing with people such as Indians General Manager Hank Greenberg, Indians owner Bill Veeck, Browns owner Mickey McBride and boxing impresario Larry Atkins.

Yockim was considered a master at making sports odds. He would make bets if he considered the wagering line to be wrong. He always bet on the underdog. He seldom went to the racetrack because he felt it was too hard to beat the horses. He loved to wager on boxing.

"He knew all the sports trivia," said Steve Kostrubanic, a former Golden Gloves champ who was Yockim's friend for many years. "He could answer any question without looking at a book." Yockim was also a fine gin rummy player. When high rollers came into town looking for a game, the denizens of Short Vincent would stake Yockim.

Like all gamblers, he lost a lot. Some say he never had much money and that he was almost broke at the end. Yockim, a lifelong bachelor, never had a car. He lived at home in Cleveland Heights with his parents, two sisters, brother-in-law and niece Edria.

Edria Mirman Ragosin fondly recalls Yockim taking her downtown as a child. "We went to a Browns game and sat in [team owner] Mickey McBride's box," she said. "We had box seats for the World Series. They were just great memories. All of his friends were so colorful. They were good people, never into drugs or anything like that."

Yockim taught his niece how to play blackjack and poker. "I learned how to do my fractions in school through him," she said.

Once, Yockim was called to testify before a federal grand jury that was investigating gambling. His lawyer, Jerry Milano, told Yockim to answer every question by saying, "I refuse to answer on the grounds it might tend to incriminate me." Milano had the words typed on a piece of paper and Yockim read them after each query. The little man was nervous and sweating. He was breathing heavily. The inquisitor, fearful that he was becoming ill, anxiously asked, "Would you like a glass of water?"

Yockim, still frightened, did not hear the question and again read automatically, "I refuse to answer on the grounds it might tend to incriminate me," sending the courtroom into convulsions of laughter.

About 30 years ago, Yockim decided to move to Las Vegas, where gambling is legal. He knew plenty of Clevelanders there, such as Billy Weinberger, the president of Caesars Palace, who had previously owned Kornman's, a first-class restaurant. "They loved my uncle out there," said Edria, who visited him on occasion with her husband. All she had to do was say, "I'm Yockim's niece," and the red carpet was laid out.

Yockim returned to Cleveland a few years ago. He had a heart ailment and wore a pacemaker. His last months were spent at the Montefiore rest home in Beachwood.

Kostrubanic visited him a couple of times each week. Yockim would talk about his days at John Adams High School, and how he was a good baseball and basketball player, blessed with speed. "We'd go out for a corned beef sandwich," Kostrubanic said. "A lot of people knew him. They would come over and shake his hand. The last time I saw him he gave me a 1980 Ring Record Book."

Another friend, Joe Amato, visited him on Super Bowl Sunday. "Make a bet that I'll die tonight," Yockim said. He was wrong that time. He lived another eight days, making small bets until the end.

He lost $40 on the New York Giants in the Super Bowl, but he was true to his code, getting three points. He always bet the underdog.

Off On Another Dream

NICK MILETI *Apr. 10, 1980*

The controversial Nick Mileti era here is over. He is a hard man to sum up, an unusual man, one who reached far higher than the ordinary mortal.

You would think that an East Side guy like Mileti, whose foreign-born father was a common laborer, would have considered himself wildly successful after buying the American Hockey League Barons and the Arena in 1968.

But that was just the beginning. Mileti soon embarked on the gaudiest spending spree in Cleveland sports history. By the time he was through, he ranked with Art Modell, Bill Veeck, Al Sutphin and Larry Atkins as the most memorable sporting entrepreneurs in the city's annals.

The funny thing is that Mileti jumped from one failure to another, always going up. He lost money with the minor league Barons, so he invented the Crusaders, a pseudo big-league hockey team.

The Crusaders floundered, but he had acquired a glamorous pro basketball franchise, the Cavaliers. While they struggled, Mileti went willy-nilly into the big-time and bought the Indians. They remained losers under his aegis.

Then, to top it off, he undertook the monumental task of building the Coliseum, the edifice for which he will always be remembered, his private pyramid.

Now Mileti is leaving the comparatively mundane world of sport, an artistic failure still. He has sold out his interest in his last team, the Cavaliers, and is going onward and upward again. This time it is for Hollywood, where he plans to make movies.

He seems to be in his rightful milieu now. Mileti was always more of an entertainer than a businessman. It always looked as though he bought all his enterprises for the sheer delight in the applause they would bring him.

It was almost as though the soft-spoken Mileti feared he could never make an impression on people by just being himself. Without the Indians, Cavs and the Coliseum, he was just another wallflower. But as the entrepreneur he was the center of attention and he reveled in that.

His biggest night came when he put together the group that bought the Indians. This was his proudest achievement. Make no mistake, Mileti saved the Indians for Cleveland.

Gabe Paul, then running the Tribe for owner Vernon Stouffer, decided to have the team play about 30 home games a year in New Orleans. There was little opposition. But along came Mileti, riding onto the scene on a white horse, banners flying. He and his investors bought the team and Mileti announced the Indians would play all their games in Cleveland, where they belonged.

The night the deal was completed, Mileti walked into the Theatrical Restaurant, home of the sporting crowd, like a conquering Caesar, to a standing ovation. That was the pinnacle for him. What a night.

(It has been said that Mileti does not deserve credit for keeping the team here, that the actual plaudits should go to Dudley Blossom, who invested the money Mileti needed to acquire the club. But Blossom, the Indians treasurer, disagrees saying, "Nick made it happen. I never even talked to Stouffer. My brother and I just gave Nick the money he needed to push him over the top.")

Those were great days for Mileti. He was always in the downtown bars, always available to fans and reporters. He was the most accessible sports mogul since Veeck's halcyon days.

Like all great salesmen, he could charm people, make them feel good. Sensing people's need for recognition, he would call them superstars. "We're all superstars," he would say.

In interviews, however, he was no Veeck. He was a lousy interview because he was too smart to ever give direct answers.

Also, he never argued with people, as though he realized it was futile to try to change a person's mind. On those rare occasions when a fan would badger Mileti at a watering hole, he would turn his head away and say nothing, a weary look on his face.

It was the same way in his businesses. When the newspaper critics began to surface, Mileti didn't fight them head-on. He simply put together a broadcasting monopoly which has never been fully appreciated or discussed.

At a time when he owned the Indians, Cavaliers and Crusaders simultaneously, Mileti also owned WWWE radio, broadcasting all of his teams' games on his own station.

He also brought in a talk show host to blabber Mileti's point of view and showcase him in fawning interviews. Mileti couldn't have had it better. It was the best propaganda machine outside Pravda.

Mileti's one big mistake was locating the Coliseum in Richfield.

Had he built it downtown, he might not have had to flee to Hollywood's land of dreams.

Wonder what he'll do next if it turns out he isn't Cecil B. DeMille?

Smooth Talker Joins the Hall

JIMMY DUDLEY *Aug. 5, 1997*

For 20 years Jimmy Dudley opened his Indians baseball broadcasts with the words: "Hello, baseball fans everywhere." When the count would come to three balls and two strikes, Dudley was sure to provide his signature line: "The string is out."

He would end each broadcast by saying; "Lots of good luck, ya heah," his friendly Southern voice dripping with honey, sugar and diamond dust.

Dudley, one of the most popular play-by-play men in Cleveland sports history, called Indians games from 1948–67. In recognition of his fine work, he was inducted into the Baseball Hall of Fame on Sunday.

Dudley, 87, who has Alzheimer's disease, could not make the trip to Cooperstown, N.Y., to accept the honor.

Angie Dudley, his wife of 47 years, had intended to represent him, but she is also in ill health. The couple live in Tucson, Ariz. Dudley's son, Douglas, gave the acceptance speech at the Hall of Fame.

"It was quite a thrill for me to speak for my dad in his absence," said Douglas, who is pastor of the Heritage Presbyterian Church in Carol Stream, Ill. "Everything went very well."

Jimmy Dudley knew he was going into the Hall of Fame. He had been notified several months ago, while he was still comparatively well. "He was thrilled," said Angie Dudley. "He said it was a dream come true."

Dudley was living at home then. For the last four months he has been getting treatment in a private home for Alzheimer's patients in Tucson.

"Physically, he's fine," said Angie Dudley. Dudley was at the microphone for the 1948 world champion Indians and the 1954 team which set the American League record with 111 victories. His "Dugout Interview" pre-game show was a staple of the era.

Dudley, a stocky, handsome man and an excellent after-dinner speaker, often told the story of the young, blind listener who sent him a fan letter and said, "Please remember, Mr. Dudley, that you're my eyes." He said he always kept that thought in his mind in his broadcasts.

Dudley partnered on Indians games with Jack Graney until 1953, Ed Edwards in 1954–55, Tom Manning in 1956, Bob Neal from 1957–61, Harry Jones from 1962–64 and then back to Neal from 1965–67.

His relationship with the late Neal created the only controversy of his career. They hated each other, never speaking. The seed of the problem lay in the fact Dudley and Neal were so much alike. Both were nationally known announcers with distinctive voices. They were natty dressers from the Bing Crosby school of haberdashery, looking good in straw hats and colorful sport coats that were always in excellent taste.

Neal, who resented playing second fiddle to Dudley, had trained to be an opera singer. Dudley, a graduate of the University of Virginia, had been a pilot in the Army Air Corps during World War II. They were definitely a cut above the ordinary play-by-play man.

Dudley, a chemistry major in college, got into sportscasting after a friend told him during a phone conversation: "With your voice, you ought to go on the radio." Dudley, who had played baseball, football and basketball at Virginia, apprenticed with Chicago Cubs announcer Hal Tutten in his first major-league job.

According to Angie Dudley, he was hired to do Indians games after the chief of Erin Brew beer, the major sponsor on the broadcasts, heard his lively, melodious voice and said: "That's the man I want to do the Indians games."

Bill Veeck, the Tribe owner at the time, hired Dudley. "Jimmy was very fond of Bill Veeck," said Angie, a former Chicago radio actress on soap operas such as Ma Perkins and Captain Midnight.

Dudley's tenure with the Tribe ended after the 1967 season, much to the chagrin of many fans. They picketed the Stadium at the opening game in 1968, holding signs that read: "Bring back Jimmy Dudley."

In 1969, Dudley was the voice of the Seattle Pilots. But he lost that job when the Pilots transferred to Milwaukee after one year. Already 60, he never worked in big-league ball again. "He was kind of lost," said Angie. "It was such a big part of his life."

Later he announced games of the Tucson Toros, worked some University of Arizona basketball games and had a radio show. He also found time to make a famed commercial for a Cleveland siding company. It ran for years and was so effective listeners could chant it from memory.

Now, his picture will be enshrined forever in the Hall of Fame.

Living by His Own Style

Jim "Mudcat" Grant *Jul. 1, 1978*

It was 8 a.m. in the Swingos Hotel coffee shop. Jim (Mudcat) Grant, television personality, sportsman and man about town, arrived for breakfast. He was in full regalia, wearing his Cleveland Indians baseball uniform.

"I'm going to Columbus this morning to talk to the Safety Patrol," he explained. "I figured I'd save a little time by wearing this." Grant is a publicist for the Indians, making talks nearly every day.

He is quite good at it. Several times I have fielded telephone calls in the sports department from people who want to tell us how much they appreciated Grant's chat with their particular group.

The calls usually go like this: Mudcat came out and spoke to our club and he was just wonderful. Everybody loved him. He was so interesting and gracious and humorous. Such a nice man. We just wanted you to know.

The Grant charisma was still intact at the breakfast table. A waitress began talking to him as though he was an old friend.

"You're a celebrity," she announced. "I've seen you on TV. What did I do to deserve this pleasant surprise?"

"Were you nice to your husband?" Grant smiled.

"No, but I broke a mirror," she said.

"Oh, well then, that's it,"said Grant. "Your bad luck is ending. You're being rewarded."

Across the room another waitress lifted a glass of water and called, "Here's to you, Mudcat." He waved back. Throughout our conversation, he was greeted by smiles and waves from customers.

Cleveland may be down on baseball and the Indians, but from what I can see, the people love Mudcat.

"This town has never let me down – never – and I've been here since 1958," he said.

The former pitcher for the Indians became a TV presence with his unique commentary on the baseball team's games from 1973 through 1976. Then Channel 8 fired him, along with his sidekick, Harry Jones. Now Grant has a new TV career, making commercials for auto dealer Ed Stinn.

The commercials, which have Grant and Stinn chatting casually, last about 30 seconds. "We film about nine of them every three or four months," said Grant. "We don't rehearse or plan what we're going to say. We just wing it."

Grant thinks he may be as well known now for those ads as he is for his sportscasting. "People come up to me and say, 'You're the man who does those car commercials with that fat man.'"

"But the kids always want me to talk the way I did on the baseball games. They ask me to say, 'Well Harry . . .' I guess I pronounce Harry Jones' name different than most people do."

In his years on the Tribe broadcasts, Grant did a lot of things differently. He didn't bother trying to imitate professional sportscasters, the way other athletes who go on the air do. He was just his unique self, colorful and warm as the Florida sun under which he was born.

Who can forget his references to "Chin Music" and Charlie Spikes. "The Bogalusa Kid," and the way he said, "All right," stretching the letters out as though savoring them. How about the way he called the town of Chardon "shar-doan"?

"I thought that was the right way to pronounce it," Grant laughed. "My sense of vowels as a Southerner is just different. Nobody ever got mad about it or tried to correct me."

"In fact, every time I'd speak in Chardon somebody would ask me. 'What's the name of our town?' I'd say, 'Shar-doan' and they'd crack up."

Grant says he received only four letters of criticism in his years on the tube for the Tribe. One came after he said that National League umpires were better than American League umpires.

Another came from a black man who said Grant should pay more attention to his English for the benefit of the ghetto kids.

"He was right, but for the wrong reason," said Grant. "You should always pay attention to your English, not just because you're talking to ghetto kids. Look, I can talk better if I want to."

At this point, Grant puffed up his chest and, in pompous stentorian tones, said, "Ladies and gentleman, now playing left field for Cleveland, Ted Cox." It was a hilarious imitation of a professional announcer.

Another critical letter arrived after a lady wrote to him for advice on breaking in a new glove. "I told her to put a grapefruit in the pocket and put the glove in water," said Grant. "But I didn't know she was going to put it in the sun to dry it. It messed up the whole glove."

"But I got tons of nice letters. I have 'em all. I still read them. It really hurt me when I was taken off the air."

Grant and Jones were canned by Bill Flynn shortly after he took over as boss of Channel 8 in early 1977. No reason was ever given for the axing. It wasn't ratings. A station official told me at the time that the baseball ratings never vary much. They go up when the team is winning and down when it's losing, no matter who the sportscasters are.

"I wish I knew why I was fired," said Grant. "Especially since we were as popular as we were. I thought I was on the way to becoming a sportscaster with a different style. That style didn't make me better, just different. I definitely think we attracted female listeners who didn't care about the game.

"There's no doubt I'd like to get back on the games," Grant continued. "I'd be willing to bet that if you go to the people, they'll tell you they want me. Ask them in your article to vote on whether they'd like to see Mudcat on the Indians games. It would be fun. I bet you'd get a super response."

It is not Grant's style to criticize people, so he was complimentary about the current Tribe TV sportscasters, Eddie Doucette and Jim Mueller. But that pair has been getting rapped somewhat by viewers who write letters to newspaper sports pages. It would be interesting to see if the fans would rather have Grant back.

Grant pointed out that there is only one black man doing play-by-play in the major leagues, Bill White of the New York Yankees.

Cleveland television has one black sportscaster, Paul Warfield of Channel 3. He hosts the sports show on weekends and gives nightly reports also. Grant was asked if he applied for that post.

"No," he said. "I wouldn't be that structured. I think if I was on a program like that, the brass would be looking at me from behind a camera and saying, 'Oh God, what's he doing now?'

"If I did that kind of show they'd have to give me leeway to do it my way. I think we could have some fun and people would go wild."

Good Guys, Bad Buys and the Lord of the Ring

LORD LAYTON *Jul. 15, 1984*

Remember Lord Layton, the professional wrestler who created a minor sensation in Cleveland 24 years ago?

He died at his home in Toronto earlier this year. Age 63. Went to the refrigerator at 2 a.m. for a glass of milk and keeled over. Massive coronary. No muss, no fuss.

Death is never easy, but it is good to hear Layton went as painlessly as he did. And it's a shame that his passing went unmentioned in the American press.

He was a good guy who brought a lot of fun to a lot of people. Besides, he raised the fine art of pro wrestling hokum to new levels during its golden era.

His carefully contrived act took place during the weekly Saturday afternoon wrestling matches which, in that time, were televised live by Channel 8. Layton, who was born in England and reared in Australia, was the ring announcer, describing the action to the audience.

He spoke in an elegant accent with perfect syntax. He was handsome, immediately likable, a cross between John Wayne and Cary Grant — wrestling's aristocrat. The name Lord fitted him, though it was bestowed by youngsters in Australia who were impressed by his size; his given name was Athol.

Layton affected the part of the naïve play-by-play man who became horrified as villainous matmen did bad things to the good guys. Few suspected he was a professional wrestler himself.

In tones of quiet shock and outrage, Layton would criticize the villains. In the interviews which followed, he could scarcely contain his disgust at having to speak to the likes of the Gallagher Brothers or the Sheik. The bad guys would insult Layton, maybe push him around. Once they threw his birthday cake to the floor.

After weeks of such buildup, the 6-5, 250-pound Layton could take no more. He accepted Mike Gallagher's challenge. A match was set for the old Arena on New Year's night, 1959. To the fans who ate up the nonsense, that would be similar today to hearing sportscaster Gib Shanley say he was going to play left tackle for the Browns so he could teach Lyle Alzado of the Los Angeles Raiders a football lesson.

Believe it or not, Layton and Gallagher drew a turnaway crowd of 12,000. Layton won, two falls to one.

The theatrics went on for weeks, with Layton also teaming with Bobo Brazil to whip the Gallaghers.

The scene became a familiar one in the early 1960s. Layton seething in controlled indignation as outlaw wrestlers hurled folding chairs over his plywood announcing desk; Layton calling for order like an oversized Peter Lawford; pushed beyond human tolerance, shucking off a tailored sports coat the size of a packing crate, and finally, Layton restoring order, meting out swift justice to the wild cheers of the crowd.

Eventually, the act went stale and Layton departed for his home in Toronto, where he had lived since 1950. He continued his show in Canada for many years, reportedly filling Maple Leaf Gardens for some shenanigans with the Sheik. His career lasted 28 years and 3,500 matches.

Layton lived in Toronto for the rest of his life. He was married with two grown children. For seven years until his death he was a goodwill ambassador for a liquor company.

He also did much work on behalf of ailing youngsters. He became a director of the Cerebral Palsy Foundation and was an illustrious potentate with the Shriners. He helped the Variety Club in Toronto in its work with handicapped children.

"He was a super guy, an outstanding man," said Reg Bovard, an official with the Variety Club. "I can't think of anyone who gave more of his time and ability to help the handicapped. He had one of the biggest funerals I've ever seen. The church was jammed with 550 people and they were standing outside."

Bovard said the convivial Layton left money in his will for his friends to have a party after his death. Some 300 showed up at a downtown Toronto theatrical club.

One of Layton's proudest moments came last Dec. 18 when the Variety Club held a sports competition for handicapped children. They came on crutches and in wheelchairs. Layton marched at the head of the parade with military bearing.

"He came in straight as a poker and took the salute," said Bovard. "There wasn't a dry eye in the house." Thirty days later he died.

On the day he died, Layton gave a luncheon speech. He seemed to be in good health. His only problem was a sore back, for which he took cortisone.

"We all miss him," Bovard said. "He could tell stories all night."

A lot of Clevelanders would have liked to say goodbye to him.

Indians – Early Years

A Tragic Figure

Louis "Chief" Sockalexis *Apr. 24, 2000*

Whether or not the Indians were named after him, the elements of tragedy are present in the life of Louis "Chief" Sockalexis, who played in 94 baseball games for the Cleveland National League club in the 1890s.

Sockalexis was a talented ballplayer whose career was ended by one of the world's oldest strikeout pitches—liquor.

The Penobscot Indian from a Maine reservation was 42 when he died in 1913 but he remains alive in the minds of baseball historians. "He has a cult following," said Cappy Gagnon of South Bend, Ind., a member of the Society of American Baseball Research. "He had his 15 minutes of fame."

Luke Salisbury of Chelsea, Mass., wrote a novel based on Sockalexis' life.

"His story is so short and so sad," said Salisbury, a professor at Bunker Hill Community College in Boston. "I suspect a lot of the interest in him comes from the fact he died young, without realizing his potential."

Sockalexis first came to public attention at Holy Cross College, where he was an outstanding skater, baseball and football player. Printed reports say he already had a drinking problem in college and that he was reprimanded by Holy Cross priests.

In recent years, Sockalexis' descendants have claimed the ballplayer did not begin drinking until he came to Cleveland. They say he became a slave to booze after playing an outstanding game and celebrating with his teammates in a tavern.

After two years at Holy Cross, Sockalexis accompanied a white teammate to sports-conscious Notre Dame University in February

1897. "I don't believe he was a university student at either Notre Dame or Holy Cross," said Larry Rutenbeck of Wichita Falls, Kan., who is working on a biography of Sockalexis. "He was just there to play ball. It was a looser time."

"He took courses like geography and reading while the other students were taking Greek and Latin," said Gagnon, director of stadium personnel at Notre Dame. "But once he set foot on campus he immediately became the best athlete in school. He was a Jim Thorpe figure."

Already 25 years old, Sockalexis was a man among the college boys. He stood 5-11, tall for that era, and weighed a muscular 185. He had great speed, having once stolen six bases in a game at Holy Cross, four of them as a designated runner for an injured teammate. Called "The Deerfoot of the Diamond," he batted left-handed and threw right-handed.

Sockalexis lasted only a month at Notre Dame. "He and a teammate were nabbed for being drunk and disorderly in a tavern," Gagnon said.

H.G. Salsinger, the late Detroit writer, quoted Notre Dame teammate William E. Hindel as saying Sockalexis and a crony were involved in a drunken fistfight with South Bend police after the two had wrecked a local establishment.

After Sockalexis left Notre Dame, he was signed by the Cleveland Spiders, whose manager, Pat Tebeau, had heard reports of his ability. One story says the Spiders squared things with the South Bend police to "get the player out of hock."

Sockalexis joined the team for spring training, which was held indoors in the Cleveland Athletic Club. The Plain Dealer stated on March 26, 1897, that Sockalexis was a gymnast who went through exercises "that would tear the ordinary man in two." Apparently, he had an unusual batting stance and swing that moved the anonymous Plain Dealer writer to mention it at least twice. On April 7 he wrote, "Sockalexis, despite the peculiar way he goes at the ball, is hitting it pretty regular."

The papers began calling the team "the Indians" in those days when team nicknames were informal. Jerry Strothers, a Cleveland Native American activist, contends the sobriquet was bestowed to make fun of Sockalexis.

J. Thomas Hetrick, author of a book on the Spiders, agrees. "The newspapers and fans ridiculed Sockalexis' ancestry," he wrote. "They said he was a descendant of Sitting Bull."

Among the myths surrounding Sockalexis is the story that he hit two homers in the opening game of 1897. The box score shows he went 0-for-3 against Louisville as Cleveland lost, 3-1, behind Cy Young. Then he got going.

"I've read that he was hitting .480," Gagnon said. "Actually, he was hitting between .320 and .340 almost all season. I know. I've gone through the box score of the whole season, game by game. He was very consistent."

He went 4-for-5, including a bases-loaded triple, against St. Louis. In New York, with the fans taunting him, he hit a home run in his first at-bat against future Hall of Famer Amos Rusie. Fans would mock Sockalexis, who played right field, with Indian war whoops and hi-yi-yi calls. "Get a tomahawk!" they would shout. It was only 21 years since the Indians defeated Custer at the Battle of the Little Bighorn and seven years after the Wounded Knee massacre. Strothers said the fans threw things at him. But he must have received some good treatment, too.

The Louisville Courier Journal reported after a game on April 24, 1897, "Sockalexis was cheered at every move he made. He caught a long fly very prettily and the spectators remarked at his grace. The crowd tried to have some fun with Sockalexis' name and imitated war whoops, to all of which the handsome Indian smiled good-naturedly." The Courier Journal said he had the attention of the "matinee girls" in the grandstand. "Isn't he cute?" one exclaimed.

Responding to a charge his teammates would get him to drink because they were jealous of him, Sockalexis in later years said, "Bosh. The white players could not do enough for me." They nicknamed him "Sock" or "Socks."

Things went well for Sockalexis until July 4, an off-day for the team. "According to legend, he went on a drunken spree," said Gagnon.

Jay Feldman, writing in SABR's Baseball Research Journal, quoted Tebeau as saying later that Sockalexis had "celebrated the Fourth by an all-night carousal in a red-light joint and had either jumped or fallen from a second-floor window."

Rutenbeck says he has no evidence the incident really happened, although it is almost always related by other Sockalexis scholars, including Hetrick.

The Cleveland newspapers of the time did not report the story, but on July 6, with the outfielder out of the lineup, The Press said, "Sockalexis has a badly sprained ankle and is almost unable to walk."

"Regardless of how he was hurt, that was the end of his career and his life," Gagnon said. "He slid downhill from there. The ankle injury cost him his speed. When he came back he was stumbling after fly balls. When he was playing regularly he could control his drinking, but it was harder when he was on the bench. He began to show up hung over. The fans got on him pretty hard."

On July 13, a Plain Dealer headline called him "A wooden Indian." The writer said Sockalexis acted as if he had disposed of too many mint juleps previous to the game.

"A Providence paper talked about his 'trysts with paleface maidens' and said that could have contributed to his demise," Salisbury said. Feldman says he was called "The Red Romeo."

Sockalexis hardly played after July 4. His entire big-league success was wrapped up in those brief 2 1/2 months of 1897. Feldman says he was fined and suspended by team owner Frank Robison. He finished the year hitting .338 in only 66 games, 94 points behind Wee Willie Keeler's league-leading mark. Sockalexis had three home runs, 42 runs batted in, 16 stolen bases and made 16 errors. "By the end of 1897 he was regarded as kind of a joke," Rutenbeck said.

He never hit another homer or stole another base. The next year he played 21 games, hitting .224, and then he vanished from the majors forever after hitting .273 in seven games in 1899. "By then he was a fat, drunken old guy," said Gagnon.

Hetrick quotes an article from the October 1898 Pittsburgh Leader, stating, "Sock swears he hasn't removed the scalp from even one glass of foamy beer since last spring, when he whooped up a dance on Superior Street in Cleveland and was discovered the next morning by manager Pat Tebeau in the act of fastening a half-Nelson to a lamppost."

Sockalexis drifted back East. He tried to play in the minors but could not make it anymore. A venture at umpiring did not last. Reports say he was jailed for vagrancy. He returned to the Indian Island reservation where he was born, working as a lumberjack and coaching youth baseball teams.

On Christmas Eve 1913, when Sockalexis was in a logging camp in Burlington, Maine, he suffered a heart attack and died. Newspaper clippings from his days in the majors were found in his shirt pocket.

The Cleveland Press never bothered to report the story of his death. The News gave it one paragraph.

The Plain Dealer and The Leader each printed the same wire

story of about four inches, with The Plain Dealer adding his picture. The Leader carried an additional four-inch story, interviewing former shortstop Ed McKean, a teammate of Sockalexis, who said, "He was a wild bird. He couldn't lose his taste for firewater. His periodical departures became such a habit he finally slipped out of the majors. He had more natural ability than any player I have ever seen, past or present."

Tainted Black

"SHOELESS" JOE JACKSON *Apr. 17, 2001*

"Shoeless" Joe Jackson lives forever in tragic baseball lore.

He was called the game's greatest natural hitter. Babe Ruth, the foremost slugger of them all, copied his perfect left-handed swing.

But Jackson ruined his life by helping the Chicago White Sox throw the 1919 World Series to gamblers, the biggest scandal in sports history. He was kicked out of baseball and died in obscurity in 1951 at 62, the eternal symbol of the unconscious genius who squanders his talent.

"Say it ain't so, Joe," is his epitaph, the plea a small boy supposedly made to Jackson after he was named as one of the cheating Black Sox.

That is all people remember about him today. It is largely forgotten that he had some of his greatest years while playing for Cleveland from 1910 to 1915.

He is the only Cleveland player to hit .400, producing a .408 mark in 1911. He also holds club season records for hits (233), triples (26) and outfield assists (32). His career .375 batting average in Cleveland is the highest in team history. He was the whole package, a fast man who could steal home and cut down runners with his powerful arm.

He lives in legend as a shy yokel, but actually Jackson had no trouble telling people how good he was. "Joe Jackson needs no press agent," Plain Dealer baseball writer Henry Edwards commented. "He believes in advertising himself."

According to "Shoeless," David Fleitz's splendid new biography of Jackson, the slugger arrived at spring training in 1912 and announced to his teammates, "Here I am, boys. Just give me a bat and

I'll put a few over the fence." Each year he would predict he would beat arch rival Ty Cobb for the batting championship, but he never did.

In later years, Jackson bragged that he bet his entire salary of $1,500 with Cleveland team owner Charles Somers in 1911. If he hit .400 he was to collect $10,000. If he was under .400, he would play for nothing. Some baseball historians say he collected the $10,000 after hitting .408, but that is probably a tall tale.

Jackson did not always have such confidence. When he first came up with the Philadelphia Athletics in 1908, the team's veterans, mostly Northerners, almost ran him out of baseball. They hazed and tormented the poor 19-year-old from South Carolina to such an extent that he quit the team several times and went home. It was only 43 years after the Civil War and there was still a residue of hate between South and North.

His Philadelphia teammates would call the illiterate Jackson "brainless," Fleitz writes.

They talked him into drinking out of finger bowls in fancy restaurants and called him "yellow," or cowardly, because he was always running home.

Connie Mack, owner-manager of the A's, offered to get Jackson a tutor to teach him to read and write, but he refused. "It don't take school stuff to play ball," he said.

Mack, feeling Jackson would never fit in on his team, reluctantly traded him to Cleveland for Bris Lord, a competent outfielder. It was one of the best deals in Cleveland baseball history.

Jackson immediately felt at home with the Cleveland club, which had a lot of Southerners. He hit from the beginning. The Plain Dealer called him "Dixie Joe" or "The General," but never "Shoeless," a term he despised. He had picked up the nickname in the minors when he played without shoes one day because his new shoes hurt.

Jackson never did learn to read and the fans would get on him, even when he was a superstar. Fleitz tells of the time he was on third base when a fan yelled, "Joe, can you spell cat?"

Jackson spit out some tobacco juice, looked at the fan and drawled, "Can you spell s— —?" using a four-letter vulgarity.

Jackson's wife, Katie, whom he married when he was 20 and she was 15, came to every game at Cleveland's League Park. She would keep score until the seventh inning, then leave for their apartment on Lexington Ave. to make dinner.

Manager Harry Davis raged at the last-place 1913 team, calling the players quitters, but praised Jackson. "He hits the ball harder than anybody I ever saw," he said.

That year, in a game against the New York Yankees, the 6-1, 178- pound Jackson became the first man to hit a ball over the roof of the Polo Grounds. The Plain Dealer said the ball carried 30 feet over the 90-foot-high grandstand, and called it a "remarkable, wonderful" feat. It was labeled the longest ball ever hit.

Years later, Cobb marveled at Jackson's talent. "The good hitters of that time choked up and punched the ball," Fleitz quotes the Georgia Peach as saying. "Not Jackson. He took a full swing. I never could have hit. 300 with that swing."

He was the first modern slugger, the precursor of today's free swingers, yet he hardly ever struck out, averaging about 20 K's a season. He struck 54 homers in that dead-ball era.

He built up his strength by holding a heavy bat level at arm's length for as long as he could and exercised his eyes by staring at a candle as long as the flame stayed in focus.

Opposing pitchers still clung to the hope he was cowardly, hitting him with pitches eight times in 1911 and 12 times in 1912. But nothing could stop Jackson. "I never pulled off the plate as long as I was in baseball," he said.

Asked the secret of his hitting, Jackson said, "It's no secret. I just wait until the ball gets right here and then I hit it."

He liked to talk about his bats as though they were living things. "Old Caroliny is one of the sweetest bats I have, but lately she's kind of balked on me," he drawled. His favorite bat was "Black Betsy," a massive 48-ounce, 36-inch instrument that was made for him by a South Carolina fan when he was 16.

Trouble started to come in 1914. He injured his leg in a slide and the knee became infected. His batting average slipped to .338. At the end of the season, Jackson began a touring vaudeville show called "Joe Jackson's Baseball Girls."

Fleitz says he reported to spring training in 1915 out of shape. He told a teammate, "I'm through after this season. I've got the stage bug."

Katie filed for divorce when Jackson left spring training for a show business appearance in Atlanta. When a sheriff tried to serve him the papers for a hearing, Jackson refused them. After the sheriff tried to put handcuffs on him, he landed two stiff rights to the officer's head, Fleitz reports. On April 12, 1915, Jackson had a nervous collapse, which was blamed on "family troubles." Katie withdrew the divorce suit and the couple lived together for the rest of their lives.

In addition to all this, Jackson was being offered big money to jump to the new Federal League. Jackson held this as a hammer over Somers, demanding a contract increase.

The financially-strapped owner finally signed him for $6,000, then traded him to the White Sox in August 1915 for Braggo Roth, Larry Chappell, Ed Klepfer and $31,500.

The Plain Dealer's Edwards said the trade would not hurt the Indians, who finished 38 games under .500. "Jackson has become a purely individual player who sacrifices teamwork," the writer said.

Jackson, increasingly infatuated with money, was pleased with the trade, saying he was looking forward to getting some "sweet World Series money." The White Sox won the World Series in 1917 and another pennant in 1919.

That was when Jackson sold out. In 1920, he told a Chicago grand jury that he had been promised $20,000, but was given only $5,000, as the Black Sox threw the 1919 Series with Cincinnati. He and seven other players were suspended from baseball for life.

Jackson wound up his career with a .356 average, third in baseball history to Cobb (.368) and Rogers Hornsby (.358).

Had he stayed in Cleveland, he would probably be in the Hall of Fame.

Jackson spent the rest of his life in his hometown of Greenville, S.C., where he owned a liquor store and laundry. The Joe Jackson Society is trying to get him into baseball's Hall of Fame.

Let's Pitch Two

EMIL "DUTCH" LEVSEN *Apr. 24, 2001*

Emil "Dutch" Levsen is not a famous pitcher. In fact, he is almost completely forgotten. If you asked 100 baseball fans to identify him, 99 would probably respond with a blank stare.

Nevertheless, Levsen delivered one of the most brilliant pitching performances in Indians history. On the afternoon of Aug. 28, 1926, the sidearming right-hander pitched all 18 innings as the Indians won a doubleheader from the Boston Red Sox in Fenway Park. He is the last major-league hurler to work two complete games of a doubleheader and win both.

To put his feat into perspective, the Milwaukee Brewers had only two complete games all of last season. Levsen, 28, pitched a four-hitter in each game, winning by scores of 6-1 and 5-1. Amazingly, he did not strike out a batter. He walked two before an announced crowd of 10,000. The first game was over in one hour and 29 minutes. Levsen took a little longer in the encore, taking 1:43.

Plain Dealer reporter Henry Edwards, who covered the games, praised the red-cheeked Levsen for his "wonderful skill and courage and his powerful right arm." He said Levsen had perfect control. The Indians used the same nine players in each game against the last-place Red Sox. Levsen had Boston hitting easy flies and grounders.

Right fielder Homer Summa caught 11 fly balls while manager-center fielder Tris Speaker grabbed seven. First baseman George Burns had 18 putouts.

Willis Hudlin, 94, of Little Rock, Ark., is one of the few people still alive who saw Levsen work the games that put him into the record book. Hudlin was a rookie pitcher with the Indians at the time.

"There was a lot of excitement," Hudlin recalled. "He knew how to pitch. His best pitch was a fastball, as I remember. But he pitched more than he should have. He put a pretty good strain on his arm."

The victories gave the 6-foot Levsen a 14-9 record. He finished with a 16-13 mark, including 18 complete games. It was his only winning season. He slipped to 3-7 the next year and to 0-3 in 1928 before retiring at age 30. His career mark was a mere 21-26.

Asked if Levsen's effort against the Red Sox ruined a career, Hudlin said, "The human arm is not made to pitch doubleheaders."

Levsen's accomplishment came with the Indians fighting for a pennant. They were in second place behind the New York Yankees of Babe Ruth and Lou Gehrig and would wind up in the runner-up spot, three games back.

The Indians featured future Hall of Famers Speaker and shortstop Joe Sewell. Burns was the American League's MVP that year, hitting .358 and rapping 64 doubles. Pitcher George Uhle led the league with 27 victories.

The doubleheader marathon was completely unplanned. In an interview with the Cleveland News 31 years later, Levsen recalled he was having such an easy time in the seventh inning of the first game that Burns yelled, "Dutch, you've got a cinch. Why don't you work the second game?"

Then Sewell shouted, "We're short of pitching, Dutch. You can help us catch the Yanks."

Showering after the opening win, several players urged Levsen, "Take a rubdown, flex your muscles and get back in there." His back was a bit sore, but he was game.

Levsen asked Speaker what he thought. "Go to it, Dutch," the Grey Eagle said. "I know you can do it."

"I was never pressed at any time and wasn't even tired after the second game," Levsen said. He had not expected to finish the night-cap but things went so smoothly he just kept going. There is no record of his pitch count, a statistic which wasn't a concern in dugouts those days.

Levsen's double duty gave Uhle, who worked 318 innings and had 32 complete games that year, an extra day of rest.

"No one will win two again," Levsen said in a 1951 interview. "No manager would allow a pitcher to try it. Pitchers in my day didn't monkey around like they do now, with screwballs, sliders and knuckleballs. There were more hard throwers in my time."

Levsen's arm went dead in spring training the next year, but he always maintained the marathon was not the cause. "I pitched fine after the doubleheader," he said. "I held the Yankees to two hits in one game. Spring training was just too much."

After retiring from baseball, the Iowa State graduate ran an ice cream and butter store in Cedar Rapids, Iowa, for about 20 years. Later, he sold life insurance and got a civil service job with the Department of Agriculture in Cincinnati. At age 73, he died on March 12, 1972, while living in a Minneapolis suburb.

"My theory is that a professional in any sport should have one lucky afternoon and I had it," he told the Minneapolis Star a few years before his death. "I still take great pride in that achievement."

The Tribe's Talented Tempest

WES FERRELL *Aug. 21, 2002*

Wes Ferrell, one of the most fascinating Indians ever, accomplished feats that are unequaled in baseball history. When you look at the way he started out, it is almost unbelievable that this Grade A character did not go on to reside in the Baseball Hall of Fame.

The strapping right-handed pitcher set a major-league record that still stands by winning at least 20 games in each of his first four full seasons, from 1929 to 1932. He was only 24 when he reached the quadruple.

Besides that, he was one of the finest hitting pitchers of all time. He rapped more home runs in his career (37) than any other hurler and hit as high as .319 in a season.

When he pitched a no-hitter for Cleveland in 1931, beating St. Louis, 9-0, he also batted in four runs with a homer and double. He hit nine homers that year, a big league record for pitchers.

But Ferrell left baseball as a classic head case, a man who could not control his emotions in his hunger to win. Trouble was as much a part of his body as his powerful right arm. Former teammate Billy Werber recalled Ferrell in remarks to the Internet's Baseball Library.

"Wes was a marvelous character," said the old third baseman. "I've seen him hit himself in the jaw with both fists and nearly knock himself out after being removed from a ballgame. He'd jump in the air and crunch the face of an expensive watch or tear cards to pieces because he wasn't getting good hands. He hated to lose at anything. He was a determined competitor, the kind you like to have on your side."

Ferrell feuded with owners, managers and umpires. Evidently he had trouble with the press, too. When he won his 20th for the fourth straight year on Aug. 21, 1932, 70 years ago today, a Cleveland writer went out of his way to subtly rap him, saying he hurled like the "great pitcher he is supposed to be."

Nine days after that victory, manager Roger Peckinpaugh suspended him for insubordination. Ferrell balked at leaving the mound when Peckinpaugh waved him off in the first inning after the Red Sox scored two runs on three hits and a walk.

Plain Dealer baseball writer Gordon Cobbledick said Ferrell jerked off his cap, pawed the dirt in fury and generally acted like a child deprived of his candy. Under an eight-column, Page One headline, another story said Ferrell, breathing invective, finally walked toward the bench and reportedly made heated remarks to Peckinpaugh, trying to show him up.

The account said his actions climaxed a series of episodes in which Ferrell tried to make it seem he was bigger than the rest of the club.

Peckinpaugh suspended him for 10 days, costing him $1,500. Ferrell was not quiet about it.

"Peckinpaugh gave me a raw deal and I'm not going to forget it," he said. "I don't care about pitching for him anymore." He came back to finish with a 23-13 record, but he and Peckinpaugh tumbled together into disaster in 1933, when Ferrell had his first bad year, going 11-12. Peckinpaugh was fired in midseason.

Ferrell rebelled again in the spring of 1934. He held out and missed all of spring training and the early part of the season, staying home in Guilford, S.C.

Ferrell twice sent back a contract that would pay him close to $12,000 if he won 20 games. The Indians suspended him and finally traded him and Dick Porter to the Red Sox on May 25, 1934, getting Bob Seeds, Bob Weiland and $25,000 in return. It was a poor deal for the Indians. Ferrell went 14-5 in Boston the rest of the year and then 25-14 in 1935.

His psyche was unchanged, however. Red Sox shortstop/manager Joe Cronin suspended him indefinitely on Aug. 21, 1936, when Ferrell left the game during a New York Yankees rally in the sixth inning. Ferrell was apparently furious because opposing pitcher Monte Pearson singled in two runs. Ferrell walked off the hill, marched through the Yankees dugout and went into the Red Sox clubhouse as players gaped. It was the second time in five days he deserted the mound.

Cronin said Ferrell had pitched his last game for the Red Sox. "I don't care if I never see him again," the manager said. "I don't care whether he goes back to Boston, North Carolina or the Fiji Islands. I'm through with him."

Ferrell was in his hotel room when writers told him he had been suspended again.

"Is that so?" he exclaimed. "Well, that isn't the end of this. I'm going to punch Cronin in the jaw soon as I can find him."

Tempers cooled after Ferrell met with Cronin and owner Tom Yawkey. The suspension was lifted after four days and Ferrell finished with a 20-15 mark.

At that point, he was still only 28 and had already won 20 six times in eight years. He appeared to be headed toward the Valhalla that only the supreme pitchers reach. But a sore arm suddenly ruined his career. His burning fastball gave way to slow curves.

He drifted to three more teams, fighting his way to a 15-10 mark in 1938 with Washington and the Yankees. But he won only three more games in his final three seasons, finishing at 193 wins and 128 losses, for a fine .601 percentage.

After his pitching career ended at 33, he went back to the minors as an outfielder. His temper remained. As a minor-league manager he was suspended for hitting an umpire and removing his team from the field, a rebel to the end.

A Terror with a Bat but a Favorite with the Fans

Joe Vosmik *Apr. 4, 1998*

William Hudec of Maple Heights was visiting his father's grave in Highland Cemetery last year. As he and his grandchildren stepped away, he noticed a nearby gravestone bearing the name of Joe Vosmik, the star outfielder for the Indians in the 1930s.

"When I saw it, I remembered all the stories my dad used to tell me about Vosmik's ballplaying," said Hudec, 57, a retired Ohio Department of Transportation employee. "The gravestone had a bat, ball and glove inscribed on it. I got caught up in his story."

Hudec began reading everything he could about Vosmik and visited baseball card shows, buying the old player's cards. He wrote a poem about him and assembled statistics of his career. He put much of the memorabilia on a laminated poster.

Today would have been Vosmik's 88th birthday, and in honor of the day, Hudec gave the poster to the ballplayer's widow, Sally Vosmik Beatty, 85, of Willoughby.

"It's absolutely fantastic, very lovely and original," Sally said. "It has a lot of work in it. Joe would have been happy."

Vosmik was one of the finest ballplayers ever born in Cleveland. The highlight of his career came in 1935, when he led the American League in triples (20), doubles (47) and hits (216). He drove in 110 runs and missed winning the batting championship by a point.

The right-handed hitter went into the final day of the season with a three-point lead over Washington's Buddy Myer in the batting race. The Indians played a doubleheader in League Park on the last day and Vosmik sat out the first game and the beginning of the second. When word came that Myer had made four hits to jump into the batting lead, Vosmik was put into the second game. He lined out in his first at-bat, bunted safely in his second and was thrown out on another bunt in his last chance.

Myer won the crown, .349 to .348.

The Indians gave Vosmik a three-year contract at $15,000 a season in appreciation of his outstanding work in 1935.

The twice-widowed Sally, who married architect Hamilton Beatty 20 years after Vosmik's death, has glowing memories of her time as a baseball wife. She recalls the black-tie parties and friendships with people such as Babe Ruth, Earl Averill, Jimmy Foxx and Lefty Grove, who was the godfather to one of the Vosmiks' three children. She still watches Indians games on television and enjoys going to Jacobs Field.

Sally, whose maiden name was Okla, first met Vosmik in a neighborhood drugstore when she was in high school. "Joe would sit on our porch and talk to me and my parents," she remembered. "He was quite a handsome guy. He had those big dimples when he smiled. People were always saying he looked like James Cagney."

Vosmik would sing the Irving Berlin song, "Always," to Sally on their dates. They married in 1936, after a seven-year courtship.

According to the old clippings, Vosmik's good looks were partly responsible for his start in professional baseball. He was playing for the Rotbart Jewelers in a sandlot all-star game in League Park and Indians General Manager Billy Evans was in attendance. He had promised to take the three best players to spring training in 1929. Evans asked his wife which players she liked. "I like that good-looking blond Viking," she replied, referring to Vosmik.

The Indians sent Vosmik to Frederick, Md., of the Blue Ridge League, where he hit .381. In 1930 he was promoted to Terre Haute, Ind., of the Three-I League, hitting .397. Coaches cured him of his lifelong habit of running on his heels.

Vosmik, a Czech-American who grew up in the Broadway-E. 55th St. area and went to East Tech, hit .320, with seven homers and 117 RBI, in his rookie year of 1931. He is one of the few players to get 100 RBI on less than 10 homers, meaning he was an excellent clutch hitter. One of the highlights of Vosmik's career came in the 1935 All-Star Game in the Stadium, when he was given a two-minute standing ovation when introduced in the starting lineup.

When the popular Vosmik was traded to the St. Louis Browns in 1937, The Plain Dealer carried the story in an eight-column headline across the top of Page One. Angry fans threatened to boycott Indians games because of the trade.

Vosmik hit .287 with 94 RBI in his last year in Cleveland. "Joe wanted to stay in Cleveland but he took the trade in stride," recalled Sally. "He said it was just a part of baseball. He never refused a child an autograph. He never let his success affect him."

The Plain Dealer editorialized, "If you couldn't get along with Vosmik, you couldn't get along with anybody." Vosmik had a big year in St. Louis, hitting .325, then was traded to Boston with its handy left-field fence. "He'll win the batting championship here," said a Boston coach. "He's got a perfect swing." Vosmik didn't quite do that, but he led the league with 201 hits and batted .324 in 1938. He finished his career in 1945 with a career .307 batting average.

After his playing days were over, he successfully managed Indians farm teams at Dayton, Oklahoma City and Tucson, Ariz. Vosmik has been inducted into the Cleveland and Ohio sports halls of fame. He died at 51 of lung cancer on Jan. 27, 1962.

A Man of Talent, Consistency, Class

Earl Averill *Aug. 7, 1996*

The Indians had an off day June 26, 1935, so players Earl Averill, Mel Harder, Joe Vosmik, Odell Hale and Willis Hudlin took their wives and children on a picnic in Orange Township.

Everybody was having a good time. Between the food and pop, Averill, 33, was happily tossing firecrackers with his four sons.

Then his brilliant career almost ended.

"Earl threw a firecracker that didn't go off," Harder recalled. "When he picked it up, it exploded."

The blast tore the flesh off the fingers of Averill's right hand and palm and severely burned his forehead and chest. The picknickers were screaming and crying.

"Vosmik and I put him in a car and took him to St. Luke's Hospital," Harder said. "It looked bad. There was a lot of blood."

Averill was stitched up for hours and missed the next six weeks of the season, including the All-Star Game, in which he was a perennial participant. Then he came back and finished with a .288 average and 19 homers, his worst season with the Tribe.

That was the only blip on a consistently smooth career that put Averill in the Hall of Fame in 1975.

An immensely popular player in his time, the late centerfielder is mostly forgotten or unknown by a new generation of baseball fans. Now he is back in the news because Albert Belle recently broke his club record of 226 home runs, which had stood for 57 years.

"He wouldn't have been upset about losing the record," Harder said. "He was a real nice guy who always enjoyed what he was doing. Everybody got along with him. He was always ready to do somebody a favor. He would always sign autographs. The fans were nuts about him."

Lillian Hanna Hudlin, a Cleveland native who married Hudlin's brother and has lived in Tulsa, Okla., for many years, said: "Earl was one of my favorite players. He was such a good sport, very well-dressed and good-looking, too."

Although Averill is No. 2 in Cleveland homers, he is still the team's career leader in runs batted in, extra-base hits, triples, total bases and runs.

In most of those departments, there are no active players close to him. He leads Belle by 377 RBI and 557 runs and has 80 more triples than Kenny Lofton.

The left-handed hitter specialized in banging the baseball against League Park's right-field wall, which was 290 feet down the line. In 11 years with the Indians, from 1929 through 1939, he batted .322, hitting more than 30 homers three times.

"When he hit the ball, it looked like a golf ball," said former pitcher Harder, 86, who won 223 games for the Indians. "He'd hit them in any park. League Park wasn't that easy for homers because of the 40-foot wall. He hit a lot of liners against the wall that would have been homers somewhere else."

"He was what we called a swing hitter," said ex-pitcher Hudlin, 90, the oldest living former Indians player, who lives in Little Rock, Ark., and won 158 games for the team. "He swung the bat like a broom, didn't use much wrist. There were very few who hit like that."

Averill did not look like a power hitter. At 5-9 and 172 pounds, he was on the small side.

General Manager Billy Evans had bought Averill from the San Francisco Seals of the Pacific Coast League for the then exorbitant price of $50,000. When Indians owner Alva Bradley saw him, he said to Evans: "You paid all that money for a midget."

Evans said: "Wait until you see him with his shirt off."

Averill, nicknamed "The Rock," had the powerful shoulders of a logger, which was one of his jobs in his hometown of Snohomish, Wash. He swung a 44-ounce bat.

Because of his high price-tag, Averill was on the spot when he joined the Indians at the age of 27. He had played semi-pro ball until 1926 before joining the Seals for three years, where he burned up the PCL. "Everybody expected a lot out of him," said Harder, his old roommate.

Averill did not disappoint, hitting a home run off Detroit lefty Earl Whitehill in his first major-league at-bat and going on to a .319 average his first year.

He just kept rolling along after that. In 1930, he hit four homers in a doubleheader against Washington and drove in 11 runs. In 1932, fearful Boston Red Sox pitchers walked him five straight times in a game.

He was picked for every All-Star Game from the inaugural contest in 1933 to 1938. His best season was 1936, when he hit .378, with a league-leading 232 hits and 126 RBI. "He was a real good centerfielder, too," Harder said. "He could cover a lot of ground and had a good arm."

The closest Averill came to controversy was when one of his homers flew over the League Park wall and hit a woman sitting in her rocking chair on the porch of her home on Lexington Ave. The irate woman sued, saying she was knocked off her rocker. Nothing came of the suit.

Nationally, his most-remembered hit came in the 1937 All-Star Game, when his liner hit the big toe of pitcher Dizzy Dean, starting the demise of the brilliant hurler. Dean tried to come back too soon, hurting his arm because he used an unnatural motion to favor the sore toe.

Clevelander Al Milnar, 82, another former Tribe pitcher of the era, recalled getting hit on the calf by an Averill liner while pitching batting practice. "He had great timing, and it was his nature to hit through the middle," Milnar said. "He apologized. He was good to young players."

Averill was thrown out of a game once, when he told an umpire in St. Louis: "I could whittle better decisions out of a stick than the ones you're making today."

He and his family lived for years in an eight-room house at 3441 Washington Blvd., Cleveland Heights, which he bought for $12,000. His top salary was $16,000, less than some players make in a game today.

In 1938, Earl Averill Day was held in the Stadium in front of about 37,000 fans. Averill received a $2,400 Cadillac and sat on its fender as it rode around the cinder track. When it passed in front of the Boston dugout, he made a deep bow, whereupon the Red Sox threw out towels in his honor.

He wound up his career with Detroit and the Boston Braves in 1940-41, then retired to Snohomish, where he worked as a motel owner and florist. Since boyhood, he was an expert on soil and flowers, especially snapdragons.

He and his wife, Loette, were married for 62 years. They originally wanted to be married when he was 17 and she was 16, but the court turned them down as being too young. Two years later, they were wed.

Life was quiet for the Averills after baseball, although one of their sons, Earl Jr., played for seven years in the major leagues. The action picked up after Averill was chosen for the Hall of Fame in 1975 by the Old-Timers Committee, when he was 73.

Then he started getting 30 to 40 letters a day requesting autographs. He always responded, even if the person did not send a self-addressed, stamped envelope.

Averill died Aug. 17, 1983, of pneumonia. He was 81.

A Hitter Retired by Pain

HAL TROSKY *Sep. 24, 1996*

Hal Trosky is one of those baseball players from long ago who has been reduced to numbers.

Casual fans never heard of him. More involved students of the game remember him as a faceless Indians slugger in the 1930s. Mostly, he is forgotten.

Lately, Trosky's name has been popping up more often in the sports pages because of the fine years Indians Jim Thome and Albert Belle are having.

One baseball writer said that Thome is producing the best Indians season by a left-handed hitter since Trosky's monster 1936 season, when he made League Park's right-field wall sing to the tune of a .342 average, 42 home runs and 162 runs batted in. Belle is on the verge of driving in more runs in a season than any Tribe hitter except Trosky in 1936.

But the Trosky story goes far beyond numbers. The first baseman was one of the most tragic figures in Cleveland baseball history.

Few hitters started out as fast as he did. He drove in more than 100 runs in each of his first six seasons with the Indians, usually averaging better than .300. A 1936 Plain Dealer story called him the best left-handed hitter to break into the American League since Lou Gehrig.

But his career came crashing down because of migraine headaches that tortured Trosky and forced his retirement at age 28. "He had those headaches every day of his life from the time he was 16," said his son, Hal Jr., 60, who has an insurance agency in Cedar Rapids, Iowa.

"I don't know how he played. They were pounding headaches, head-splitting. The Indians tried everything to help him. They sent him to every clinic and hospital.

"For years and years, people sent in cures to try to help him. We heard all the old wives' tales. He tried molasses and vinegar. Nothing helped."

Mel Harder, 87, one of Trosky's teammates, said: "He'd lie down in the trainer's room and then go out and play. It's a shame he had those headaches. He was a really nice person, a good family man, a good hustler and not a bad fielder. Lord knows how far he would have gone in baseball if it wasn't for the headaches."

"He kept it to himself," said Willis Hudlin, 90, the oldest living former Indians player. "He was a happy-go-lucky guy."

Migraines affect the vision. One day, when there was a runner on first base, Trosky asked Harder, who was pitching, not to throw to first to hold on the runner. "I'm afraid I won't see the ball," Trosky said.

"Dad's career ended when a pitcher threw a fastball an inch

under his chin and he never moved," Hal Jr. said. "The umpire told him the ball almost hit him. Dad dropped his bat and walked off the field." That was in 1941.

"A fellow can't go on like this forever," Trosky said, speaking of the headache pain. "If I can't find some relief, I'll have to give up and spend the rest of my days on my farm in Iowa." He said the headaches lessened in intensity when he was away from baseball during the winter.

Trosky briefly attempted comebacks with the Chicago White Sox in 1944 and 1946, then hung 'em up for good. He finished his career with 228 homers and 1,012 RBI.

His son said Trosky found a migraine cure in the 1950s, when he gave up dairy products and chewing tobacco. "He was allergic to them," the younger Trosky said. "After that, he was much better. He was a farmer all his life, but then he sold the farm and sold rural real estate the rest of his life. He spent his time among the people he knew and liked best. He was a friendly, outgoing man."

He also scouted for the White Sox for about a decade.

Trosky's Cleveland career was marked by a controversy. In 1940, he was perceived as the ringleader of the Indians' rebellion against hated manager Oscar Vitt. A large group of Indians players went to see club owner Alva Bradley in his office in the Marion Building on W. 3rd St. and asked him to fire Vitt.

When news of the story broke, the Indians were ridiculed throughout baseball for the rest of the season as the "Cleveland Cry Babies." When they played in Detroit, Tigers fans put baby bottles on top of their dugout roof and wheeled a baby buggy onto the field. Trosky missed the meeting with Bradley to attend his mother's funeral, but when he came back to the Indians the next day, he was greeted with boos.

"The biggest shock of my life was coming into the ballpark and hearing myself practically getting booed out of the Stadium," Trosky said. "This is one of the saddest days of my life. They've got me down." That was the first season Trosky failed to reach 100 RBI, winding up with 93.

Cleveland News writer Ed McAuley called Trosky "the most sensitive athlete I have ever known." McAuley recalled an occasion in which Trosky quoted verbatim a facetious comment on his fielding that appeared in his column five years earlier.

Franklin Lewis, the aggressive Cleveland Press sports columnist, called Trosky "a worry wart who cannot give his best efforts when upset." Lewis said Trosky worried too much about world affairs and "became a neurotic who was caught between a mental fog and a physical bog."

During the "Cry Baby" storm, when he was getting booed throughout the league, Trosky called writers into the dugout to deny he was the leader of the rebellion.

The Vitt affair was far out of character for Trosky, a man once described by a writer as a person "so easy to get along with it ought to be practically illegal to have trouble with him."

Trosky's original name was Troyavesky, a mixture of Polish, German and Bohemian. The 6-2, 200-pound blond grew up in the village of Norway, Iowa, where he won the high school's popularity contest. He and his wife, Lorraine, went to school together starting in kindergarten. She watched him play marbles and they waded together in Prairie Creek. Trosky, a saxaphonist, and Lorraine, a pianist, played musical duets such as "Sleepy Time Down South," "Good Night, Sweetheart," and "Nola."

They didn't date until they were 18, when they went to see a Johnny Mack Brown movie. They also would drive 30 miles to see University of Iowa basketball games.

When they were married in 1933, Norway's entire population of 300 was at the reception.

Trosky became a Cleveland sensation in his rookie year of 1934, when he hit .330 with 35 homers. He was paid $3,000 that year. "I've always been the low-salary man on every club I've been with," Trosky said. "Some of the fellows think I'm tight because I don't spend money like they do, but I just haven't got it to spend."

The old Cleveland News, in a feature article, called him "one of the handsomest athletes who ever broke into the American League." The article continued, noting his symmetrical build: "He looks like a hero of the Tarzan type." Another story said he looked like movie star Errol Flynn.

His nicknames were "Prince Hal," "Handsome Hal," and "Hoot." As a rookie, he got some advice from Babe Ruth. Trosky was holding the New York Yankees star on first base with Gehrig at bat. "You better go back to the grass, kid," Ruth said. "This guy hits the ball pretty hard."

Trosky continued to hold Ruth on, whereupon Gehrig lined a ball chest high at the first baseman. He managed to get a glove on it, but the force of the ball tore his glove off, and the ball landed down the right-field line. Ruth went to third and then made a laughing gesture to Trosky, as if to say, "I told you so."

When his son, Hal, was born in Shaker Heights in 1936, Trosky was asked if he would like him to become a ballplayer. "The little guy can become anything he darn pleases," Trosky said. "If you haven't the natural ability to play baseball, it doesn't matter if you want to or not."

Hal Jr. did become a ballplayer, making it to the White Sox as a pitcher for one game in 1958.

Another son, 14-month-old Jim, was operated on at Babies and Childrens Hospital in Cleveland to recover a piece of bacon that had lodged in his lung. The bacon had gone down his windpipe, rather than the esophagus. The operation was successful. (Jim is now a pilot.)

When Trosky had his banner year in 1936, he was paid $7,500. At the time of his retirement, he was up to $19,000, second on the team only to Feller.

As skilled as he was, Trosky never made the American League All-Star team. That was because his first-base competition was comprised of Hall of Famers Gehrig, Jimmie Foxx and Hank Greenberg. Trosky, irked that he was never selected for the All-Star teams by Yankees manager Joe McCarthy, always drove hard to do well against New York.

"It was tragic he had to stop playing," said his son, Hal Jr. "His best years were ahead of him. But he never looked back. Back then, you just felt lucky to have played the game." Trosky died June 18, 1979, from a heart attack at age 66. Lorraine, 84, lives in an assisted-care center in Cedar Rapids.

Though Only 17, He Was Ready to Pitch

BOB FELLER *Aug. 23, 1996*

The 1930s were a great time for teenage celebrities. The movies had Shirley Temple, Judy Garland, Mickey Rooney and Deanna Durbin. Radio had Bobby Breen.

Baseball's adolescent marvel was the Indians' Bob Feller, the most precocious pitcher in major-league baseball history. Using a frightening fastball and a violent curve, Feller had 107 victories by age 22, including three straight years when he averaged 25 wins a season.

He created a sensation in his first major-league start, when he was 17 years old. Rapid Robert dominated the St. Louis Browns, striking out 15 and throwing a six-hitter for a 4-1 victory in League Park on Aug. 23, 1936. Today is the 60th anniversary of that game.

Feller had already shown himself capable of handling major-leaguers when he struck out eight St. Louis Cardinals in a three-inning exhibition game stint on July 6 that year. Nevertheless, Indians manager Steve O'Neill played it safe as Feller stepped to the mound to face the Browns, sending Denny Galehouse to the bullpen to warm up simultaneously.

O'Neill's conservatism was understandable. Feller was still a high school student, having completed the 11th grade in his hometown of Van Meter, Iowa, only a couple of months earlier. In another month he would be going back to school for his senior year. Feller had done well in brief relief appearances with the Indians since his mugging of the Cardinals in that exhibition, but he was still wild. And the fatherly O'Neill could not forget he was 17. Feller soon ended O'Neill's fears. Hurling to young catcher Charley "Greek" George, he struck out the side in the first inning, getting Lyn Lary, Moose Solters and Beau Bell.

Galehouse sat down and never got up again. Feller struck out Lary and Solters three times each, got Sam West and Ollie Bejma twice apiece and Bell, Jim Bottomley, Angelo Giuliani, Ed Coleman and opposing pitcher Earl Caldwell once. He just missed tying Rube Waddell's American League record of 16 strikeouts.

The Plain Dealer put the story of the chubby-cheeked Feller's effort on the top of Page One and called it "the greatest pitching debut in big league history."

"I knew Dizzy Dean had the major-league record of 17 strikeouts," Feller said after the game. "I didn't know what the AL record was, but it wouldn't have made any difference because I gave it all I had.

"I was worried my arm would tire around the sixth or seventh inning, but it held up fine."

After the game Feller was besieged by autograph seekers, then went to a movie with his roommate, center fielder Roy "Thunder" Weatherly. "He was mobbed by fans wherever he went," The Plain Dealer reported.

Feller showed no signs of tension in the game. But that was not true of his patron, Indians General Manager Cy Slapnicka, the man who signed him and brought him to the Tribe before he pitched a day in the minor leagues.

"I was so worried I must have lost five pounds watching the boy," Slapnicka said. "But I feel great now."

Sixty years later, Hall of Famer Feller recalls: "I was never really nervous in a game. I knew if I got hit I'd get them next time. It didn't bother me that Galehouse was warming up. I remember the crowd [about 10,000] was behind me, but I really didn't hear anything. The main thing I was trying to show was that Slapnicka was right." Feller, 77, could not recall if his teammates gave him extra encouragement because of his youth, but said, "They were happy I won. Hal Trosky [first baseman and a fellow Iowan] was always a big booster of mine. He'd say, 'Just get the ball over the plate.' Greek George was a good, smart catcher. He'd come to the mound and talk. And the umpires were usually behind me. I remember Red Ormsby, when he was in the infield, would say, 'This guy can't hit. Just put it over.'"

Giuliani, 83, who was the catcher for the Browns and had one single that long-ago day, recalled the speed and power of the young Feller. "He could throw the ball 100 miles per hour consistently," said Giuliani from his home in St. Paul, Minn. "He had a high leg kick and his performance was awesome for a kid that age." Feller had an even more spectacular effort later in his rookie season, tying the major-league record with 17 strikeouts in a 5-2 victory over Philadelphia on Sept. 13, 1936. He was still 17.

After the season he went back to high school in Van Meter as a bona fide celebrity. He says his old schoolmates treated him no differently. "The only difference was I couldn't play high school basketball anymore because I was a professional." Feller attended school until it was time to go to spring training in New Orleans. A tutor accompanied him and he was able to get his high school diploma. Then there was no stopping him on the way to the Hall of Fame, except for the four-year detour that took him into the Navy during World War II at the peak of his career. He wound up with a 266-162 record. It is reasonable to estimate he might have had another 80 were it not for the war.

One of Baseball's All-Time Screwballs

JOHNNY ALLEN *Jul. 9, 1978*

Forty-one years after his sensational 1937 season with the Indians and 19 years after his death, Johnny Allen, one of baseball's all-time screwballs, is back in the news.

The spectacular performance of lefty Ron Guidry, who won 13 straight games for the New York Yankees before losing for the first time Friday, has baseball buffs reminiscing about the stunning 15-1 season Allen put together for the '37 Indians.

Allen, a right-hander with a flaming fastball and temper to match, won his first 15 games that summer before losing on the last day of the campaign. His resulting .938 percentage remains the best in American League history.

Allen won his 15th game on the final Thursday of the season, beating Chicago, 6-4. Then he came back with two days of rest, on Sunday, to try for his 16th straight.

A crowd of 21,500 came to old Briggs Stadium to watch Allen bid to go into the record books. But he lost, 1-0, when an undistinguished southpaw, Whistling Jake Wade, chose that day to throw a one-hitter. It was one of only 27 games Wade won in eight years in the majors.

Allen hurled a tidy five-hitter and surrendered the only run in the first inning, after Pete Fox doubled to the right field corner with one out. Charley Gehringer, who won the batting championship that year with a .371 average, popped to Odell Hale, but Hank Greenberg singled to left for the run. It was High Hank's 183d run batted in, one short of Lou Gehrig's league record.

The Indians' only chance to win came in the seventh inning, when Lyn Lary walked and Hal Trosky grounded a single over second base. With two out, Julius Solters was hit by a pitch, but then Bruce Campbell lined to Gee Walker in left.

The time of the game was one hour, 35 minutes. The Plain Dealer reported that the crowd gave ovations to Allen and Wade throughout the contest.

The loss kept Allen from tying the league mark of 16 straight victories in a season, which is held by Walter Johnson, Lefty Grove, Schoolboy Rowe and Smokey Joe Wood. The National League record for a season is 19 straight, held by Rube Marquard of the 1912 New York Giants.

However, Allen's 17 consecutive triumphs in 1936-37 are still a league record, matched only by Baltimore's Dave McNally in 1968-69. The NL mark is 24 in a row, by Carl Hubbell of the Giants, also in 1936-37.

Allen's work in '37 is all the more remarkable because he suffered from appendicitis much of the year. The illness caused him to miss a month of pitching at the start of the season.

Then, on June 19, when his record was 4-0, he underwent an emergency appendectomy. "He will be out for two months and will probably be of little value to the team for the rest of the season," wrote Gordon Cobbledick, then Plain Dealer baseball writer.

But Allen came back in a month, roaring.

Allen's remarks following his 1-0 loss to Detroit in that historic '37 finale have been lost to posterity. But it can safely be assumed they were furiously unprintable. He never lost a game. Someone else always lost it for him."

Maybe the fiery Allen had something there. In 12 tumultuous years in the majors, he won 142 games and lost only 75. His 1938 salary of $20,000 was the highest paid to any pitcher save Hubbell, who was getting $24,000.

But as good as he was on the mound, he was known more for his escapades. He battled umpires, teammates, managers and sportswriters. He was especially critical of the men in blue. "There ain't any of them blankety-blanks that's any good," he said.

In his first year with the Indians, on June 4, 1936, Allen was fined $250 by manager Steve O'Neill after a 1-0 loss to Boston's Wes Ferrell. After the game Allen was in a typically boisterous mood in the Brunswick Hotel, rapping teammates and Cleveland sportswriters.

He climaxed the evening by throwing a ladder down a corridor, damaging wall plaster with a swinging lantern, and tossing a fire extinguisher at the wine steward.

The most famous of his adventures happened on June 7, 1938, also in Boston. The Red Sox protested that he was pitching with a tattered shirt sleeve and umpire Bill McGowan ordered him to change his sweatshirt.

Allen refused and walked straight to the clubhouse. He never came out. Manager Oscar Vitt went in to find him. The furious Allen informed him he would pitch no more that day, whereupon Vitt fined him $250.

Allen insisted he would never pitch again if he couldn't wear the shirt, which he had been using all year. But league officials were just as insistent that the torn sleeve interfered with batters' vision.

Alva Bradley, the Indians' owner, came to the rescue. He told Allen that the Higbee Co. wanted to buy his shirt and put it on display.

"Okay," said the mercenary Allen. "But let me see a check first." Bradley paid him $250 for the shirt, exactly the amount Allen had been fined.

The solution was perfect. The Higbee people were happy because people were flocking to their store to see the famed garment. The Indians were happy because they had their ace back. And Allen was happy because he had defied the establishment and gotten away with it.

Later that year Allen came up with a sore arm and had to have an operation. That finished him as a great pitcher, but he stuck around the majors through 1944, remaining as irascible as ever.

After his playing days were over he joined his old enemies and became, of all things, an umpire. He never advanced beyond the low minors, but ballplayers said that he wasn't particularly quarrelsome. He died on March 20, 1959, at age 53.

A Star Who Fared, Then Faded

JEFF HEATH *May 1, 2001*

It was impossible to ignore Jeff Heath. He was the kind of ballplayer who was always in the news.

The left fielder, recently named one of the 100 greatest Indians players, had two wildly successful seasons with the bat, putting up the kind of numbers that bring Cooperstown to mind. He was built like Hercules. He could scare a catcher when he came speeding home with the winning run and he excelled at holding out and calling management cheap.

But he was popular with his teammates and the press, especially when he was hitting.

Memory recalls a spring training photo from the 1940s in which Heath is swimming on his back, merrily spewing a stream of water out of his mouth in the pose of a human fountain.

Heath was always good for spring training stories. In 1940 in Fort Myers, Fla., he offered teammate Joe Krakauskas $5 if he would jump into the swimming pool with his suit on. Krakauskas immediately dove in. A reporter asked him how he could be so stupid. "I put one over on Heath," the pitcher replied. "It'll cost me only 50 cents to get the suit pressed. I'll be ahead $4.50."

Veteran Cleveland fan Alan Hart recalls Heath signing autographs for children after games and then taking a bunch for a ride in his convertible.

As one of the leaders of the Tribe's 1940 rebellion against hated manager Oscar Vitt, Heath took his share of abuse on the road, where fans put baby bottles on the Cleveland dugout and called the players crybabies.

A fan in Washington, getting into the act, threw a teddy bear at Heath on the field. Hart says Heath laughed, picked it up and hugged it.

But Heath had a hot temper. It was on display for two straight days in August 1939. Heath struck out against Boston's Denny Galehouse and threw his bat in frustration. It bounced 10 feet in the air and glanced off Cleveland Press editor Louis Seltzer, who was sitting in a front-row box. Umpire Bill McGowan threw Heath out of the game.

When the angry Heath came into the dugout, his best friend, pitcher Johnny Broaca, tried to calm him down. According to The Plain Dealer report that day, Heath said, "Mind your own business or I'll knock your block off."

Broaca, who had been on the boxing team at Yale University, removed his glasses and took up the challenge. A skirmish followed. "We had trouble breaking it up," recalled former teammate Harry Eisenstat, 85. "They really went at it."

The next day, after Heath left the tying run on base by fouling out in the ninth inning, a fan in the front row heckled him. Heath responded with a punch.

"It was just another blunder in a season full of mistakes," Heath said after the game. "He yelled at me, 'Why don't you throw your bat into the stands again?' I hurt my hand when I punched him."

At his peak, Heath could hit as well as anybody. In 1938, when he was 23, he hit .343, losing the batting title to Jimmy Foxx by six points. He led the league in triples with 18, hit 21 homers and drove in 112 runs. His slugging average of .602 trailed only Hall of Famers Foxx and Hank Greenberg, and beat Joe DiMaggio's .581.

"Heath had all the tools," recalled Lou Boudreau, 83, Heath's teammate and manager. "He was strong and fast."

But Heath slipped to .292 the next year and .219 in 1940 under the tyrannical Vitt, who believed Heath could be a superstar if he tried harder. This gave Heath a reputation as a loafer.

The Plain Dealer's Gordon Cobbledick, while acknowledging Heath's curious temperament, said he was the most misunderstood player in baseball. Cobbledick wrote that Heath, far from being lazy, would take batting practice for 35 minutes after a game.

In 1941, with Vitt gone, Heath stormed back and had a tremendous season. He was fourth in the league in hitting (.340), third in slugging (.586), second in total bases (343), second in RBI (123), second in hits (199), first in triples (20), and third in stolen bases (18). He became the first American Leaguer (George Brett is the other) to hit 20 doubles, triples and homers in the same season.

Ted Williams hit .406 and DiMaggio hit in 56 straight games that same year. Heath had more hits, triples and steals than both, and more RBI and total bases than Williams.

He never approached that kind of splendor again, although he hit .300 four more times. He retired in 1949 as a good, but not great, player.

Boudreau feels Heath never lived up to his potential. "He'd work hard, but he'd give up," Boudreau said. "He didn't have that drive. He couldn't make adjustments at the plate."

Hall of Famer Bob Feller, 82, who roomed with Heath, says the left fielder never took baseball, or life, seriously. "But he wasn't a carouser," Feller said. "He did not dissipate. He just didn't plan ahead."

In Eisenstat's view, Heath had trouble accepting failure. "If he'd go 0-for-4, he'd complain that the pitcher wasn't really that good," Eisenstat said. "He'd keep talking about it. I'd tell him to forget it. That was yesterday. When he had a bad day, he wasn't the nicest guy to be around."

Heath would never allow teammates to use his bats. "There are only so many hits in a bat," he would say.

He pounded League Park's 290-foot right-field wall in his biggest years, and could drive the ball into its roomy left-center field for triples.

Heath never liked the old Stadium, with its enormous outfield that stretched to 470 feet in dead center and 435 feet in the power alleys. He complained to Ed McAuley of the old Cleveland News that management should put up a fence to cut down the acreage. (Two years later, he was traded and the fence became a reality.)

After the 1945 season, when he hit .305, the Indians sent him to Washington for outfielder George Case, the reigning stolen-base king of baseball. Heath had one last hurrah with the National League champion Boston Braves of 1948, hitting .319 with 20 homers. He would have played against the Indians in the World Series that year, but he broke his leg on a slide into home in the final week of the season. He hit .306 in 36 games the next year before retiring at age 34.

In 1952, Franklin Lewis of the Cleveland Press, calling Heath one of his favorite characters, asked him if he would have done anything different in his career if he had it to do over. "I wouldn't gag around as much," Heath said. "I shouldn't have popped off. It's all right for the little guys to talk loud, but not a big ox like me."

Heath died in Seattle in 1975 at age 60 after a heart attack, his career a monument to what might have been.

Retired Indian Recalls an Era

AL MILNAR

Aug. 11, 1985

After the baseball strike and greed of last week, it was nice to visit the old player.

Al Milnar is a symbol of contrast between the modern athletes and those of the past. He never rode in a limousine. He never had an agent or received $44 a day in meal money.

The thought of striking when he played was as foreign as jumping over the 60-foot right field fence at old League Park.

Milnar was pretty good, winning 18 games for the Indians and making the All Star team in 1940.

But when he retired, he didn't get a $30,000-a-year pension to help him struggle through the rest of his life.

Instead, Milnar had to go to work, just like any normal person. For 22 years he was a security guard at Fisher Body. "It was a very good job," he says.

His salary was short of the $800,000 a year made by that troubled football star, Tony Dorsett. But he never went bankrupt, as Dorsett has. Life has been just fine for the 70-year-old left-hander.

For 27 years he and his wife, Anne, have lived in an impeccable brick house on the Euclid-Cleveland border. They raised their three children there. The plants and grass look as though they were groomed by a professional landscaper. "I like garden work, " Milnar says modestly.

He is tall with the muscular arms you sometimes see on a lean man. He doesn't say much, but he smiles a lot. He is a likable Gary Cooper type.

"He plays golf every Monday and Wednesday," says Anne. They have been married 47 years. "They go out at 8 in the morning and don't come back until 5. Sometimes they go all the way to Pennsylvania."

"I shoot about 90," says Milnar. "I like to walk. Sometimes we stop for a beer after. There's eight or 12 of us."

You suspect that he might be critical of the mercenary ballplayers for striking. But he isn't. "They're all doing it now," he shrugs, "even the teachers and police. Every athlete wants to get the most out of it."

Milnar's 14-12 and 18-10 seasons in 1939 and 1940 would have made him a millionaire today, but he holds no regrets. "We weren't smart enough to have agents," he laughed. His top salary was $12,500.

It is a trick of life that players get more money today, when it is generally agreed that baseball quality is down. In 1934 Milnar won 22 and lost 12 with New Orleans, the Indians' top farm team. The next year, he was even better, going 24-5.

"The Indians still wouldn't bring me up," he said. "Today they bring up a guy if he's 1-3."

Can you imagine how the Tribe would be salivating if it had a 24-5 hurler at Maine today?

Milnar started at Zanesville of the Mid-Atlantic League at $75 a month in 1933. His neighbors gave him a party in a huge hall when he departed. Frank Lausche, later to be Cleveland mayor, Ohio governor, and U.S. senator, spoke. Milnar was awarded a going-away gift of a 16 mm camera, which he still has.

Oh yes, he was an idol then. Next time you young folk feel sorry for an old-timer, remember that he might have had his glory days, too.

Milnar was born and raised on E. 39th St. and St. Clair, where his parents had a confectionery. His Yugoslavian-born father considered him a problem child because he was always playing ball, no matter how often he was spanked.

The memories come racing back as Milnar leafs through his scrapbook. He received a $200 bonus for defeating the Yankees, 2-1, in 11 innings. He scored the winning run, too, singling and coming home on a drive off the League Park wall by Hal Trosky. That couldn't happen in these imbecilic days of the designated hitter.

Once the high-kicking lefty had a no-hitter for eight and two-third innings against Detroit. Doc Cramer, a good singles hitter, broke it up.

"I read once that Phil Rizzuto said I was the first pitcher he ever saw throw a slider," recalled Milnar. Rizzuto is a former Yankee shortstop who is now a sportscaster.

"Phil is wrong," said Milnar. "If I ever see him, I want to tell him. Johnny Allen (his Indians teammate) taught me to throw a slider and he learned it from George Blaeholder. Everybody accused Allen of throwing spitters, but he was really throwing sliders. I know Rizzuto batted against Allen."

Milnar displayed a picture of Joe DiMaggio hitting a single against him at League Park in 1941. It was the final hit the Yankee Clipper got during his famous 56-game hitting streak. The next night he was stopped at the Stadium.

"I saw Joe a few years ago and told him I had that picture," said Milnar. "He told me he had the same one."

Milnar got up from the couch and went into another room. "Here's my pride and joy," he said. It was a bat from the 1940 All Star game, bearing the names of his distinguished teammates. Several of them are now in the Hall of Fame.

Milnar had a 57-58 lifetime record over eight years, but he can always say he once trod the field with the greatest players in baseball.

The grandfather of seven is one of the forgotten players. The Indians, the Wahoo Club and SMACO, the sports media organization, don't seem to know he's alive. They never invite him to their old-timers affairs.

"If they don't invite you, what can you do?" said Milnar. "They pass up me and Oscar Grimes (another old Tribesman) all the time. I would really have liked to go to that golf outing they had for Mike Garcia a few weeks ago."

Let's hope they remember Milnar next time. He gave a lot of people some warm memories.

Enshrinement Eludes Harder Again

MEL HARDER *Mar. 1, 2000*

It is 12:30 in the afternoon on what will turn out to be another countdown to disappointment for Mel Harder. The legendary Indians pitcher is sitting at a table in his condominium in Chardon, writing letters.

"I get stacks of mail," he says. "People ask me everything, like how I pitched to Babe Ruth."

From his demeanor, it is impossible to tell the importance of this day in Harder's life. In a few hours, he will learn if he has finally been elected to baseball's Hall of Fame by the 15-man Veterans Committee.

Dom DiMaggio, Bill Mazeroski and Gil Hodges are rumored to be Harder's chief rivals for induction.

"I hope I get picked," says Harder, 90, who had a 223-186 record for the Indians from 1928 to 1947. But he refuses to get his hopes too high. He has been hurt too many times before, even if he won't admit it.

"If I don't get in it'll be like losing a ball game," he says. "When I lost a game I didn't let it bother me. I handled it then and I'll handle it now.

"If I get in, it won't change me."

Ted Williams, the great Boston star, has been leading the drive to get Harder elected. "I feel pretty good about that," Harder says. "I knew Ted to say hello to, but that's about it. I had pretty good luck pitching to him."

The curveballer did even better against Joe DiMaggio. The Hall of Famer batted .140 against Harder in his career.

The old right-hander thinks back to 1928, when he joined the Indians as a 17-year-old youth who weighed only 140 pounds. The story is that the Indians told Harder to drink milk shakes to put on some weight, but he remembers it differently. "After games the players would go to a bootlegging place on Woodland Avenue," he recalled. "They always invited me along. I'd always have two beers. That and a few hamburgers got me up to 168 that first year."

Harder's memory drifts back to the great players of his time. He admired pitchers Ted Lyons, George Uhle and Herb Pennock, watching all their moves. "They were all smart," he says. He recalls that roommate Eddie Montague told him he would have to develop a curve if he was to make it in the big leagues. Harder listened. Soon, he was snapping off a good hook. He recalls his four All-Star game appearances, in which he did not give up a run in 13 innings. That makes him the most successful All-Star pitcher ever.

Harder remembers that he was a pretty good hitter for a pitcher. "I used to get five or six doubles a year," he says. "I hit four homers." He pulled everything to left.

At 1 p.m., the doorbell rings. It is Harder's next-door neighbor, Dorothy Gigliotti, who brings the widower soup. "Eat, eat," she says. "Sometimes I've got to poke him."

Harder is having some health problems. He has trouble moving around because his legs ache and he cannot eat solid food.

A few minutes later, Curtis Danburg of the Indians' publicity staff arrives. He is there to set up interviews for Harder's election. "When is the Hall of Fame induction?" Harder asks. "In July," Danburg says.

"Good," says Harder. "I've got a little time to heal up. Either that or I'll be twice as bad."

Shortly, there are six media people in the condo, along with Harder's grandson, Dan Itschner, a school principal. The group settles before the TV set in the living room to get the news, which is due around 2 p.m.

"Larry Dolan (new Indians owner) sat in this chair I'm in the other day," says Harder. "We had a good talk. I told him it was an honor to meet him. He said, 'It's an honor to meet you.'"

Harder and the media have a pleasant chat about baseball. It is easy to forget the Hall of Fame vote. Harder recalls that Walter Johnson, the great pitcher, was one of his favorite managers. He had his best years pitching under Johnson, winning 20 in 1934 and 22 in 1935. Finally, at 2:44, the phone rings. Everybody stops talking. The caller is a sportscaster who tells Danburg he heard Mel did not make the Hall. The news is relayed. Harder gives a nervous laugh and sits impassively, with no expression.

Danburg makes a call and comes back to say, "Nobody was elected. The votes were split."

Harder says with a laugh, "That's amazing. If they can't come to a decision, they should keep voting until they do."

True to his word, the old pitcher takes it like a losing ball game. "Well, next year, you never know," he says. "It's disappointing, but the more I think about it, I'm just lucky to be alive. I've been through too many rough things to worry about it."

The media people shake Harder's hand and offer condolences. "Sorry," says Harder. "The party's over." The visitors leave, each pondering how harsh life can be.

Postscript: Harder died on Oct. 20, 2002 at 93. He wore the Indians uniform as a pitcher and coach for 36 years, longer than anybody in team history.

"Tell Her I'm All Right"

RAY CHAPMAN *Aug. 4, 1995*

When Ray Chapman, 29, woke up on the morning of Aug. 16, 1920, he had just about everything a young man could want.

He was the accomplished shortstop of the first-place Cleveland Indians and one of the most popular players in the American League.

Less than a year earlier, he had married Kathleen Daly of Cleveland, whose father was the president of the East Ohio Gas Co. They were expecting their first child. Mr. Daly was having a splendid house built for the young couple in East Cleveland.

Eighteen hours later, Chapman was dead, killed by a pitch from Carl Mays of the New York Yankees that hit him on the left temple. He remains the only player in major league history to die from injuries suffered during a game.

Chapman's death was the central event of the Indians' march to the 1920 pennant and World Series victory over Brooklyn.

It was the first and most complex of the Indians' three pennants. It had elements of triumph, heartbreak and corruption that were not present on the Cleveland champions of 1948 and 1954.

The 1920 Indians were led by one of Cleveland's great sports heroes, center fielder and manager Tris Speaker, who hit .388, second in the league to George Sisler of St. Louis, who hit .407.

Only 32, Speaker was gray-haired and was called the Grey Eagle. Until the 1960s, when he was displaced by Willie Mays and Joe DiMaggio, Speaker was routinely placed in the all-time greatest outfield by sports writers, alongside Ty Cobb and Babe Ruth.

Other outstanding players on the club were pitchers Jim Bagby, Stan Coveleskie and Ray Caldwell, who combined for 75 victories;

third baseman Larry Gardner, who led the club in runs batted in; stalwart catcher Steve O'Neill, later an Indians manager; right fielder Elmer Smith, the cleanup hitter who had 12 home runs, most on the team, and second baseman Bill Wamby, who was to make the only unassisted triple play in World Series history that fall.

Chapman, who was hitting .303, was the team's best bunter and base stealer.

It was a hectic pennant race between the Indians, New York Yankees and the Chicago White Sox, who had thrown the World Series to gamblers the previous year, but had not yet been found out.

The Indians were on top, a half game ahead of the Yankees, when the two teams met in the Polo Grounds on the fatal day. They had a 3-0 lead when Chapman led off the fifth inning against Carl Mays, a submarine pitcher who had a reputation for knocking down hitters.

He threw a fastball that struck Chapman with such force that it bounced back to Mays. To some fans, it looked like a bunt. Players from both teams ran to his side.

The Plain Dealer reported that Chapman stood up, shrugged off assistance, and began to stagger toward the clubhouse in centerfield, flanked by two teammates. But when he approached second, his knees buckled and the teammates put their arms around his shoulders and carried him to the clubhouse.

Chapman asked for his wedding ring, which he had given to the trainer for safekeeping before the game, according to Mike Sowell's fine book, "The Pitch That Killed."

At St. Lawrence Hospital, barely able to talk, he said, "Don't call Kate. I don't want her to worry. But if you do, tell her I'm all right."

Those were his last words.

His skull was fractured, with the bone pressing against the brain. His pulse was down to 40. Doctors operated, beginning about 12:30 a.m. Chapman died about 4:40 a.m.

Kathleen Chapman, 26, arrived in New York that same morning. "I feared something would happen," she said. "We had been too happy and it couldn't last."

She went to Speaker's room in the Ansonia Hotel. Other players were there. Speaker, who had been the best man at their wedding, looked at her, unable to speak.

"He's dead, isn't he?" Kathleen said. Speaker nodded and she fainted, said Sowell.

Outfielder Jack Graney, another of Chapman's best friends, wept openly and said that Mays should never be allowed to pitch again. First baseman Doc Johnston said Mays should be "strung up," according to Sowell.

Some players on other teams said Mays should be banned from baseball and threatened to boycott games against the Yankees. The Cleveland Press said Mays should retire and called for banning of the beanball.

The distraught Mays was in seclusion in his apartment, then was called to the New York police station. "I'd do anything to undo what happened," he told the district attorney, who ruled the death accidental. Speaker agreed it was an accident.

Chapman's body lay in state at the home of his in-laws at 13573 Euclid Ave. "People came to pay their respects all night," recalled Margaret Chapman Joy, 91, Chapman's sister, who was 16 then.

Graney and Speaker were so grief-stricken that neither could attend the funeral in St. John's Cathedral, Mrs. Joy remembered. "The crowds were so big we could barely get in," she said. Teammates O'Neill and Smokey Joe Wood were among the pallbearers.

Thousands of people massed around the church at E. 9th St. and Superior Avenue. Flags were at half-staff all over the city. Chapman was buried in Lakeview Cemetery.

The Indians went into the doldrums after the tragedy, losing six of eight games. Sparked anew by rookies Joey Sewell, who replaced Chapman at short, and pitcher Walter "Duster" Mails, who won seven games without a loss down the stretch, they rallied to win the pennant by two games over Chicago.

They received a big break in the last week of the season, when it was announced that eight White Sox players had been indicted for throwing the 1919 World Series and would not play anymore that season. The Indians were a half-game ahead of Chicago at the time.

On the eve of the World Series against Brooklyn, The Plain Dealer ran a drawing of Chapman on Page 1, looking down from the clouds at his teammates and saying, "Carry on."

The Indians won the Series, five games to three.

Mrs. Joy has some great memories of her brother. "We were very close," said the retired schoolteacher who lives in Huntington, West Virginia. "He was 13 years older than me, but he was a wonderful brother."

Chapman often treated Joy to trips to Cleveland and other American League stops. She recalled the unfailing good humor for which Chapman was noted. "He could mix with anyone," she said.

"He was very musical and liked to sing and dance. He had a lot of friends in show business, like Al Jolson, William S. Hart and Will Rogers. He loved the theater. Once in New York, he took me to an Al Jolson show, and when we sat down, Jolson stopped the performance and said, 'Hi, Chappie.'"

Mrs. Joy recalled that one of Chapman's Cleveland managers, either Joe Birmingham or Lee Fohl, said that Chapman did not have to play one inning to earn his salary.

"He had such great spirit," she said. "One winter, he sold shoes for an old friend. He said Ray was the best salesman he ever had. After the season, our neighbors in Herrin, Illinois, said they could always tell when Ray was home because they'd hear him whistling."

Chapman, a tenor, was noted for singing such songs as "Dear Old Girl," with a quartet of Indians that included O'Neill, Graney and Wood. Chapman once won an amateur singing contest.

Mrs. Joy described Chapman's wife, Kathleen, as a "lovely, cultivated girl." "They had a beautiful home on Euclid Ave.," she remembered. "I stayed there several times. We would go to the games in a chauffeured limousine. That was all new to us. Ray never even had a car before. Once he was riding with Mr. Daly and another man who turned out to be the secretary of the Navy."

"Kathleen was never the same after Ray died," she said. "Neither was my mother. She lived another 40 years, but she never got over it. Ray was her favorite. I don't think Kathleen ever went to another baseball game."

On Feb. 27, 1921, about six months after Chapman's death, Kathleen gave birth to a daughter.

Two years later, Kathleen married a cousin, who was an oilman. On April 21, 1928, she died in Los Angeles after swallowing a poisonous fluid. She was in the company of her mother, who had been with her as she tried to recover from a nervous breakdown. The family said she took the poison accidentally. She was 34.

The Chapmans' daughter went to live with her grandmother and died on April 27, 1929, during a measles epidemic. She is buried with her mother in the Daly family plot in Calvary Cemetery in Cleveland.

"The whole family was wiped out in a very short time" said Mrs. Joy, who last visited Chapman's grave in Lakeview five years ago.

"Ray is there all by himself," she said. "He loved Cleveland. He thought it was just a wonderful place. So did I. I still look in the papers to see how the Indians are doing."

Acknowledgments

Special thanks to Patti Graziano, director of The Plain Dealer News Research Center, and her staff, including librarian Mary Ann Cofta, David Jardy, Brian Zawicki and John Golonka, for their help through the years, and to Plain Dealer news researchers Jo Ellen Corrigan and Cheryl Diamond for their contributions.

Thanks also to the staff of the Cleveland State University Library Special Collections department and University Archives, including director Bill Barrow and archivists Bill Becker and Joanne Cornelius, for their help researching the photos.

And thanks to Plain Dealer Sports Editor Roy Hewitt, Deputy Sports Editor Mike Starkey and the rest of the PD sports staff for all the help, support and encouragement.

Index

Photograph numbers are indicated with a "P" (e.g., P123); photographs are arranged sequentially on non-numbered pages in two sections.

About the Author

Bob Dolgan has written thousands of columns, articles, and feature stories about sports for *The Plain Dealer* during the past six decades. His writing has also appeared in *The Sporting News*, *Baseball Digest*, and *Golf Digest*. He was named one of the top 10 sports columnists in America by the Associated Press Sports Editors in 1985, and has won many other national, state, and local sportswriting awards. Since 1995, he has written frequently about sports history for *The Plain Dealer*, including contributions to a nationally recognized 1997 series on black baseball players and a 2001 series on the 100th anniversary of the Cleveland Indians. In 1999 he was inducted into the Cleveland Journalism Hall of Fame. He is also co-author of *The Polka King*, with Frank Yankovic. A Cleveland native and a graduate of John Carroll University, he lives in Willoughby Hills, Ohio.